Securities and Financial Derivatives

Part 1: Securities, Markets and Investment Advice
● ● ● ● ● ● ● ● ● ● ● ● ● ● ● ● ● ●

The Official Learning and Reference Manual

APPROVED WORKBOOK

4th Edition, October 2007

This Workbook relates to syllabus version 8.0 and will cover examinations from 19th November 2007 to 31st March 2009.

THIS WORKBOOK HAS BEEN EXTENDED

PROFESSIONALISM | *INTEGRITY* | *EXCELLENCE*

SECURITIES AND FINANCIAL DERIVATIVES

Welcome to the Certificate in Securities and Financial Derivatives study material for the Securities & Investment Institute's *Certificate Programme*. This manual has been written to prepare you for the Securities & Investment Institute's Securities and Financial Derivatives examination.

PUBLISHED BY:

Securities & Investment Institute
© Securities & Investment Institute 2007
8 Eastcheap
London EC3M 1AE
Tel: 020 7645 0600
Fax: 020 7645 0601

This is an educational manual only and the Securities & Investment Institute accepts no responsibility for persons undertaking trading or investments in whatever form.

While every effort has been made to ensure its accuracy, no responsibility for loss occasioned to any person acting or refraining from action as a result of any material in this publication can be accepted by the publisher or authors.

All rights reserved. No part of this publication may be reproduced, stored in a retrieval system, or transmitted, in any form or by any means, electronic, mechanical, photocopying, recording or otherwise without the prior permission of the copyright owner.

Warning: Any unauthorised act in relation to all or any part of the material in this publication may result in both a civil claim for damages and criminal prosecution.

A Learning Map, which contains the full syllabus, appears at the end of this workbook. The syllabus can also be viewed on the Institute's website at www.sii.org.uk and is also available by contacting Client Services on 020 7645 0680. Please note that the examination is based upon the syllabus. Candidates are reminded to check the Content Update area of the Institute's website (www.sii.org.uk) on a regular basis for updates that could affect their examination as a result of industry change.

Workbook version: 4.2 (October 2007)

FOREWORD

Learning and Professional Development with the SII

The SII is the leading professional body for the securities and investment industry in the UK. 40,000 of its examinations are taken each year in the UK and around the world. This learning manual (or 'workbook' as it is often known in the industry) provides not only a thorough preparation for the appropriate SII examination, but is a valuable desktop reference for practitioners. It can also be used as a learning tool for readers interested in knowing more, but not necessarily entering an examination.

The SII official learning manuals ensure that candidates gain a comprehensive understanding of examination content. Our material is written and updated by industry specialists and reviewed by experienced, senior figures in the financial services industry. Exam and manual quality is assured through a rigorous editorial system of practitioner panels and boards. SII examinations are used extensively by firms to meet the requirements of the UK regulator, the FSA. The SII also works closely with a number of international regulators which recognise our examinations and the manuals supporting them.

SII learning manuals are normally revised annually. It is important that candidates check they purchase the correct version for the period when they wish to take their examination. Between versions, candidates should keep abreast of the latest industry developments through the Content Update area of the SII website. SII is also pleased to endorse the workbooks published by 7City Learning and BPP for candidates preparing for SII examinations.

The SII produces a range of elearning revision tools such as *Revision Express*, *Regulatory Refresher* and *eIAQ* that can be used in conjunction with our learning and reference manuals. For further details, please visit www.sii.org.uk

As a Professional Body, 41,000 SII members subscribe to the SII Code of Conduct and the SII has a significant voice in the industry, standing for professionalism, excellence and the promotion of trust and integrity. Continuing professional development (CPD) is at the heart of the Institute's values. Our CPD scheme is available free of charge to members, and this includes an on-line record keeping system as well as regular seminars, conferences and professional networks in specialist subject areas, all of which cover a range of current industry topics. Reading this manual and taking an SII examination is credited as professional development within the SIICPD scheme. To learn more about SII membership visit our website at www.sii.org.uk

We hope that you will find this manual useful and interesting. Once you have completed it you will find helpful suggestions on qualifications and membership progression with the SII.

Ruth Martin
Managing Director

Contents

Chapter 1:   Securities   1

Chapter 2:   New Issues   45

Chapter 3:   Primary & Secondary Markets   81

Chapter 4:   Settlement   119

Chapter 5:   Special Regulatory Requirements   131

Chapter 6:   Accounting Analysis   141

Chapter 7:   Risk and Reward   169

Abbreviations   181

It is estimated that this workbook will require approximately **100** hours of study time.

INTRODUCTION

As an introduction we will look at the Financial Services Industry within both local and global economy.

Stock markets and investment instruments are not unique to one country. There is increasing similarity in the instruments that are traded on all world markets and in the way that trading and settlement systems are developing.

Financial Services Industry

The world economy is growing rapidly, becoming increasingly integrated and interdependent as trade and investment flows rise. It is important, therefore, to understand the core role that the industry undertakes within the economy and some key features of the global financial services sector.

Role of the Financial Services Industry

The financial services industry in developed countries is a major contributor to the economy. In the UK, for example, the activities of investment banks and firms headquartered in the City of London provide considerable employment and overseas earnings for the economy.

The financial services industry provides the link between organisations needing capital and those with capital available for investment. An organisation needing capital might be a growing company, and the capital might be provided by individuals saving for their retirement in a pension fund. It is the financial services industry that channels money invested in pension funds, life assurance policies, collective investment schemes etc to organisations that need it, and provides transmission, payment, advisory and management services.

The financial services industry plays a critical role in all advanced economies and the services it provides can be broken down into three core functions:
- Investment Chain - savers and borrowers are brought together, bringing finance to business and opportunities for savers to use their savings. The efficiency of this chain is critical in allocating capital to the most profitable investments, raising productivity and improving competitiveness in the global economy.
- Risk - in addition to the opportunities that the investment chain provides for pooling investment risks, the financial services sector allows other risks to be managed effectively and efficiently through the use of insurance and increasingly sophisticated derivatives. These tools help business cope with global uncertainties as diverse as the value of currencies, the incidence of major accidents or devastating weather conditions and protect households against everyday contingencies.
- Payment Systems – payment and banking services operated by the financial services sector provide the practical mechanisms for money to be managed, transmitted and received quickly and reliably. It is an essential requirement for commercial activities, for participation in international trade and investment. Access to payment systems and banking services is a vital component of financial inclusion for individuals.

Global Financial Services Industry

The scale and importance of the financial services industry to the global economy is shown by reports issued by various organisations at the end of 2005.

Figures issued by the World Federation of Exchanges showed that the total value of shares quoted globally, reached US$41 trillion whilst according to the Bank for International Settlements the total value of global bonds in issue reached US$46 trillion. The hedge fund industry is estimated to be worth US$1 trillion and turnover in the Foreign Exchange Markets is in the region of US$2.5 trillion a day.

The USA and Europe dominate the investment markets with over US$40 trillion of funds under management:-

US$bn	Europe	US
Pensions	3,621	12,119
Insurance	6,002	5,465
Mutual Funds	6,002	8,905
Total	15,625	26,489

Industry Participants
The type of organisations operating in Financial Services is varied. An understanding of their roles is important to understand how the industry is organised and interacts.
The following sections detail the functions of the main participants within the industry.

Wholesale and Retail Business
Within the financial services industry there are two distinct areas, namely the wholesale institutional sector and the retail sector.

- the main functions of the wholesale financial sector are:
- International banking – cross-border banking transactions
- Equity markets — the trading of quoted shares
- Bond markets — the trading of government or corporate debt
- Foreign exchange — the trading of currencies
- Derivatives — the trading of options, swaps, futures and forwards
- Investment banking — tailored banking services such as undertaking mergers and acquisitions, equity trading, fixed income trading and private equity
- Custody – looking after shares and bonds
- Fund management — managing mutual, pension and insurance pooled funds
- Insurance — re-insurance, major corporate insurance, captive insurance and risk-sharing insurance

- the retail sector focuses on services provided to personal customers including:
- Retail banking – traditional range of deposit accounts, lending and credit cards
- Pensions – provision of investment accounts specifically designed to capture savings during a person's working life and provide benefits on retirement
- Investment services – a range of investment products ranging from execution only stock broking to full wealth management services and private banking
- Insurance – provision of a range of life insurance and protection solutions for areas such as medical insurance, critical illness, income and mortgage protection

The Wholesale Sector

INTERNATIONAL BANKING
International banking refers to banking activities that involve cross-border transactions.

EQUITY MARKETS
Equity markets are the best known of financial markets and facilitate the trading of shares in quoted companies. Although a number of well known stock exchanges – London Stock Exchange, NYSE, NASDAQ, Euronext, Deutsch Börse currently dominate the markets, exchanges in other markets are growing fast. In addition, other methods of trading shares are growing in importance with the potential for exchanges in their current shape to be bypassed.

BOND MARKETS
The bond markets are larger both in size and value of trading than equity markets. Investments traded range from domestic bonds issued by companies and governments to international bonds issued by companies, governments and supra-national agencies eg, World Bank.

Although the US has the largest bond market, trading in international bonds is predominantly undertaken in European markets.

FOREIGN EXCHANGE MARKETS
Europe is the largest market for foreign exchange, accounting for over half of total global trading. Most of that activity takes place in the UK which accounts for around a third.

The rate at which one currency is exchanged for another is set by supply and demand. For example, if there is strong demand from Japanese investors for US assets, such as property or bonds and shares, the US Dollar would rise in value.

Foreign exchange (Forex) rates tend to reflect:
- Prospects for growth; and
- Comparative interest rates.

Forex rates will have a substantial impact on businesses that engage in international trade.

As a result, there is an active market, provided by the major banks, enabling companies to deal with inflows and outflows of overseas currencies. Historically, most deals were arranged by telephone, however electronic trading is becoming increasingly prevalent.

The **spot** rate is the rate quoted by the bank for the exchange of one currency for another immediately, although for large commercial transactions the underlying cash is not available until two business days have elapsed.

The **forward** rate is the rate quoted by the bank for the exchange of one currency for another at some agreed future date. Companies entering into forward transactions will know how much an overseas currency will cost or generate in advance. This will enable the companies to plan and budget more accurately.

DERIVATIVES MARKETS

Derivatives markets trade a range of complex products based on underlying instruments. Financial derivatives include currencies, interest rates, equities, and credit risk, whilst commodity derivatives include agricultural, metals and energy.

Derivatives based on these underlying elements are available on both the Exchange Traded Market and the Over the Counter Market (OTC).

Turnover in US and European derivatives increased fourfold between 2000 and 2005 with US exchanges accounting for over half of global turnover. The largest of the exchange traded derivatives markets is the Chicago Mercantile Exchange.

Europe dominates trading in the OTC derivatives markets with the UK enjoying the largest share of foreign exchange derivative turnover. Based on the value of the notional amounts outstanding, the OTC derivatives markets are about four times the size of stock quoted on stock exchanges.

Interest rate derivatives contracts account for three-quarters of outstanding derivatives contracts, mostly through interest rate swaps. In terms of currencies the interest rate derivatives market is dominated by the euro and the dollar.

INVESTMENT BANKS

Investment banks provide advice and arrange finance for companies who want to float on the stock market, raise additional finance by issuing further shares or bonds, or carry out mergers and acquisitions. They also provide services for those who might want to invest in shares and bonds, in particular pension funds and asset managers.

Typically, an investment banking group provides world-wide some or all of the following services, either in divisions of the bank or in associated companies within the group:

- Corporate Finance and advisory work, normally in connection with new issues of securities for raising finance, take-overs, mergers and acquisitions
- Banking, for governments, institutions and companies.
- Treasury dealing for corporate clients in currencies, with financial engineering services to protect them from interest and exchange rate fluctuations
- Investment management, for pension funds, charities, private clients, either via direct investment for the more wealthy or via unit and investment trusts. In larger firms, the value of funds under management runs into many billions of pounds.
- Securities trading, in equities, bonds, derivatives and offering broking and distribution facilities

Only a few investment banks provide services in all areas. Most others tend to specialise and concentrate on a few product lines. A number of banks have diversified their range of services in response to the downturn between 2000 and 2002 by developing businesses such as proprietary trading, servicing hedge funds or making private equity investments.

CUSTODIAN BANKS
Custodians are banks that specialise in safe custody services - looking after portfolios of shares and bonds on behalf of others, such as fund managers, and pension funds.

The activities they undertake include:
- Holding assets in safekeeping such as equities and bonds
- Arrange settlement of any purchases and sales of securities
- Collect income from assets, namely dividends in the case of equities and interest in the case of bonds
- Provide information on the underlying companies and their annual general meetings
- Manage cash transactions
- Perform foreign exchange transactions where required and
- Provide regular reporting on all their activities to their clients

The custody business is now dominated by a small number of global custodians who are often divisions of investment banks. Generally, they also offer other services to their clients, such as stock lending, measuring the performance of the portfolios and maximising the return on any surplus cash.

FUND MANAGEMENT (ASSET MANAGEMENT)
Fund Management is the investment management of portfolios for pension funds, insurance companies and mutual funds.

Other areas of fund management include private wealth management and provision of investment management services to institutional entities such as, companies, charities and local government authorities.

The area also includes hedge funds, which are one of the fastest growing forms of institutional asset management.

INSURANCE MARKETS
Insurance markets specialise in the management of risk, one of the three principal functions of the financial services industry.

In 2004 the world market was worth US$3.2 trillion based on the number of premiums written with the majority being life insurance premiums. The EU and USA are the largest players in the insurance market.

Lloyd's of London is the largest insurance organisation in the world. It is said that anything can be insured on Lloyd's, from mainstream assets such as buildings, to footballers' legs and master wine tasters' taste buds.

The Retail Sector

Private individuals use a variety of financial services firms depending on the level of their assets. Many benefit from pensions and health insurance provided by their employers, others use the services provided by companies such as those listed below.

RETAIL BANKS

Retail, or high street, banks provide services such as taking deposits from, and lending funds to, retail customers, as well as providing payment and money transmission services. They may also provide similar services to business customers.

Historically, these banks have tended to operate through a network of branches located on the high street, but increasingly they also provide internet and telephone banking.

As well as providing traditional banking services, larger retail banks also offer products such as asset management, pensions and insurance.

SAVINGS INSTITUTIONS

As well as retail banks, most countries also have savings institutions that started off by specialising in offering savings products to retail customers but now tend to offer a similar range of services to banks.

PENSION FUNDS

Pension funds are one of the key methods by which individuals can make provision for retirement.

Taken overall, pension funds are large, long-term investors in shares, bonds and cash. Some also invest in physical assets like property. To meet their aim of providing a pension on retirement, the sums of money invested in pensions are substantial.

STOCKBROKERS

Stockbrokers arrange stock market trades on behalf of clients. They may advise investors about which individual shares or bonds they should buy or, alternatively, they may offer execution-only services.

Like fund managers, firms of stockbrokers can be independent companies, but more usually they are divisions of larger entities, such as investment banks. They earn their profits by charging fees for their advice and commissions on transactions.

INVESTMENT MANAGERS

Fund managers, also known as investment managers, run portfolios of investments for others. They invest money held by pension funds, insurance companies and others. Some are independent companies; others are divisions of larger entities like insurance companies or banks.

Fund managers will buy and sell shares, bonds and other assets in order to increase the value of clients' portfolios. They can conveniently be sub-divided into 'institutional' and 'private client' fund managers.

Institutional fund managers work on behalf of institutions, for example, investing money for a company's pension fund, or an insurance company's fund or managing the investments in a unit trust.

Private client fund managers invest the money of relatively wealthy individuals. Individual institutional funds typically provide the fund managers with larger sums of money than do private clients.

The fund managers make a profit by charging their clients for managing their money; their charges are often based on a small percentage of the fund being managed.

PRIVATE BANKING

Private banks provide a full range of services for their clients including: wealth management, estate planning, tax planning, insurance, lending, lines of credit, etc.

Private banking can be onshore and offshore. Although both are largely the preserve of wealthy individuals, offshore banking means banking under a different financial regulatory regime to the one in place in a person's home country. Offshore banking also refers to the breadth of investment opportunities available under these different countries' regimes.

The annual World Wealth Report, published by Merrill Lynch Cap Gemini estimated that the value of funds managed on behalf of 9.5 million high net worth individuals is around US$37.2 trillion in 2007.

The distinction between private and retail banks is gradually diminishing as private banks reduce their investment thresholds in order to compete for this market and high street banks expand their services to attract the "Mass Affluent" and high-net worth individuals.

INSURANCE COMPANIES

One of the key functions of the financial services industry is to allow risks to be managed effectively.

Protection planning is a key area of financial advice and the insurance industry provides a wide range of products to meet almost all potential scenarios. These products arrange from payment protection policies designed to pay out in the event that an individual is unable to meet repayments on loans and mortgages to medical policies designed to cover hospital bills or pay out in the event of a critical illness.

Insurance companies also market a wide range of investment products and have recently been large players in the structured products market by offering guaranteed stock market related bonds.

Insurance companies collect premiums in exchange for cover provided. The UK insurance industry is the largest in Europe and 3rd largest globally. In 2005, £31 billion of general premiums and £87 billion of long term premiums were collected. This premium income is used to buy investments like shares and bonds and as a result, the insurance industry controls 17% of London Stock Market. The insurance company will subsequently realise investments to pay any claims that may arise on the various policies. In addition to the participants in the Wholesale and Retails Sectors there are:-

THIRD PARTY ADMINISTRATORS

The Third Part Administrator (TPA) undertakes investment administration e.g. settlement and custody on behalf of other firms and specialise in this area of the investment industry.

The number of firms and the scale of their operations have grown with the increasing use by firms of outsourcing. The rational behind outsourcing has been that it enables a firm to focus on the core areas of its business and leave another firm to complete associated functions which it can process more efficiently.

TRADE BODIES
The investment industry is a dynamic, rapidly changing business and requires cooperation between firms to ensure that the views of various sections of the industry are represented and that cross-firm developments can take place to create an efficient market in which those firms can operate.

This is essentially the role of the numerous trade bodies that exist across the world's financial markets. In the UK, the trade bodies of particular relevance to the investment industry are the Association of Investment Companies (AIC), the Association of Private Client Investment Managers (APCIMS), the Futures and Options Association (FOA), the Investment Management Association (IMA) and the London Investment Banking Association (LIBA).

SECURITIES

1.	SHARES	4
2.	DEBT INSTRUMENTS	9
3.	GOVERNMENT DEBT	19
4.	CORPORATE DEBT	26
5.	EUROBONDS	32
6.	OTHER SECURITIES	33
7.	FOREIGN EXCHANGE	37
8.	PRIME BROKERAGE AND EQUITY FINANCE	40

This syllabus area will provide approximately 22 of the 100 examination questions

Shares and Bonds

As a broad introduction to this chapter, it is useful to provide a reminder of the essential differences between the two major types of security: shares (or equities) and bonds.

Investors in **bonds** essentially hold an IOU (I owe you) from another organisation, such as a company. The bond investors:

- loan money to an organisation in return for an **agreed rate of interest**;
- have an **agreed date** on which they get their money back;
- can **sue** the issuer of the bond if the interest on the bond isn't paid;
- can **sue** the issuer of the bond if repayment doesn't occur.

Investors in **equities** hold a stake in the company. The equity investors:

- purchase a small piece, or **share**, of a company;
- cannot be certain that they will receive **dividend payments**;
- cannot be certain of the **amount of dividend** that they will receive;
- could **lose** everything if the company fails.

Securities like shares and bonds take one of two main forms: registered and bearer. The form determines how an investor would prove ownership of a particular investment.

> **Example**
>
> Mr X owns 100 shares in Marks and Spencer plc. If a burglar breaks into Mr X's house and steals Mr X's share certificates, can he pretend that he owns the Marks and Spencer shares and sell them?
>
> Fortunately, the answer is no.

The answer to the above example is no because shares in the UK are held in registered form. This means that the certificate is simply evidence of ownership. The proof that counts is the name and address held on the company's share register.

Some securities come in **bearer** form. Unlike registered securities, with bearer form securities the **physical possession** of the certificate is the proof of ownership.

Bearer securities are easier to transfer since there is no register. They can simply be handed over. However, this does raise a few problems:

- it is difficult for the authorities to monitor ownership, making them attractive investments for **money launderers**;
- the issuing company has difficulty knowing who to send dividend or interest payments to;
- physical **security** of the certificates is of greater importance and can increase the cost of holding the investment.

Examples of securities that are usually held in bearer form that will be encountered later in this chapter are **Eurobonds** and **American Depositary Receipts (ADRs)**.

1. SHARES

Introduction - Types of Share

Shares can be divided into two categories: ordinary shares and preference shares. Every company has ordinary shares in issue. In addition to the ordinary shares, some companies issue preference shares.

The performance of **ordinary shares** is closely tied to the fortunes of the company. Holders of ordinary shares have the right to **vote** on key decisions and receive dividends. Some companies have more than one class of ordinary shares (perhaps distinguishing between **A** ordinary shares and **B** ordinary shares), where one class of shares does not provide voting rights and are, therefore, referred to as **non-voting shares**.

Preference shares are less risky than ordinary shares and potentially less profitable. Holders, generally, do not have the right to vote on company affairs, but they are entitled to receive a **fixed dividend** each year (as long as the company feels they have sufficient profits). These dividends must be paid before any dividends to ordinary shareholders; hence the term **preference**. Although preference shares tend to be non-voting, it is common for preference shareholders to become entitled to vote in the event of no dividend being paid for a 'substantial' period of time. Precisely how long 'substantial' is will be detailed in the company's constitution.

1.1 Features of Ordinary Shares

> **LEARNING OBJECTIVES**
>
> 1.1.1 know the principal features and characteristics of ordinary shares and non-voting shares: 'A' ordinary shares; preference shares; bearer shares; partly paid shares and calls; ranking for dividends; ranking in a liquidation; voting rights; purpose of non-voting shares

The ordinary shareholders of a company take the greatest risk. If the company is liquidated, they will only receive any pay out if there is money remaining after satisfying all of the other claims from creditors, bondholders and preference shareholders.

If the company is sufficiently profitable, the ordinary shareholders may receive dividends. Dividends for ordinary shareholders are proposed by the directors and generally ratified by the shareholders at the Annual General Meeting (AGM). However, the ordinary shareholders will only receive a dividend after any preference dividends have been paid.

Each ordinary share is typically given the right to vote at AGMs and Extraordinary General Meetings (EGMs), although sometimes voting rights are restricted to certain classes of ordinary shares. Such different classes of shares (often called 'A' ordinary and 'B' ordinary shares), are created to separate ownership and control, as illustrated in the following example:

> **Example**
>
> ABC plc is a small, successful, privately owned company with two founding directors each holding 500 ordinary shares of its total issued ordinary shares of 1000 shares. ABC plc needs more investment for expansion and the company agrees to issue 200 new shares to venture capitalists. However, the venture capitalists require control over the company as a condition of their investment.
>
> This is achieved by creating a second class of ordinary shares. The founding directors' shares become non-voting 'A' shares and the venture capitalists hold voting 'B' shares. The result is that although the founding directors hold non-voting 'A' shares, they still own most of the company (1,000 shares of the total 1,200 shares), but control is now exercised by the venture capitalists since it is their 'B' shares that have votes.

Each shareholder has the right to vote at both an AGM and EGM but may, if they so wish, appoint a third party, or proxy, to vote on their behalf. A proxy may be an individual or group of individuals appointed by the board of directors of the company to formally represent the shareholders who send in proxy requests, to vote the represented shares in accordance with the shareholders' instructions.

Each ordinary share has a **nominal value**, which represents the minimum amount that the company must receive from subscribers on the issue of the shares. Occasionally the company may not demand all of the nominal value at issue, with the shares referred to as being **partly-paid**. At some later date, the company will **call** on the shareholders to pay the remaining nominal value.

Most ordinary shares are registered, meaning that the issuing company maintains a register of who holds the shares. Shares issued by a company that does not maintain a register are known as **bearer shares** - they can be transferred to other investors by simply handing over the certificate. For registered shares, a transfer requires a change of entry in the shareholders' register.

1.2 Types of Preference Share

LEARNING OBJECTIVES

1.1.2 understand the differences and principal characteristics of the following classes of preference shares: cumulative; participating; redeemable; convertible

Preference shares can come in a variety of forms.

- **Cumulative**: a cumulative preference shareholder will not only be paid this year's dividend before any ordinary shareholders' dividends, but also any unpaid dividends from previous years.
- **Redeemable**: these are preference shares that enable the company to buy back the shares from the shareholder at an agreed price in the future. The shares from the company's perspective, are similar to debt. The money provided by the preference shareholders can be repaid, removing any obligation the firm has to them.
- **Participating**: one drawback of preference shares, when compared to ordinary shares, is that if the company starts to generate large profits, the ordinary shareholders will often see their dividends rise, whereas the preference shareholders still get a fixed level of dividend. To counter this some preference shares offer the opportunity to participate in higher distributions.

- **Convertible**: in this case, the preference shareholder has the right, but not the obligation, to convert the preference shares into a predetermined number of ordinary shares. For example, perhaps one preference share can be converted into two ordinary shares. This is another method of avoiding the lack of upside potential in the preference shares, compared to ordinary shares.

Note that a particular preference share may exhibit more than one of these features.

1.3 Stock Indices

> **LEARNING OBJECTIVES**
>
> 1.1.3 know the broad composition and geographical scope and use of the following stock indices: DJ STOXX; FTSE Eurofirst 300; MSCI World; FTSE 100; Dow Jones Industrial Average; Nikkei Stock 225; Hang Seng

There are thousands of companies that are listed and traded on various stock exchanges around the world. Stock indices such as the FTSE 100 and the Dow Jones Industrial Average are produced so that existing and potential investors can get a snapshot of the way share prices are generally moving. These stock indices are calculated by specialist firms such as FTSE International (that originated as a joint venture between the Financial Times and the stock exchange in London) and Dow Jones Indexes (part of the Dow Jones Company, which also publishes the Wall Street Journal). Each index can be thought of as an 'average' share price of its constituents, as illustrated in the example below.

> **Example - The FTSE 100**
>
> The FTSE 100 is a stock index based on the share prices of the largest 100 companies listed on the London Stock Exchange. It started at a base level of 1000 points in January 1984, meaning that the value of the 100 constituent companies at that time equated to 1000 index points. As the value of the constituent companies increase (or decrease), the FTSE 100 will increase (or decrease). So, if the value of the constituents grew by 10% in the first 9 months following the index publication date, the index would have risen to 1100 index points.
>
> At the time of writing, the FTSE 100 stands at 6660 index points.

The following indices are covered within the syllabus, and the table below provides their broad composition and geographical scope.

Index name	Composition	Geographical Scope
FTSE 100	Largest 100 UK companies listed on the LSE and measured by market capitalisation	UK
Dow Jones Industrial Average	30 large US companies selected by the editors of the Wall Street Journal	USA
Nikkei Stock 225	225 large and regularly traded Japanese companies traded on the Tokyo Stock Exchange	Japan
Hang Seng	38 companies listed on the Hong Kong Stock Exchange selected on the basis of market value, turnover and financial performance	Hong Kong/China
DJ Stoxx	A family of indices, based around the DJ Stoxx Global 1800 index that consists of 600 largest capitalisation companies from each of 3 regions - Europe, Americas and Asia/Pacific	Global developed markets
MSCI World	A market capitalisation based index including companies from 23 countries, totalling approx 1700 companies	Global developed markets
FTSE Eurofirst 300	300 largest listed companies by market capitalisation from across Europe	Europe

These stock market indices are used both as a gauge of the market and as a performance benchmark. If the index is going up, the prices of the constituents will generally be increasing, and the market will be described as going through a 'bullish' phase. In contrast, if the index is falling, the prices of the constituents will generally be decreasing and the market will be described as going through a 'bearish' phase.

The use of an index as a performance benchmark is illustrated in the following example:

> **Example**
>
> An investor holds a small number of large listed Japanese shares. Over the course of the year, the value of her shares has increased by 8%. The investor considers this a good performance because, over the same period, the Nikkei 225 has only increased by 5%. The investor's portfolio has 'outperformed' the market.

1.4 Tax Credits on UK Dividends

LEARNING OBJECTIVES

1.1.4   understand the use of a tax credit on a dividend

If a UK resident receives dividends on shares held, he will probably be subject to UK income tax. However, dividends received are deemed to have already suffered tax at 10% before they are received. This is called the 'tax credit' on the dividends and means that the investor only has to pay further income tax if he is a higher rate (40%) tax payer. The effect of this credit under the applicable rules is that no income tax is payable by any recipient of dividends whose total income is below the higher rate tax level, after adding in the grossed up value of those dividends. It is not a proper credit because, for example, a non-taxpayer cannot recover it. Where the dividends are received by higher rate payers, then additional tax of 25% of the amount paid becomes payable, equivalent to 32.5% of the grossed up value minus the tax credit. Note that it is not 40%.

This is illustrated in the following example:

Example

Mr X Ample is a higher rate (40%) taxpayer and has 100 shares in ABC plc. ABC pays a dividend of 90 pence on each share. Mr Ample will receive £90 (90 pence x 100 shares) and, as far as the tax authority is concerned, he will be considered as having received £100 and having paid tax of £10 already. The £100 is referred to as the 'gross dividend' and the £90 received is the 'net dividend'. Since he is a higher rate taxpayer, Mr Ample will have to pay a further 25% of the net dividend to complete his tax due and payable.

In summary, Mr X Ample:

Received 90p x 100 shares the 'net dividend'	=	£90
Tax credit = 10/100 of the net dividend	=	£10
'Gross dividend entitlement	=	£100
Tax due = 32.5% (10% tax credit + 25% of dividend payment received) x £100	=	£32.50
Deemed paid by way of the tax credit	=	(£10)
Remaining to be paid	=	£22.50

2. DEBT INSTRUMENTS

2.1 Features and Characteristics

LEARNING OBJECTIVES

1.2.1 know the principal features and characteristics of debt instruments

As seen at the start of this chapter, a bond is essentially an IOU (I owe you) issued by an organisation (the borrower, or issuer), in return for the money lent to it.

The **nominal value** (or par value) of a bond is the amount that the borrower will pay back to the holder of the bond on maturity.

The **issuer** of a bond is important. If a company issuing a bond was considered high-risk, it will need to offer a high rate of interest on the bond to attract investors.

The **redemption date** of a bond is the date on which the borrower agrees to pay back the nominal value of the bond. It is also referred to as the date on which the bond matures, ie, the **maturity date**.

A bond's **coupon** is the interest rate that the borrower pays to the bondholder, expressed as a percentage of the nominal value. In diagrammatic form:

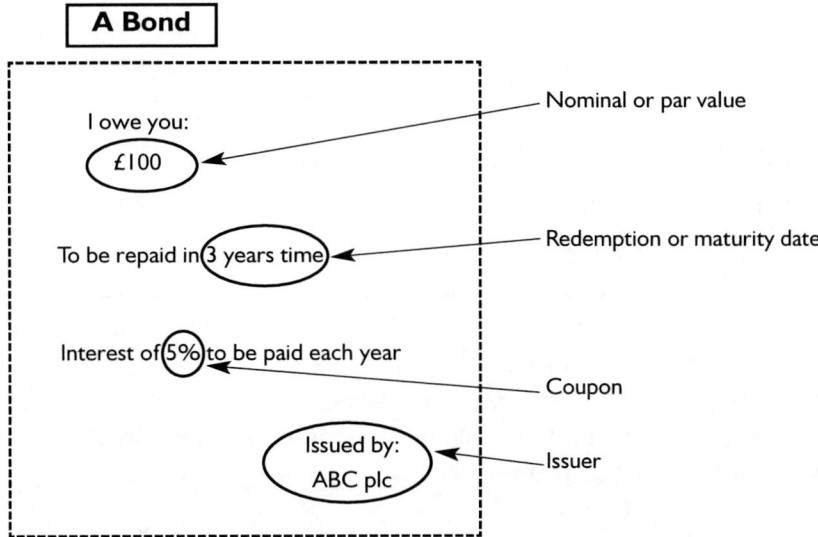

2.2 Yields

LEARNING OBJECTIVES

1.2.2 understand the uses and limitations of the following: flat yield; gross redemption yield (using internal rate of return); net redemption yield; modified duration; calculation of price change; convexity

Introduction

The yield is a measure of the percentage return that an investment provides. For a bond, there are three potential ways yields can be calculated: the flat yield (also known as the interest or running yield), the gross redemption yield and the net redemption yield.

Flat Yield

The **flat yield** only considers the coupon and ignores the existence of any capital gain (or loss) through to redemption. As such, it is best suited to short-term investors in the bond, rather than those investors that might hold the bond through to its maturity and benefit from the gain (or suffer from the loss) at maturity.

The calculation of the flat yield is as follows:

Flat yield = (annual coupon/price) x 100

For example, the flat yield on a 5% gilt, redeeming in 6 years and priced at £104.40, would be:

(5/104.40) x 100 = 4.79%.

Exercise 1

i. Calculate the flat yield on a 4% gilt, redeeming in 8 years and priced at £98.90

ii. Calculate the flat yield on a 7% gilt, redeeming in 3 years and priced at £108.60

The answers to this exercise can be found at the end of this chapter.

Using the flat yield, it is simple to see how a change in interest rates will impact bond prices. If interest rates increase, investors will want an equivalent increase in the yield on their bonds. However, because the coupon is fixed for most bonds, the only way that the yield can increase is for the price to fall. This is the inverse relationship between interest rates and bond prices. **When interest rates rise, bond prices fall and vice versa.**

Gross Redemption Yield (GRY)

The **Gross Redemption Yield** is a fuller measure of yield than the flat yield, because it takes both the coupons and any gain (or loss) through to maturity into account. As such, it is more appropriate for long-term investors than the flat yield. In particular, because it ignores the impact of any taxation (hence gross redemption yield), this measure of return is useful for non-taxpaying, long-term investors such as pension funds and charities.

The calculation of the GRY utilises the approach covered in section 2.6 of this chapter to arrive at the present value of a gilt. It is the 'internal rate of return' of the bond. The internal rate of return is simply the discount rate that, when applied to the future cash flows of the bond, produces the current price of that bond.

Net Redemption Yield (NRY)

The **Net Redemption Yield** is similar to the gross redemption yield, in that it takes both the annual coupons and the profit (or loss) made through to maturity into account. However, it looks at the after-tax cash flows rather than the gross cash flows. As a result it is a useful measure for tax paying, long-term investors.

The coupon received from gilts is generally taxable, but any gain made on redemption (or subsequent sale) is not taxable. This makes gilts with a low coupon attractive to higher rate taxpayers, as the price will be lower than par, resulting in a substantial part of the return coming in the form of a tax-free capital gain.

Modified Duration

It is clear that if interest rates rise the price of fixed-rate debt instruments (eg, most gilts and many corporate debt issues) falls, and vice versa.

If an investor thinks that interest rates are going to fall in the future, then investing in fixed interest securities is a good idea because, if the investor is correct, their price will rise.

However, some fixed-interest securities will be more responsive to a movement in interest rates than others. They will all rise in value when interest rates fall, but some will probably rise by more than others. The ones that rise the most are the more **volatile** securities.

All other things being equal, a lower coupon bond will be more volatile to a change in interest rates than a higher coupon bond. Similarly, all other things being equal, a longer dated bond will be more responsive than a shorter dated bond.

To identify which bonds are more volatile, **volatility measures** can be used.

The one measure of volatility required for this examination is **modified duration**.

The modified duration of a particular debt instrument shows the **expected change in its price**, given a **specified change in interest rates**. The higher the modified duration, the more the price of that instrument will move. The modified duration is the approximate percentage change in the price of a bond, brought about by a 1% change in the interest rate. If a bond is priced at £95.84 and its modified duration is 1.02, what is the approximate price after an increase in interest rates by one percentage point?

If interest rates increase, the bond's price will fall by 1.02/100 x £95.84 = £0.98

If interest rates rise by one half of a percentage point, the bond price will fall by 1.02/100 x £95.84 x 0.5 = £0.49.

Convexity

If market interest rates (and, therefore, required yields) move by a small amount, then modified duration is fairly accurate in predicting the change in a bond's price. However, when rate changes are large, modified duration tends to underestimate the rise in prices (if rates fall) and overestimate price falls (when rates increase).

These errors are due to the relationship between yields and prices being curved rather than a straight line. Modified duration assumes a straight line relationship, and making the adjustment for convexity will refine the anticipated price change given a particular movement in yield.

Diagrammatically, the relationship between the modified duration based estimate and the convexity adjustment can be seen in the following graph:

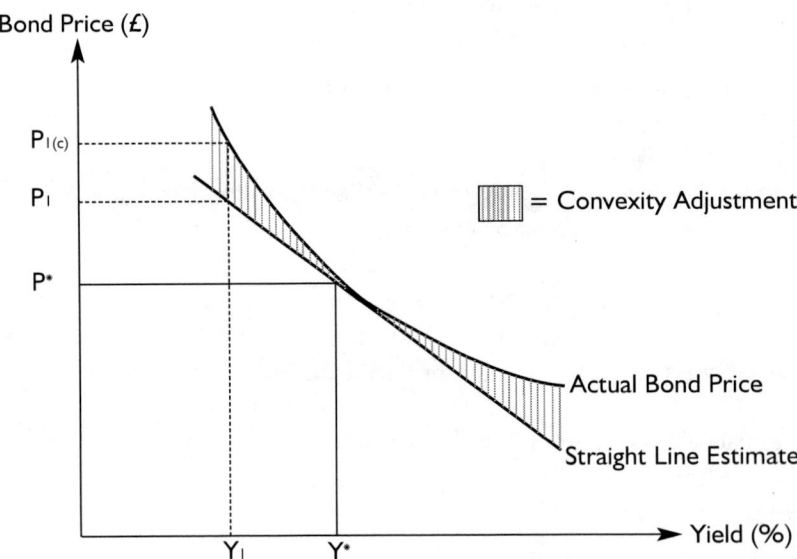

If a bond was currently priced at P* with a gross redemption yield of Y*, and the interest rates on the market and required yield fell to Y_1, then modified duration would estimate the price would rise to P_1. The actual price rise would be greater, and would be captured by applying the convexity adjustment to increase the price rise to $P_1(c)$.

2.3 Corporate Debt

LEARNING OBJECTIVES

1.2.3 be able to calculate simple interest income on corporate debt and conversion premiums on convertible bonds

Introduction

Corporate debt is simply money that is borrowed by a company that has to be repaid. Generally, corporate debt also requires servicing by making regular interest payments. Corporate debt can be subdivided into money borrowed from banks via loans and overdrafts, and directly from investors in the form of IOU (I owe you) instruments, typically bonds.

Debt finance is less expensive than equity finance because investing in debt finance is less risky than investing in the equity of the same company. The interest on debt has to be paid and is paid before dividends, so there is more certainty. Additionally, if the firm were to go into liquidation, the holders of debt finance would be paid back before the shareholders receive anything. For investors in bonds, firms like Standard and Poor's capture the comparative riskiness of the issuer and the bond in their credit ratings.

However, raising money via debt finance does present dangers to the issuing company. The lenders are often able to claim some or all of the assets of the firm in the event of non-compliance with the terms of the loan - for instance, a bank providing mortgage finance would be able to claim the property as security against the loan.

Interest on Corporate Debt

Interest on bonds is calculated by reference to the coupon rate, coupon frequency and nominal value.

Exercise

For example, XYZ plc has issued bonds paying an annual 8% coupon and maturing in 2020. The bonds are currently priced at 106 – meaning investors have to pay £106 for each £100 of nominal value.

If an investor were to buy £5000 nominal value, the bonds would cost £5300 (£5000 x 106/100). The interest income for the investor each year would be nominal value times the coupon rate - £5000 x 8% = £400.

If the interest was paid semi-annually, then the annual payment would be split into two portions.

Convertible Bonds

Some corporates issue bonds with conversion rights, known as 'convertible' bonds. Convertible bonds give the holder of the bond the right, but not the obligation, to convert into a predetermined number of ordinary shares of the issuer. Given this choice, the holder will choose to convert into shares if, at maturity, the value of the shares they can convert into exceeds the redemption value of the bond. Because there is this upside potential to the value of a convertible bond if the share price rises, and the downside protection of the redemption value if the shares do not perform well, convertible bonds generally trade at a premium to their share value. The calculation of the **premium** is shown by the following example.

Example

A convertible bond issued by XYZ plc is trading at £114. It offers the holder the option of converting £100 nominal into 25 shares. The shares of XYZ are currently trading at £3.90. To calculate the premium, first work out the share value of the conversion choice.

For £100 nominal value, that is £3.90 x 25 shares = £97.50

The bond is trading at £114, so the premium in absolute terms is £114 - £97.50 = £16.50.

It is more usual to express it as a percentage of the conversion value:

(£16.50/£97.50) x 100 = 16.9%

Exercise 2

The convertible bonds issued by ABC plc are trading at £110. Each £100 nominal value offers the holder the option of converting into 15 ordinary ABC plc shares. The ordinary shares of ABC plc are currently trading at £6.40. What is the conversion premium, expressed in percentage terms?

The answer can be found at the end of this chapter.

Convertible bonds enable the holder to exploit the growth potential in the equity whilst retaining the safety net of the bond. It is for this reason that convertible bonds trade at a premium to the value of the shares they can convert into. If there were no premium, then there would be an arbitrage opportunity for investors to buy the shares more cheaply via the convertible than in the equity market.

Usually, convertible bonds are issued where the price of each share is set at the outset and that price will be adjusted to take into account any subsequent bonus or rights issues. Given the share price, it is simple to calculate the conversion ratio - the number of shares that each £100 of nominal value of the bonds can convert into.

$$\text{Conversion ratio} = \frac{\text{Nominal value}}{\text{Conversion price of shares}}$$

> **Example**
>
> For example, £100 nominal value of a convertible bond is able to convert into shares at £4.46 each.
>
> The conversion ratio = £100/£4.46 = 22.42 shares

If the issuing company has a 1 for 1 bonus issue, then the conversion price would halve and the conversion ratio would double.

2.4 Spreads

> **LEARNING OBJECTIVES**
>
> 1.2.4 understand the concept of spreads and be able to convert spread over a Government benchmark to a LIBOR-based spread

Commentators often refer to **spreads** in the bond markets. A **spread** is simply the difference between the yield available on one instrument and the yield available elsewhere. It is usually expressed in **basis points**, with each basis point representing 1/100 of one percent.

Spreads are commonly expressed as spreads over government bonds. For example, if a 10 year corporate bond is yielding 6% and the equivalent 10 year gilt is yielding 4.2%, the spread over the government bond is 6% - 4.2% = 1.8% or 180 basis points. This spread will vary, mainly as a result of the relative risk of the corporate bond compared to the gilt, so for a more risky corporate issuer, the spread will be greater.

Spreads are also calculated against other benchmarks, such as the published interest rates represented by LIBOR (the London Inter-Bank Offered Rate). Because the government is less likely to default on their borrowings than the major banks (that provide the LIBOR rates), the spread of instruments versus LIBOR will generally be less than the spread against government bonds. In the earlier example, if the equivalent LIBOR rate was 4.5%, the spread over LIBOR would be 6% - 4.5% = 1.5% or 150 basis points, compared to the 180 basis point spread over government bonds.

2.5 The Yield Curve

LEARNING OBJECTIVES

1.2.5 understand the role of the yield curve and the relationship between price and yield with reference to the yield curve (normal and inverted)

Introduction

In the UK government bond market, there is a range of gilts available with various periods until maturity. By plotting the gross redemption yields of these gilts on a graph, with yields on the **Y** axis and time remaining on the **X** axis, a pattern emerges. The line of best fit across these points is the **yield curve**. It shows the yields available to investors in gilts over different time horizons. The yield curve provides a useful tool for comparison - for example, if 10 year gilts yield 4%, then a 10 year corporate bond should provide a higher yield to compensate investors for the additional default risk they face.

The Normal Yield Curve

Typically, the shape of the yield curve is upward sloping to the right, as shown below:

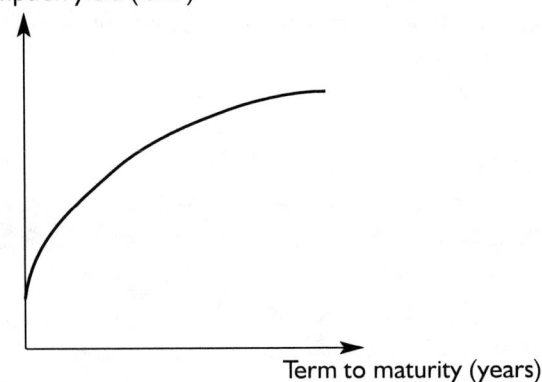

This is known as the **normal yield curve**, and its shape captures the fact that investors have a **liquidity preference**: they prefer more rather than less liquidity. As a result of this, they are willing to accept a lower yield on more liquid, short-dated gilts, and demand a higher yield on less liquid, longer-dated gilts. Given the same coupon rate, the price of a short-dated gilt will be higher than a longer-dated gilt, resulting in a higher yield for the longer-dated gilt than the equivalent shorter-dated gilt.

The Inverted Yield Curve

Occasionally, the yield curve may not exhibit its normal, upward sloping to the right shape. Instead, it might be downward sloping to the right, known as the inverted yield curve.

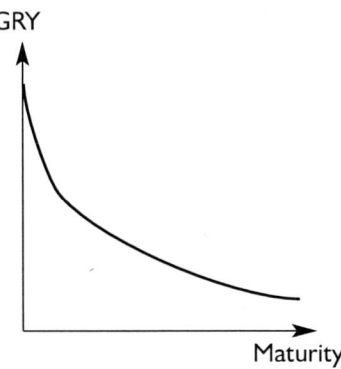

Clearly, in an inverted yield curve scenario, yields available on short-term gilts exceed those available on long-term gilts. This occurs when there is an expectation of a significant reduction in interest rates at some stage in the future. The consequence of this is that, when investing in longer-term gilts that will be outstanding when the interest rates fall, the investor is willing to accept a lower yield. For shorter-term gilts that will not be outstanding when the interest rate falls, the investor is demanding a higher yield.

The existence of an inverted yield curve does not remove any liquidity preference, but the impact of the anticipated interest rate fall outweighs the effect of the liquidity preference.

Inflation and The Yield Curve

Within the required yields on bonds is the investors' anticipation of inflation. If inflation is expected to increase, then the yields demanded by investors need to reward them for the anticipated inflation - so the yield curve would be expected to rise.

Paradoxically, when the Bank of England is concerned about inflationary pressures and increases short-term interest rates to counter the danger, the impact on medium and long-dated bonds can be that the yields fall. This is because the investors have confidence that in the medium term, inflationary pressures will be removed by the pre-emptive actions of the Bank of England Monetary Policy Committee.

2.6 The Present Value of a Bond

LEARNING OBJECTIVES

1.2.6 be able to calculate the present value of a bond (maximum 2 years) with annual coupon and interest income

Introduction

Money has a **time value**. That is, money deposited today will attract a rate of interest over the term it is invested. £100 invested today at an annual rate of interest of 5% becomes £105 in one year's time. The addition of this interest to the original sum invested acts as compensation to the depositor for forgoing £100 of consumption for one year.

The time value of money can also be illustrated by expressing the value of a sum receivable in the future in terms of its value today, again by taking account of the prevailing rate of interest. This is known as the sum's **present value**. So, £100 receivable in one year's time, given an interest rate of 5%, will be worth £100/1.05 = £95.24 today, in present value terms. This process of establishing present values is known as **discounting**, the interest rate in the calculation acting as the discount rate.

Discounting

The value today, or the present value, of a lump sum due to be received on a specified future date, can be established by discounting this amount by the prevailing rate of interest.

To arrive at the present value of a single sum, receivable after n years, when the prevailing rate of interest is r, simply multiply the lump sum by the following:

$$1/(1 + r)^n$$

Referring back to the earlier example, £100 receivable in one year's time, given an interest rate of 5%, would have a present value of:

$$£100 \times 1/(1+r)^n = £100 \times 1/1.05 = £100 \times 0.9524 = £95.24$$

If £100 were due to be received in two years' time, then the present value would be:

$$£100 \times 1/(1+r)^2 = £100 \times 0.907 = £90.70$$

The present value calculations can be used to derive the price of a bond, given the appropriate rate of interest and the cash flows.

Imagine £100 nominal of a two-year bond paying annual coupons of 10%. Given an appropriate rate of interest, the sum of the present values will provide the logical price for the bond.

Using an interest rate of 5% per annum, the following present values emerge:

Time	Cash flow	Discount factor	Present value
End of year one	£10	1/1.05	9.52
End of year two	£110	$1/1.05^2$	99.77
Sum of the individual present value = Price of the bond			£109.29

> **Exercise 3**
>
> What would be the price of the bond if interest rates were:
>
> (a) 6%?
>
> (b) 4%?
>
> The answers can be found at the end of the chapter.

3. GOVERNMENT DEBT

Introduction

Most developed countries have active markets for bonds issued by their government. For example, 'gilts' are bonds issued by the UK Government. They are issued to cover the Government's borrowing needs and the UK Treasury has created an executive agency called the Debt Management Office (DMO) to issue, service and manage gilts on its behalf.

As with other bonds, gilts are issued with a given nominal value that will be repaid at the bond's redemption date and a coupon rate representing the percentage of the nominal value that will be paid to the holder of the bond each year. Obviously different gilts can have different redemption dates and the coupon is payable at different points of the year (generally at semi-annual intervals).

> **Example**
>
> Gilts are denoted by their coupon rate and their redemption date, for example 6% Treasury Stock 2028. The coupon indicates the cash payment per £100 nominal value that the holder will receive each year. This payment is made in two equal semi-annual payments on fixed dates, six months apart. An investor holding £1,000 nominal of 6% Treasury Stock 2028 will receive two coupon payments of £30 each, on 7 June and 7 December each year, until the repayment of the £1,000 on 7 December 2028.

3.1 Classes of Government Debt

> **LEARNING OBJECTIVES**
>
> 1.3.1 know the principal features and characteristics of the following classes of Government debt: short-, medium-, long-dated; dual-dated; undated

Government debt, such as UK gilts, can be divided into three classes:

- Short-, medium- and long-dated;
- Dual-dated;
- Undated.

Short-, Medium- and Long-Dated Gilts

These are the simplest form of UK Government bonds and constitute the largest proportion of the gilts in issue. They are fixed coupon gilts with fixed redemption dates and are subdivided by the Debt Management Office into three, based on the period of time that remains until the gilt matures.

- Short - less than seven years to redemption;
- Medium - between seven and fifteen years to redemption;
- Long - over fifteen years to redemption.

For example, 6% Treasury Stock 2028 would be classified as a long-dated gilt because more than 15 years remain until it reaches its redemption date of 7 December 2028.

Dual-Dated Gilts

These gilts have two specified redemption dates and the Debt Management Office can choose to repay the gilt at any point between the two dates. The maturity classification applied to dual-dated gilts is short-, medium- or long-dated depending upon the time remaining to the later of the two dates.

> **Example**
>
> For example 5% Treasury 2020 - 2024 would enable the DMO to choose to redeem the gilt at the earliest in 2020, and at any time up to the later date of 2024. What would make the government redeem early or late?
>
> The answer is dependant upon the interest rates at the time. If in 2020 the interest rate that the DMO would have to pay to provide the funds for redemption were only 4%, then it would redeem at the earliest point - saving 1% per annum. In contrast if the interest rate were greater than 5%, the DMO would not redeem, potentially until it was forced to in 2024.

Undated Gilts

There are a small number of gilts for which the redemption is at the discretion of the government. Examples include 3.5% War Loan and 2.5% Consolidated Loan Stock (commonly referred to as 2.5% Consol's). They are some of the oldest gilts outstanding and because they all have comparatively low coupons, there is little incentive for the government to redeem them. On issue, these gilts did have a date attached to them, but it was followed by 'aft', meaning that it is the date on, or after, which the government can choose to redeem. If the government issued a gilt with a date of 2022 aft, it could choose to redeem the gilt at any stage after 2022, effectively making the gilt undated.

3.2 Interest Rates and Accrued Interest

> **LEARNING OBJECTIVES**
>
> 1.3.2 understand the following features and characteristics of Government debt: redemption price; interest payable; accrued interest; effect of changes in interest rates

As seen, government bonds such as UK gilts specify a redemption value (the nominal value of the bond) that will be repaid at the end of the bond's life and a coupon. The coupon is the amount of interest paid to the holder of the bond each year.

Gilts are quoted on the basis of the price a buyer would pay for £100 nominal value.

> **Example**
>
> For example, Treasury 6% 2028 might be trading at 108, so a buyer would have to pay £108 for each £100 nominal value. Why would the buyer be willing to pay more than £100? The answer lies in the available interest rate across the financial markets. If the interest rate available on deposited funds was lower than the coupon rate on the gilt, then that gilt would be a relatively attractive investment and its price would be pushed upwards until the return it offered was in line with other investments.

So, as interest rates across the financial markets decrease, the quoted price of gilts will increase. Conversely, if interest rates increase, the quoted price of gilts will decrease. In summary, there is an inverse relationship between gilts prices and interest rates.

Bonds' quoted prices are **clean prices**, ie, they are exclusive of interest. If a gilt is purchased between interest payments, an adjustment is made to arrive at the amount of cash required to cover the interest element as well. This is known as the accrued interest and it is the amount of interest earned by the bond's seller since the last coupon payment. The price including the accrued interest is the **dirty price**.

Accrued interest is paid to compensate the seller for the period during which the seller has held the gilt, but for which they receive no interest from the bond's issuer. Having only held the gilt for part of the interest-earning period, the seller receives a pro-rata share of the next coupon from the purchaser.

> **Example**
>
> So, if the £5,000 nominal of 6% Treasury 2028 mentioned above was sold by the original owner exactly halfway between the semi-annual coupon payments at a clean price of £126.46, the settlement would involve the following sum:
>
> Clean price: £126.46 x £5,000/£100 = £6,323
>
> Plus, accrued interest: £5,000 x 6% x 6/12 x ½ = £75
>
> Dirty price paid by the buyer to the seller = £6,398

The accrued interest in the gilts market is calculated using the **actual/actual day count convention**. In other words, the seller is compensated for the interest on the basis of the actual number of days that have elapsed since the last coupon was paid, divided by the total number of days in the actual period.

The DMO will pay the coupons to the registered holder of the gilt at each coupon payment date. However, because of the possibility of ownership changes just before the coupon payment date, there is a period prior to each coupon payment date when a gilt is dealt without entitlement to the impending coupon payment (known as the **ex-dividend** period). For most gilts this period is **seven working days** prior to the coupon payment date. For the remainder of the year the gilt is described as trading **cum-dividend**.

3.3 Index-Linked Debt

LEARNING OBJECTIVES

1.3.3 understand the following features and characteristics of index linked debt: index-linking; the retail price index and index-linking; effect of the index on price, interest and redemption; return during a period of zero inflation

Index-linked bonds (such as index-linked gilts) differ from conventional bonds in that the coupon payments and the principal are adjusted in line with a published index of price inflation, such as the UK Retail Prices Index (RPI). This means that both the coupons and the principal on redemption paid by these bonds are adjusted to take account of inflation since the bond's issue. Assuming inflation is positive, the nominal amount outstanding of an index-linked bond is less than the redemption value the government will pay on maturity.

To calculate the inflation adjustment, two index figures are required: that applicable to the stock when it was originally issued and that relating to the current interest payment. For UK gilts, the RPI figures used are those applicable eight months before the relevant dates (eg, for a December coupon, the previous April RPI data is used). This indexation lag is required so that the size of each forthcoming interest payment is known at the start of the coupon period, thereby allowing accrued interest to be calculated.

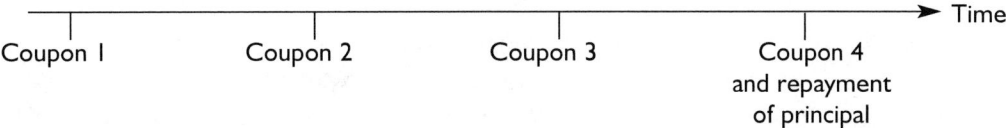

Each payment is uplifted by multiplying by:

$$\frac{\text{RPI 8 months previously}}{\text{RPI 8 months prior to issue}}$$

Every six months the coupon payment on an index-linked gilt consists of two elements:

- Half of the annual real coupon, and
- An adjustment factor to uplift the real coupon to take into account inflation (as measured by RPI increases post issue).

The uplifted redemption payment is calculated in a similar fashion, using the RPI eight months earlier and the RPI applicable to the original issue date.

> **Example**
>
> For example, 2% index linked 2035 pays semi annual coupons on 26 January and 26 June each year. An investor holding £20,000 nominal will receive 2% of £20,000 x 6/12 = £200 each half year plus the RPI uplift.
>
> At the redemption date in 2035, the investor will receive £20,000 uplifted by the RPI increases since issue.

Because these bonds are uplifted by increases in the relevant price index, they are effectively inflation proof. In times of inflation, they will increase in price and preserve the purchasing power of the investment.

In a period of zero inflation, index linked bonds will pay the coupon rate with no uplift and simply pay back the nominal value at maturity.

3.4 Treasury Bills

> **LEARNING OBJECTIVES**
>
> 1.3.4 understand the features and characteristics of Treasury bills: issuer; purpose of issue; minimum denomination; normal life; no coupon and redemption at par; redemption

Introduction

As well as issuing bonds to fund the government's long-term borrowing needs, developed countries also manage the liquidity needs of the government. This is done primarily through issuing short-term IOUs known as 'Treasury bills'.

Definition, Uses and Principal Features

Treasury bills (T-bills) are short-term loan instruments, guaranteed by the government, with a maturity date of less than one year at issue. Generally, they are issued with either one month (28 days), three months (91 days) or six months (182 days) to redemption, with the three month T-bill the most common. They pay no coupon, and consequently are issued at a discount to their nominal value, the discount representing the return available to the investor.

For example, UK Treasury bills are issued at weekly auctions, known as 'tenders', held by the DMO at the end of the week (usually a Friday). These tenders are open to bids from a group of eligible bidders which include all of the major banks. The bids are tendered competitively - only those bidding a high enough price will be allocated any Treasury bills and they will pay the price that they bid. The bids must be for a minimum of £500,000 nominal of the Treasury bills, and above this level bids must be made in multiples of £50,000. In subsequent trading, the minimum denomination of T-bills is £25,000.

Since they are guaranteed by the government, Treasury bills provide a very secure investment for market participants with short-term investment horizons. The return on a Treasury bill is wholly dependant upon the price paid.

> **Example**
>
> For example if a purchaser paid £990,000 for £1,000,000 nominal of a three month Treasury bill, the return will be the gain made of £10,000. As a percentage of invested funds the return is:
>
> £10,000/£990,000 x 100 = 1.01% over three months

3.5 International Government Bonds

LEARNING OBJECTIVES

1.3.5 know the features and characteristics of international bonds: settlement periods; coupons; terms and maturities

The following table highlights the way government bonds are referred to and classified across the major economies of the world, and the settlement period for any market transactions that might take place after the bonds were issued.

Country	Name	Coupon Frequency	Maturity	Settlement Period
United States	Treasury bonds (T-bonds)	semi-annual	over 10 years	T+1
	Treasury notes (T-notes)	semi-annual	2 to 10 years	T+1
	Treasury bills (T-bills)	no coupon paid	Less than 1 year	Trade date
France	OAT	annual	7 to 30 years	T+3
	BTAN	annual	2 to 5 years	
Germany	Bund	annual	over 10 years	T+3
	Bobl	annual	5 years	
	Schatze	annual	up to 2 years	
Japan	Japanese Government Bond (JGB)	semi-annual	long (10 years, most common), super long (20 years)	T+3

4. CORPORATE DEBT

4.1 Secured Debt

LEARNING OBJECTIVES

1.4.1 know the principal features and uses of secured debt: fixed charges and floating charges; asset-backed securities; mortgage-backed securities

Investors in corporate debt face the risk that the issuer will not be able to pay the interest and/or the principal amount. If this were to happen, it is known as default. One way for the corporate borrower to lessen the risk of default is to issue secured debt, where the debt offers the company's assets as a guarantee. There are two ways of doing this:

- **fixed charge** - the debt carries a fixed charge over a particular company asset, eg, a building;
- **floating charge** - the debt is secured against a group of the company's assets. In the event of default, a floating charge crystallises over the available assets.

Bonds issued with a fixed charge are generally referred to as 'debentures'.

Asset-Backed Securities

Asset-backed securities are bonds that are backed by a particular pool of assets. These assets can take several forms, such as mortgage loans, credit card receivables and car loans. The rock star David Bowie issued asset backed securities on the future royalties that would be generated from his music.

The assets provide the bondholders' security, since the cash generated from them is used to service the bonds (pay the interest), and to repay the principal sum at maturity. Such arrangements are often referred to as the **securitisation** of assets.

Diagrammatically:

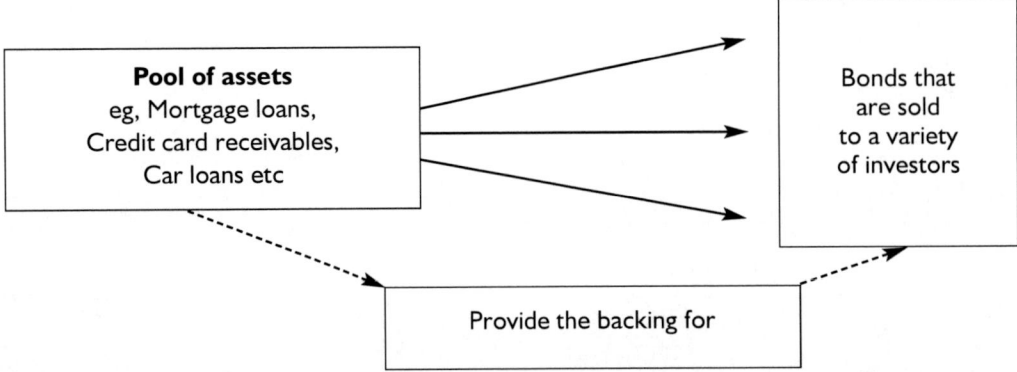

Mortgage-Backed Securities

Mortgage-backed securities are one example of asset backed securities. They are created from mortgage loans made by financial institutions like banks and building societies. Mortgage-backed securities are bonds that are created when a group of mortgage loans are packaged (or pooled) for sale to investors. As the underlying mortgage loans are paid off by the homeowners, the investors receive payments of interest and principal.

The mortgage-backed securities market began in the US, where the majority of issues are made by (or guaranteed by) an agency of the US Government. The Government National Mortgage Association (commonly referred to as 'Ginnie Mae'), the Federal National Mortgage Association ('Fannie Mae') and the Federal Home Loan Mortgage Corporation ('Freddie Mac') are the major issuers. These agencies buy qualifying mortgage loans, or guarantee pools of such loans originated by financial institutions, securitise the loans and issue bonds. Some private institutions, such as financial institutions and house builders, issue their own mortgage-backed securities.

As with other asset backed securities, mortgage-backed securities issues are often sub-divided into a variety of classes (or 'tranches'), each tranche having a particular priority in relation to interest and principal payments. Typically, as the underlying payments on the mortgage loans are collected, the interest on all tranches of the bonds is paid first. As loans are repaid, the principal is first paid back to the first tranche of bondholders, then the second tranche, third tranche etc. Such arrangements will create different risk profiles and repayment schedules for each tranche, enabling the appropriate securities to be held according to the needs of the investor. Traditionally, the investors in such securities have been institutional investors, like insurance companies and pension funds, although some are attracting the more sophisticated individual investor.

Further Details in relation to Asset-Backed Securities

As mentioned above, the investors in asset-backed securities have recourse to the pool of assets, although there may be an order of priority between investors in different tranches of the issue.

The precise payment dates for interest and principal will be dependant on the anticipated and actual payment stream generated by the underlying assets and the needs of investors. Asset-backed securities based on a pool of mortgage loans are likely to be longer dated than those based on a pool of credit card receivables. Within these constraints, the issuers of asset backed securities do create a variety of tranches to appeal to the differing maturity and risk appetites of investors.

Many asset-backed securities utilise a 'special purpose vehicle' (or SPV) in order to lessen the default risk that investors face when investing in the securities. This SPV is often a trust, and the originator of the assets, such as the bank granting the mortgage loans, sells the loans to the SPV and the SPV issues the asset backed bonds. This serves two purposes:

1. The SPV is a separate entity from the originator of the assets, so the assets leave the originator's financial statements to be replaced by the cash from the SPV. This is often described as an 'off balance sheet' arrangement because the assets have left the originator's balance sheet.

2. The SPV is a standalone entity, so if the originator of the assets were to suffer bankruptcy, the SPV would still remain intact with the pool of assets available to service the bonds. This is often described as 'bankruptcy remote' and enhances the credit worthiness of asset backed securities, potentially giving them a higher rating than the originator of the assets.

Diagrammatically:

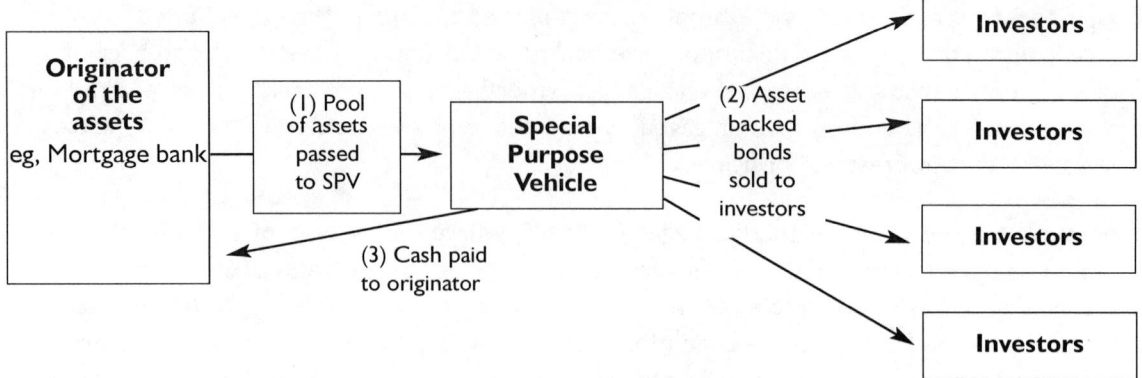

4.2 Unsecured Debt

LEARNING OBJECTIVES

1.4.2 understand the principal features and uses of unsecured debt: subordinated; guaranteed; convertible bonds

Unsecured debt is not secured against any of the company's assets, so the holder has no special protection against default. To compensate the holder for the additional risk, the coupon on an unsecured bond, or the interest on unsecured bank borrowing, will be higher than on equivalent secured borrowings.

Subordinated debt is not secured and the lenders have agreed that, if the company fails, they will only be reimbursed when other creditors have been paid back, and then only if there is enough money left over. Interest payments on subordinated borrowings will be higher than those on equivalent unsecured borrowings that are not subordinated. This is simply because of the additional default risk faced by subordinated lenders.

Guaranteed debt is where a guarantee is provided by someone other than the issuer. The guarantor is typically the parent company, or another company in the same group of companies as the issuer.

As seen earlier, convertible bonds give the holder of the bond the right, but not the obligation, to convert into a predetermined number of ordinary shares of the issuer.

The following table summarises the characteristics of subordinated, guaranteed and convertible bonds as compared to an unsecured bond issued by the same company:

	Subordinated bond	**Guaranteed bond**	**Convertible bond**
Normal life	No difference: Typically 7 to 30 years to maturity		
Ranking in a liquidation	Below unsecured bonds	Alongside other unsecured bonds	Alongside other unsecured bonds
Risk and rating	Greater risk of default, so a lower credit rating	Little risk of default due to the guarantee, so a higher credit rating	No difference to unsecured bonds
Coupon	Likely to be higher than unsecured bonds	Likely to be lower due to the guarantee	Potentially lower due to the upside potential of the share price
Benefits to the issuer	Attractive regulatory treatment for financial institution issuers	Guarantor is lowering the cost of the debt finance	Upside potential of the shares restricts the cost of the debt and the possibility of conversion removes the need to principal repayment

Fixed coupon bonds are issued with a fixed rate of coupon. If interest rates rise, the fixed coupon becomes less attractive and the price of the bond falls. The opposite is true of an interest rate fall. As for government bonds, the interest is always calculated by reference to the nominal value of the bond, so a £1,000 nominal 5% ABC corporate bond will pay £50 per annum to the holder.

Floating rate bonds are bonds where the coupon rate varies. The rate is adjusted in line with published, market interest rates. The published interest rates that are normally used are based on London Inter-Bank Offered Rates (LIBOR). LIBORs are the average rates at which banks in London offer loans to other banks. The British Bankers' Association (BBA) publishes LIBORs for different currencies and time periods each day. Typically, a margin is added to the LIBOR rate, measured in basis points, each basis point representing one hundredth of one percent. A corporate issuer may offer floating rate bonds to investors at 3-month sterling LIBOR plus 75 basis points. If LIBOR were at 4%, then the coupon paid would be 4.75%, with the additional 75 basis points compensating the investor for the additional risk of the company collapsing.

4.3 Credit Ratings

LEARNING OBJECTIVES

1.4.3 understand the principal features and uses of credit ratings: rating agencies; impact on price; use of credit enhancements; difference between investment grade and sub-investment grade bonds

Bondholders face the risk that the issuer of the bond might default on their obligation to pay interest and the principal amount at redemption. This so-called 'credit risk' - the probability of an issuer defaulting on their payment obligations and the extent of the resulting loss - can be assessed by reference to the independent credit ratings given to most bond issues.

The three most prominent credit rating agencies that provide these ratings are Standard & Poor's, Moody's and Fitch. Bond issues subject to credit ratings can be divided into two distinct categories: those accorded an investment grade rating and those categorised as non-investment grade or speculative. The latter are also known as 'high-yield' or 'junk' bonds. Investment grade issues offer the greatest liquidity. The table below provides an abridged version of the credit ratings available from the three agencies.

Although the three rating agencies use similar methods to rate issuers and individual bond issues, essentially by assessing whether the cash flow likely to be generated by the borrower will comfortably service, and ultimately repay its debts, the rating each gives often differs, though not usually significantly so.

	Standard & Poor's	Moody's	Fitch
Investment Grade	AAA to BBB	AAA to BAA3	AAA to BBB
Non-Investment Grade	BB+ to C	BA1 to C	BB+ to C
Already In Default	D	-	DDD to D

Occasionally, issues such as asset-backed securities are credit enhanced in some way to gain a higher credit rating. The simplest method of achieving this would be through some form of insurance scheme that will pay out should the pool of assets be insufficient to service or repay the debt.

4.4 Commercial Paper

LEARNING OBJECTIVES

1.4.4   know the principal features and uses of Commercial Paper: issuers; investors; discount security; unsecured; rating; normal life

Zero coupon bonds pay no interest. Instead, they promise to pay just the nominal value at redemption. Because there is no other possible form of return, investors will pay less than the nominal value when they buy zero coupon bonds, with their return coming in the form of the difference between the price they pay for the bond and the amount they receive when the bond is redeemed. The bond is said to be issued at a **discount** to its face value, with the discount providing all of the return on a zero coupon bond.

Discount securities, such as zero coupon bonds, are attractive investments for an investor looking for a fixed sum at some set date in the future. Because the investor is looking for a set, single sum, he does not want to worry about reinvesting regular interest payments.

Commercial paper is a money market instrument, issued by a company. The money market is the term for the market involving cash deposits and short-term instruments that are issued with less than one year to their maturity. Commercial paper is the corporate equivalent of a government's treasury bill. It is typically zero coupon, issued at a discount to nominal value, offers no security and has a life of around three months.

Large companies issue commercial paper to assist in the management of their liquidity. Rather than borrowing directly from banks, these large entities run commercial paper programmes that are placed with institutional investors.

The various companies' commercial paper is differentiated by credit ratings - where the large credit rating agencies like Standard and Poor's and Moody's assess the stability of the issuer.

5. EUROBONDS

5.1 Principal Features and Uses

> **LEARNING OBJECTIVES**
>
> 1.5.1 understand the principal features and uses of Eurobonds: issued through syndicates of international banks; concept of continuous pure bearer; immobilised in depositories; ex-interest date; accrued interest; interest payments

Essentially, eurobonds are international bond issues. They are a way for an organisation to issue debt without being restricted to their own domestic market. They are generally issued via a syndicate of international banks. Generally, eurobond issuers do not keep a record of the holders of their bonds; the certificates themselves are all that is needed to prove ownership. This is the concept of bearer documents, where the holder of the certificates (the bearer) has all the rights attached to ownership. Eurobonds are issued in bearer form and, because they are issued internationally, they are largely free of national regulation. Eurobonds have been innovative in their structure to accommodate the needs of issuers and investors. There are 'plain vanilla', fixed coupon bonds that normally pay the coupons once a year. Additionally, there are zero-coupon bonds and other forms of eurobond such as floating rate bonds and bonds with coupons that increase over time ('stepped bonds').

An absence of national regulation means that eurobonds can pay interest gross, making the buyer responsible for paying their own tax and avoiding 'withholding tax' (tax being withheld in the country of origin). Initially, eurobonds were aimed at wealthy individuals, but as the market has grown they have increasingly become investments held by institutional investors.

As bearer documents, it is important that eurobonds are kept safe, and this is often achieved by holding the bonds in depositaries, particularly those maintained by Euroclear and Clearstream. When the bonds are deposited in these organisations they are described as being 'immobilised'. Immobilisation does not mean that the bonds cannot be transferred in secondary market transactions, it simply means that the bonds are safely held within a reputable depositary and a buyer is likely to retain the bonds in their immobilised form.

As the eurobond market has grown, a self-regulatory organisation has been formed that oversees the market and its participants - the International Capital Market Association (ICMA).

Settlement and accrued interest conventions have been established for the secondary market. Settlement is on a 'T+3' basis and accrued interest is calculated on the basis of 30 days per month and 360 days per year ('30/360' basis).

The following table highlights the major features of eurobonds:

Feature	Detail
Form:	Bearer
Interest payments:	Gross
Tax:	Taxable but untaxed at source
Trades matched through:	TRAX system
Trades settled through:	Euroclear or Clearstream
Settlement period:	Trade day plus three
Trading mechanism:	Over-the-counter (OTC)

6. OTHER SECURITIES

6.1 Depositary Receipts

> **LEARNING OBJECTIVES**
>
> 1.6.1 know the principal features and characteristics of Depositary Receipts: American Depositary Receipts; Global Depositary Receipts; transferability; means of creation including pre-release facility; how registered; rights attached; dividends; transfer to underlying shares

Depositary Receipts (DRs) come in two broad forms – American Depositary Receipts (ADRs) and Global Depositary Receipts (GDRs).

The United States is a huge pool of potential investment. Therefore, substantial non-US companies may want to attract US investors to raise funds. American Depositary Receipts (also known as ADRs) facilitate this process, indeed they were created to make it easier for Americans to invest in overseas companies. Global Depositary Receipts (GDRs) are depositary receipts that are identical to ADRs, except that they are marketed to appeal to a broader base of investors, some of whom may be based outside of America. Both ADRs and GDRs are negotiable certificates evidencing ownership of shares in a corporation from a country outside of the USA. Each DR has a particular number of underlying shares, or is represented by a fraction of an underlying share. This can be illustrated by the following example:

> **Example**
>
> Volkswagen AG (the motor vehicle manufacturer) is listed in Frankfurt. It has two classes of shares listed - ordinary shares and preference shares. There are separate ADRs in existence for the ordinary shares and preference shares. Each ADR represents 0.2 individual Volkswagen shares.

DRs are typically created (or 'sponsored') by the foreign corporation (Volkswagen in the above example). They will liaise with an investment bank regarding the precise structure of the DR, such as the number or fraction of shares represented by each DR. A 'depositary' bank will then accept a certain number of underlying shares from the issuer, create the DRs to represent the shares and make these DRs available to US, and potentially other, investors, probably via local brokers. This creation process for an ADR is illustrated by the following diagram:

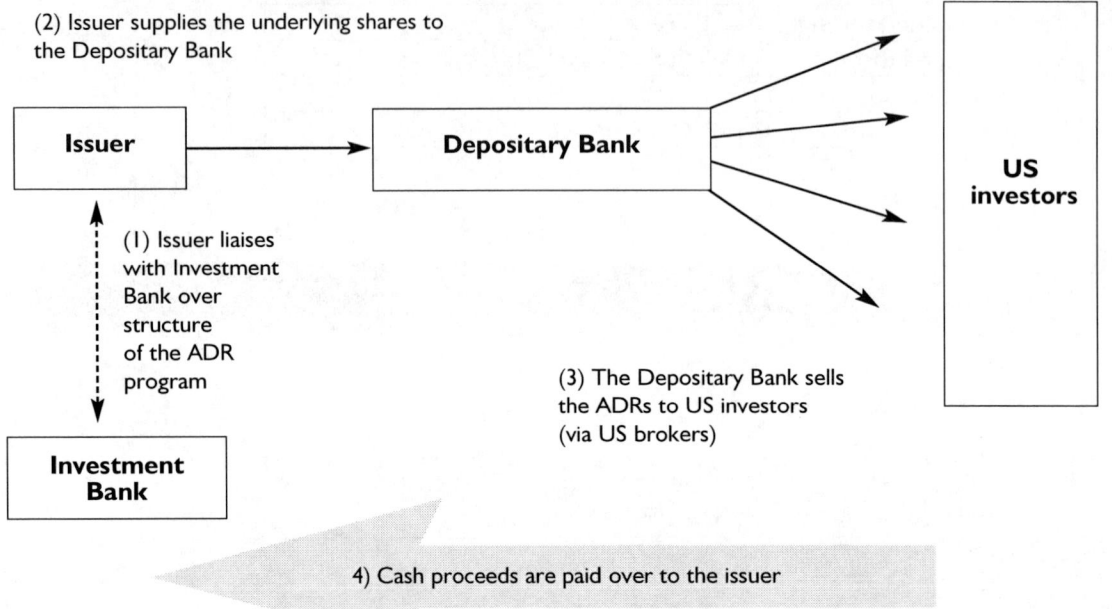

One characteristic of DRs that must also be considered is **pre-release trading** (or **grey** market trading).

When an DR is being created, the depositary bank receives notification that, in the future, the shares will be placed on deposit. As long as the depositary bank holds cash collateral, even though the shares are not yet on deposit, the depositary bank can create and sell the receipt (the DR) at this time. Effectively, investors are buying a receipt that entitles them to all the benefits of a share that will, in the future, be held on deposit for them.

The DR can be treated in this way for up to three months before the actual purchase of the underlying shares.

The shares underlying the DR are registered in the name of the depositary bank, with the DRs themselves transferable as bearer securities. The DRs are typically quoted and traded in US dollars and are governed by the trading and settlement procedures of the market on which they are traded.

The **depositary bank** acts as a go-between for the investor and the company. When the company pays a dividend, it is paid in the company's domestic currency to the bank, which then converts the dividend into **dollars** and passes it on to the DR holders. The US investor need not concern himself with currency movements. Furthermore, when an DR holder decides to sell, his DRs will be sold on in dollars. This removal of the need for any currency transactions for the US investor is a key attraction of the DR.

DR holders are **entitled to vote**, just like ordinary shareholders, except that the votes will be exercised via the depositary bank.

If the DR represented a UK company's shares, there are tax ramifications in the form of **stamp duty**. The UK tax authority, Her Majesty's Revenue & Customs (HMRC, formerly the Inland Revenue) levies a tax known as stamp duty on share purchases, at 0.5% of the price paid to purchase shares.

However, because DRs may trade outside the UK, in the US, there is n**o stamp duty charged on the purchase** of an DR. Instead, HMRC charges a one-off fee for **stamp duty of 1.5%, when the DR is created**.

If an investor wanted to sell his DRs, he could do so either by selling them to another investor as a DR, or by selling the underlying shares in the home market of the company concerned. The latter route would involve cancelling the DR by delivering the certificates to the depositary bank. The depositary bank would then release the appropriate number of shares in accordance with the instructions received.

6.2 Warrants

> **LEARNING OBJECTIVES**
>
> 1.6.2 know the rights, uses and differences between warrants and covered warrants: what are warrants; what are covered warrants; benefit to the issuing company and purpose; issue by a third party; right to subscribe for capital; affect on price of maturity and the underlying security; detachability; exercise and expiry; the calculation of the conversion premium(discount) on a warrant (warrant price + exercise priceminus the share price)

Traditionally, a warrant is an instrument issued by a company that allows the holder to subscribe for shares in that company at a fixed price over a fixed period. A typical warrant might have a life of several years.

Warrants are listed and traded on stock exchanges. If the holder decides to exercise, the company will issue new shares.

> **Example**
>
> Warrants are available in a (fictional) investment company, Cambridge Investment Trust plc. Cambridge Investment Trust plc shares are currently trading at 77 pence each, and warrants are available giving the investor the right to buy shares at £1 each, up until 2010. The warrants are trading at 4p each.

In the above example, the warrants 'expiry' date is in 2010 and its 'exercise price' is 100p.

What are the advantages to the company, such as the fictional Cambridge Investment Trust plc encountered above, that persuade them to issue warrants? Clearly, the sale of warrants for cash will raise money for the company, and if the warrants are exercised, then further capital will be raised by the company. Similarly to call options, holding the warrant does not entitle the investor to receive dividends or to vote at company meetings, so the capital raised until the warrant is exercised could be considered as free.

Obviously warrants offer a highly geared investment opportunity for the investor, and warrants are often issued alongside other investments, rather than sold in their own right.

> **Example**
>
> For example, CBC plc is attempting to raise finance by issuing bonds. Their advisors inform them that they could issue bonds paying a coupon of 6% pa, or lower it to 5% pa if they give away a single warrant with each £100 nominal of the bonds. The warrants are detachable from the bonds - in other words the investors could decide to sell their warrants or keep them, regardless of whether they retain the bonds.

Covered Warrants

Another type of warrant is a **covered warrant**. These are warrants issued by firms (usually investment banks), rather than the company whose shares the warrant enables the investor to buy. They are offered in the form of call warrants (giving the investor the right to buy), or put warrants (giving the investor the right to sell). In the UK, covered warrants are traded on the London Stock Exchange.

Warrant Price Behaviour

Warrants (including covered warrants) are highly geared investments. A modest outlay can result in a large gain, but the investor can lose everything. Their value is driven by the length of time for which they are valid (their 'maturity' or period until expiry) and the value of the underlying security.

There is a relatively simple method of looking at the price of one warrant relative to other warrants – using the **conversion premium**. The conversion premium is the price of the warrant plus the exercise price required to buy the underlying share less the prevailing share price.

For example, calculating the conversion premium for the Cambridge Investment Trust encountered above:

Warrant price	= 4p
Plus exercise price	= 100p
Less share price	= 77p
Conversion premium	= 27p

Note that if the resultant figure was a negative, the warrant would be trading at a 'conversion discount'.

7. FOREIGN EXCHANGE

7.1 Introduction

> **LEARNING OBJECTIVES**
>
> **1.7.1** know the principal features and uses of spot, forward and cross rates: quotation as bid-offer spreads; forwards quoted as bid-offer margins against the spot; quotation of cross rates

The foreign exchange market (or 'forex' or 'FX') is the collective way of describing all the transactions in which one currency is exchanged for another, anywhere in the world. There is no physical exchange for the currency market in London, it is purely **over-the-counter (OTC)** and dominated by the banks.

There are two types of transaction conducted on the foreign exchange market:

- **spot transactions** are immediate currency deals that are settled within two working days;
- **forward transactions** involve currency deals that are agreed for a future date at a rate of exchange fixed now.

As we will see in the next section, both spot and forward rates are quoted by dealers in the form of a buying rate (the bid) and a selling rate (the offer). The spread between these two prices enables the foreign exchange dealer to make a profit.

The users of the foreign exchange market fall into two broad camps.

First, the foreign exchange transactions driven by international trade. If a Japanese company sells goods to a US customer, they might invoice the transaction in US dollars. These dollars will need to be exchanged for Japanese yen by the Japanese company and this is the foreign exchange transaction. The Japanese company may not be expecting to receive the dollars for a month after submission of the invoice. This gives them two choices:

i. They could wait until they receive the dollars and then execute a 'spot' transaction

ii. They could enter into a forward transaction to sell the dollars for yen in a month's time. This would provide them with certainty as to the number of yen they will receive and assist in their budgeting efforts.

The second reason for foreign exchange transactions is for speculative transactions. If an investor felt that the US dollar was likely to weaken against the euro, he could buy euros in either the spot or forward market to profit if he is right.

Generally, exchange rates around the world are quoted against the US dollar. A **cross rate** is any foreign currency rate that does not include the US dollar. For example, the GBP/JPY (Great Britain pound/Japanese yen) is a cross rate. Obviously such a cross rate will be of particular interest to companies doing international business between the constituent countries, for example, a UK company selling goods or services to Japanese consumers, and receiving payment in yen.

7.2 Spot and Forward Transactions

LEARNING OBJECTIVES
1.7.2 be able to calculate spot and forward settlement prices

A typical sterling/dollar spot quote might look something like this:

GBP\USD spot rate 1.8055 - 1.8145

Buyer's rate: £1 buys $1.8055

Seller's rate: $1.8145 buys £1

The buyer's rate and seller's rate refer to buying and selling dollars respectively. The difference between the buyer's and seller's rates is generally referred to as the bid-offer spread. It enables the bank offering the deals to make money.

How much would an investor expect to get if the above spot rate is applied? If the investor wanted to sell $50,000 for pounds sterling, he would get £27,556. This is based on the sellers rate of $1.8145:£1.

Exercise 4

Using the same spot rates as above:

i. How much would Mr A receive in £s for $100,000?

ii. How much would Mr X receive in $s for £70,000?

The answers can be found at the end of the chapter.

The forward market is almost exactly the same as the spot market, except that currency deals are agreed for a future date, but at a rate of exchange fixed now. These rates of exchange are not directly quoted. Instead, quotes on the forward market state how much must be added to, or subtracted from, the present spot rate.

For example, the three month GBP/USD quote might be as follows:

spot $1.8055 - $1.8145

three months'   forward 1.00 - 0.97c pm

pm stands for **premium**. It is used when the dollar is going to be more expensive relative to £ sterling in the future. It is deducted from the quoted spot rate in order to arrive at the forward rate. So your £1 will buy fewer dollars in three months' time and if you have dollars in three months' time, the bank will sell you more £ sterling per dollar than they will now. The premium is quoted in cents, unlike the spot rate, which is quoted in dollars. So 1.00 pm is a premium of 1 cent or 0.01 dollars. And 0.97 pm is a premium of 0.97 cents or 0.0097 dollars.

Certificate in Securities and Financial Derivatives - Part 1

The three month forward quote is, therefore:

three month forward $1.7955 - $1.8048

Alternatively the three month forward rate might exhibit a discount, rather than a premium, for example:

spot   1.8055 - 1.8145

three months forward   0.79 - 0.82c dis

dis stands for **discount**. The discount is used when the dollar is going to be cheaper relative to £ sterling in the future. It needs to be added to the quoted spot rate to arrive at the forward rate. £1 will buy more dollars in three months' time and if you have dollars in three months' time, the bank will sell you less £ sterling per dollar than they will now. The three month forward quote is therefore:

three month forward $1.8134 - $1.8227

Exercise 5

i. Using the same spot rate of $1.8055 - $1.8145, what would the one year forward rate be given the following:

One year forward   3.98 - 3.85c pm

ii. How many dollars would an investor receive in a year's time, if he were to agree to sell £1m in a one year forward transaction?

The answers can be found at the end of the chapter.

Interest Rate Parity

The quoted forward rate premium or discount is not a random view of where the market thinks the exchange rate will be in the future. It is driven by its relationship with interest rates available for deposits and borrowings in the respective currencies. If the so-called 'interest rate parity' relationship does not hold, then there is a potential for arbitrageurs to exploit the forward rates to make guaranteed profits. This is best illustrated by looking at a simple example:

Example

The spot rate between US dollars and £ sterling is currently £1 equivalent to $1.80 (ignoring the bid-offer spread). The annual interest rate available for borrowing or depositing cash is 2% in the US and 4.5% in the UK. What is the one year forward rate?

The forward rate should be based on the spot rate ($1.80 = £1), adjusted for the interest rates.

$1.80 now attracts interest at 2% pa, so in a year it will become $1.80 x 1.02 = $1.836.

£1 now attracts interest at 4.5% pa, so in a year it will become £1.00 x 1.045 = £1.045.

The forward rate should be based on $1.836 being equivalent to £1.045, or 1.836/1.045 = $1.757 per £1.

If the forward rate were not at this level, then arbitrageurs could exploit the inequality between spot, interest rates and forward rates.

8. PRIME BROKERAGE AND EQUITY FINANCE

8.1 Prime Broker services

LEARNING OBJECTIVES

1.8.1 know the main services provided by an equity and fixed income prime broker, including: securities lending and borrowing; leverage trade execution; cash management; core settlement; custody

'Prime brokerage' is the term given to a collection of services provided by investment banks to their hedge fund clients. Hedge funds are investment funds that are typically only open to a limited range of investors. They tend to follow complex investment strategies, often involving derivatives. However, amongst the more straightforward strategies adopted is the equity long/short strategy. This involves taking both long positions in equities (in other words buying shares) and, at the same time, committing to sell equities that are not held by the fund (described as selling short). The hope is that the gain in one half of the strategy (the long or the short) will more than cover the loss on the other half of the strategy (the short or the long). Selling short inevitably means that the fund will need to 'borrow' the securities it has sold until the position is unwound.

The typical services that are provided by a prime broker include the following:

1. **Securities lending and borrowing:** for example, to cover short positions in a long/short strategy.
2. **Leveraged trade execution:** in other words undertaking trades on the fund's behalf that are partly financed by borrowed funds.
3. **Cash management:** maximising the return that is generated from cash held by the fund.
4. **Core settlement:** taking the necessary steps to make sure that any securities purchased become the property of the fund, and the appropriate cash is received for any sales made of the fund's securities in a timely manner.
5. **Custody:** keeping the securities held by the fund safe, and processing any corporate actions promptly and in accordance with the fund's wishes.

8.2 Sources of Equity Finance

> **LEARNING OBJECTIVES**
>
> 1.8.2 know the use of the main sources of equity financing: stock borrowing and lending; repurchase agreements; collaterised borrowing; rehypothecation (tri-party repos); synthetic financing

In order to finance and create positions in equity required by their hedge fund clients, prime brokers have a number of possibilities:

1. **Stock borrowing and lending.** Prime brokers can arrange the appropriate shares to be borrowed to cover the hedge fund's short positions and also use the fund's long positions to lend to others and provide additional returns to the fund as a result.

2. **Repurchase agreements.** Repurchase agreements (or repo) are essentially where the prime broker arranges the sale of securities owned by the fund for cash, whilst agreeing to buy back the equivalent securities later for a slightly inflated price. The increase in price is effectively the borrowing cost of the cash, and is often referred to as the 'repo rate'.

3. **Collateralised borrowing.** Prime brokers advance cash to the customer against the security of a first fixed charge over the customer's portfolio. In the event of the customer's default, this gives the prime broker a right of recourse against the charged assets for the amounts owing to it. The availability of the portfolio as collateral in this way should enable the bank to provide loans at more competitive rates than would be the case with an unsecured loan.

4. **Rehypothecation.** In addition to holding collateral and having a charge over the fund's portfolio, the prime broker might also require a right to re-charge, dispose of or otherwise use the customer's assets which are subject to the security, including disposing of them to a third party. This is commonly described as a 'right of rehypothecation'. When assets have been rehypothecated, the assets become the property of the prime broker as and when the prime broker uses them in this way, for instance by depositing rehypothecated securities with a third-party financier to obtain cheaper funding, or by lending the securities to another client.

5. **Synthetic financing.** This is where the prime broker will create exposure to particular securities by using derivatives, like swaps, rather than directly buying and holding the securities themselves. This route is generally substantially cheaper than outright purchases.

EXERCISE ANSWERS

Answers to Exercise 1

(i) Calculate the flat yield on a 4% gilt, redeeming in 8 years and priced at £98.90

$$(4/98.90) \times 100 = 4.04\%.$$

(ii) Calculate the flat yield on a 7% gilt, redeeming in 3 years and priced at £108.60

$$(7/108.60) \times 100 = 6.45\%$$

Answers to Exercise 2

The share value of the conversion choice is currently 15 x £6.40 = £96

The bond is trading at £110, so the premium is £14 per £100 nominal value.

Expressed as a percentage 14/96 x 100 = 14.6%

Answers to Exercise 3

(a)

Time	Cash flow	Discount factor	Present value
End of year one	£10	1/1.06	9.43
End of year two	£110	$1/1.06^2$	97.90
Sum of the individual present value = Price of the bond			£107.33

(b)

Time	Cash flow	Discount factor	Present value
End of year one	£10	1/1.04	9.62
End of year two	£110	$1/1.04^2$	101.70
Sum of the individual present value = Price of the bond			£111.32

Answers to Exercise 4

Using the spot rate $1.8055 - $1.8145:

(i) How much would Mr A receive in £s for $100,000?

Using the seller's rate of $1.8145, Mr A would receive: 100,000/1.8145 = £55,111.60

(ii) How much would Mr X receive in $s for £70,000

Using the buyer's rate of $1.8055, Mr X would receive 70,000 x 1.8055 = $126,385

Answers to Exercise 5

(i) Spot rate $1.8055 - $1.8145

One year forward 3.98 - 3.85c pm

One year forward rate $1.7657 - $1.7760

(ii) How many dollars would an investor receive in a year's time, if he were to agree to sell £1m in a one year forward transaction?

Using the buyer's rate = $1.7657 x £1m = $1,765,700

NEW ISSUES

1.	THE PRIMARY AND SECONDARY MARKETS	47
2.	STOCK EXCHANGES	48
3.	LONDON STOCK EXCHANGE	51
4.	AIM LISTING	53
5.	LISTING SECURITIES	55
6.	BOND OFFERINGS	68
7.	SECONDARY ISSUES AND BUYBACKS	74
8.	ROLE AND RESPONSIBILITY OF MARKET MAKERS FOR NEW ISSUES	75

This syllabus area will provide approximately 18 of the 100 examination questions

1. THE PRIMARY AND SECONDARY MARKETS

1.1 Primary versus Secondary

LEARNING OBJECTIVES

2.1.1 know the principal characteristics of, and the differences between, the primary and secondary markets. In particular: the role of the listing authority; users of the primary market and why; users of the secondary market and why

Stock exchanges, like the London Stock Exchange in the UK and NYSE Euronext in the US, are simply organised marketplaces for issuing securities and then trading those securities via their members. All stock exchanges provide both a primary and a secondary market.

1. The **primary** market, or the new issues market, is where securities are issued for the first time. The primary markets exist to enable issuers of securities, such as companies, to raise capital and enable the surplus funds held by potential investors to be matched with investment opportunities the issuers offer. It is a crucial source of funding. The terminology often used is that companies 'float' on the Stock Exchange when they first access the primary market. The process that the companies go through when they float is often called the 'initial public offering' (or IPO). As we will see later in this chapter, companies can use a variety of ways to achieve flotation, such as offers for investors to subscribe for their shares (offers for subscription).

2. The **secondary** market is where existing securities are traded between investors, and the stock exchanges provide a variety of systems to assist in this, such as the London Stock Exchange's SETS system that is used to trade the largest companies' shares. These systems provide investors with liquidity, giving them the ability to sell their securities if they wish. The secondary market activity also results in the ongoing provision of buy and sell prices to investors via the exchange's member firms.

Each jurisdiction has its own rules and regulations for companies seeking a listing, and continuing obligations for those already listed. For example, in the UK, there is the **United Kingdom Listing Authority (UKLA)** which is a division of the Financial Services Authority (FSA). The formal description of the UKLA is that it is **the competent authority for listing** - making the decisions as to which companies' shares and bonds (including gilts) can be admitted to be traded on the London Stock Exchange (LSE). The rules are contained in a rulebook called the **Listing Rules**, often referred to as the purple book because it has a purple cover.

It is the UKLA that sets the rules relating to becoming listed on the LSE, including the implementation of any relevant EU directives. The LSE is responsible for the operation of the exchange, including the trading of the securities on the secondary market, although the UKLA can suspend the listing of particular securities and, therefore, remove their secondary market trading activity on the Exchange.

In a similar way in the US, the Securities and Exchange Commission (SEC) requires companies seeking a listing on the US exchanges (such as NYSE Euronext and NASDAQ) to register certain details with the SEC first. Once listed, companies are then required to file regular reports with the SEC, particularly in relation to their trading performance and financial situation.

2. STOCK EXCHANGES

2.1 Purpose and Role

> **LEARNING OBJECTIVES**
>
> 2.2.1 know the purpose, role and main features of the major stock exchanges
>
> (see the syllabus learning map at the back of the book for the full learning objective)

As seen above, stock exchanges provide trading systems to enable listed securities to be bought and sold in the secondary market. Primarily these exchanges provide liquidity to existing and potential investors, enabling existing investors to sell their securities and allowing potential investors to become actual investors by purchasing securities. Furthermore, because these exchanges concentrate trading activity on their systems, the prices at which trades are done is the 'market price' at any given time. This is described as the 'price formation' process.

Stock exchanges offer membership to investment banks and firms of stockbrokers. Becoming a member of an exchange enables these banks and stockbrokers to be involved in secondary market trades. This involvement will be in one of two ways:

1. As broker. Brokers simply arrange deals for their clients, as well as potentially giving advice to their clients as to which securities they should buy, sell or retain. In return for arranging (and potentially advising), the brokers will earn a commission that is typically calculated as a set percentage of the value of the deal. Acting as a broker is often described as 'dealing as agent', and firms of stockbrokers tend to act as brokers on the stock exchanges.

2. As dealer. In contrast to brokers, dealers actually buy or sell securities. If a client wants to sell shares, a dealer may buy those shares; if another client wants to buy shares, a dealer may sell those shares. Acting as a dealer is often described as 'dealing as principal', because the dealer is taking a principal position by either buying, or selling the securities. It is the investment banks that tend to act as dealers on the stock exchanges.

Historically, stock exchanges were physical locations where the members would gather. The brokers would bring orders from their clients and arrange deals with the dealers on the floor of the exchange. Where the deals are arranged verbally on the floor of the exchange, the method of trading is described as 'open outcry'. However, stock exchanges have introduced electronic systems to execute deals, and the physical exchange floor is increasingly unusual. Today the majority of the world's major stock exchanges run secondary market trading systems that are solely 'electronic'.

The major exchanges around the world are detailed in the following table alongside the country (or countries) they operate within, and a brief outline of their trading systems:

Exchange	Country/countries	Trading system
Deutsche Börse	Germany	Electronic
London Stock Exchange	UK	Electronic
NASDAQ	US	Electronic
NYSE Euronext	US and Europe	Electronic plus some open outcry in Wall Street
Tokyo Stock Exchange	Japan	Electronic

2.2 Securities Listed

LEARNING OBJECTIVES

2.2.2 understand the different types of securities listed and why: Ordinary shares; Preference shares; Global Depository Receipts; Corporate bonds; Government bonds

The types of securities listed on stock exchanges include shares, bonds and depositary receipts; all three are listed to attract investors through a combination of prestige, the associated publicity and liquidity.

Companies that have preference shares as well as ordinary shares can list both on the exchange. Listed bonds include those issued by companies and by government. Depositary receipts in the form of either american depositary receipts (ADRs) on the US exchanges and global depositary receipts (GDRs) elsewhere are both popular ways of attracting overseas investors, in addition to domestic investors.

2.3 Advisers

LEARNING OBJECTIVES

2.2.3 know the role of advisors: Listing Agent; Corporate Broker

In order to have its securities listed, the company concerned will have to appoint certain advisers. The precise requirements and roles are laid down in the local regulations that apply to the particular exchange. Generally, the advisors will include both a listing agent (at the initial public offering stage) and a corporate broker (both at IPO and afterwards).

The **listing agent** is alternatively referred to as the 'sponsor'. The role is to ensure that the company is suitable for a listing, as well as advising the company generally in relation to the listing, and liaising with the exchange and the listing authority on the company's behalf. Additionally, the listing agent will co-ordinate the activities of other advisers working on behalf of the company, such as accountants and solicitors. The firm acting as listing agent is typically an investment bank or a firm of stockbrokers.

The **corporate broker** may be the same firm as the listing agent. The responsibilities of the corporate broker are to act as an interface between the company on the one hand, and the stock market and investors in the company's securities on the other. In particular, the corporate broker advises the company on 'market conditions' – the way existing and potential investors are viewing the company in relation to its peers, and the general direction of the market.

2.4 Issuer's Obligations

LEARNING OBJECTIVES

2.2.4 know the Issuer's obligations: Corporate governance; Reporting

An issuer that is planning to have its securities listed will have to undertake certain obligations. Like the requirements for advisers, the precise obligations can vary across jurisdictions, but they always include obligations in relation to corporate governance and reporting.

Corporate governance is the way a company (the corporate) manages and controls it activities (governs itself). In particular, it is expected (and, in some jurisdictions, required) that the listed companies have put in place appropriate corporate and management structures. Examples include reducing the influence of a single individual by splitting the roles of chairman and chief executive of the company, appointing a reasonable proportion of non-executive directors to the board, and having a suitably qualified finance director.

Reporting requirements are designed to make sure that existing and potential investors are kept informed of progress and developments at the listed company. For example, it is particularly important that financial information is provided regularly and that the information is reliable. So, listed companies are generally required to provide audited annual accounts and less detailed half-yearly, or perhaps quarterly, reports.

3. LONDON STOCK EXCHANGE

3.1 Regulatory Framework

LEARNING OBJECTIVES

2.3.1 know the regulatory framework for the LSE: Companies Act; FSA; Exchange Rule Book

The regulatory framework that lies behind the way that the LSE operates includes three major constituents: the law (in particular the Companies Act), the requirements of the Financial Services Authority (FSA) and the rules laid down by the Exchange itself (in its rule book).

The **Companies Act** details the requirements for companies generally, such as the requirement to prepare annual accounts, the need to have accounts audited and for Annual General Meetings. Of particular significance to the London Stock Exchange are the Companies Act requirements to enable a company to be a public limited company (plc), since one of the requirements for a company to be listed and traded on the Exchange is that the company is a plc.

The **Financial Services Authority** has to give its recognition before an exchange is allowed to operate in the UK. It has granted recognition to the LSE and, by virtue of this recognition, the exchange is described as a recognised investment exchange (RIE). In granting recognition, the FSA assesses whether the exchange has sufficient systems and controls to run a market. Furthermore, the FSA (through its division – the UK Listing Authority, or UKLA) lays down the detailed rules that have to be met before companies are admitted to the official 'list' that enables their shares to be traded on the exchange.

The **London Stock Exchange** also has its own rules in relation to who can access its systems and become members of the exchange, as well as how those members must behave when trading on the exchange.

3.2 Criteria for Listing

LEARNING OBJECTIVES

2.3.2 know the admissions criteria for listing: trading record; amount raised; percentage in public hands; market capitalisation; payment of a fee

The LSE has established two markets for company securities: the **official list** and the **Alternative Investment Market (AIM)**. The official, or full, list is the senior market, indeed often it is referred to as the 'main market' - entry rules are stringent, ensuring that only companies of a high quality can be involved. AIM was created to provide a market for smaller, less well-established companies. As we will see later in this chapter, the admission requirements of AIM are less stringent.

The criteria for admission to the official list are set out in the Listing Rules and, as we have seen, this rulebook is maintained by the UK Listing Authority, itself a division of the FSA.

The main rules contained in the Listing Rules for admission to the full list are:

- every company applying for a listing must be a public limited company (a plc) and must be represented by a **sponsor** (alternatively referred to as a 'listing agent'), which will usually be an investment bank, stockbroker, law firm or accountancy practice. The sponsor provides a link between the company and the UKLA, guiding the company through the listing process;
- the expected market capitalisation of the company should be at least **£700,000**;
- the company should have a trading record of at least **three years**;
- at least 25% of the company's shares should be in public hands, or be available for public purchase. The term **public** excludes directors and their associates and anyone who holds 5% or more of the shares.
- the company and its advisors must publish a **prospectus**, a detailed document providing potential investors with the information required to make an informed decision on the company and its shares.
- the company must restrict its ability to issue **warrants to no more than 20%** of the issued share capital.
- listing is not free, and a further requirement before a company's shares can be admitted to the Official List is that the appropriate fee has been paid.

Once listed, companies are expected to fulfil the Stock Exchange's **continuing obligations**. For example, they are obliged to issue a **half-yearly report** in addition to annual accounts, and they have to notify the market of any new, price-sensitive information.

4. AIM LISTING

4.1 Introduction

LEARNING OBJECTIVES
2.4.1 understand the different types of securities listed and why: Ordinary shares; Preference shares

The Alternative Investment Market (AIM) is the LSE's market for companies that are not ready for the official list, but want to open up channels for their shares to be issued and subsequently traded. It admits both ordinary shares and preference shares.

4.2 AIM Listing Criteria

LEARNING OBJECTIVES
2.4.2 know the admissions criteria: appointment and role of a nominated advisor; appointment and role of a broker; transferability of shares; no minimum shares in public hands; no trading record required; no shareholder approval needed; no minimum market capitalisation

In contrast to the official list, where access is via application to the UKLA and the UKLA's listing rules must be complied with, AIM companies application and regulations are set by the LSE. AIM companies are usually smaller than their fully listed counterparts and the rules governing their listing are much less stringent. There is no restriction on market value, percentage of shares in public hands or trading history and no shareholder approval is required.

The main requirements for a company's shares to be admitted to the AIM are two-fold:

1. That there is no restriction of the transferability of the shares.
2. That the AIM company appoints two experts to assist them:
   a. **the nominated adviser.** The nominated adviser can be thought of as an exchange expert, advising the company on all aspects of AIM listing rules and compliance;
   b. **the broker.** AIM companies' shares are usually less liquid than those of fully listed companies; it is the broker's job to ensure that there is a market in the company's shares, facilitate trading in those shares and provide ongoing information about the company to interested parties. (As with the full market, the LSE imposes similar continuing obligations on AIM companies).

There are also certain other aspects in relation to AIM companies and the broker and nominated adviser:

- the broker and adviser can be the same firm; they are often firms of stockbrokers or accountants;
- if a company ceases, at any time, to have a broker or adviser, then the firm's shares are suspended from trading;
- if the company is without a broker or adviser for a period of one month they are removed from AIM.

4.3 AIM Issuer's Obligations

LEARNING OBJECTIVES

2.4.3 know the issuer's obligations: Corporate governance; Reporting

Companies considering admission onto the AIM must meet the **corporate governance requirements** of the market. Broadly, the companies are required to have independent non-executive directors on the board to represent the interests of outside shareholders.

Once a company has been admitted onto the AIM market, that company takes on certain **reporting requirements**. These require the preparation and distribution of both annual and interm (half-yearly) accounts to shareholders, as well as announcing any price-sensitive information in an orderly manner

4.4 AIM Regulatory Framework

LEARNING OBJECTIVES

2.4.4 know the regulatory framework for AIM: London Stock Exchange; AIM Rules; Companies Act; FSA

As with the overall exchange, there are three major constituents to the regulatory framework for AIM: the law (in particular, the Companies Act), the requirements of the FSA, and the rules laid down by the Exchange itself (in its own rulebook).

As we have seen, the **Companies Act** details the requirements for companies generally, such as the requirement to prepare annual accounts, the need to have accounts audited and for Annual General Meetings. As with the LSE generally, the Companies Act requirements to enable a company to be a plc are particularly important because one of the requirements for a company to be listed and traded on AIM is that the company is a plc.

The **Financial Services Authority's** recognition of the London Stock Exchange as an RIE enables the LSE to set up the submarket that is AIM. However, the nominated adviser role removes the need for any UK Listing Authority involvement.

The **London Stock Exchange** also has its own rules in relation to AIM. There is a rulebook for the companies admitted to the market ('the AIM rules for companies'), and a rulebook for the nominated advisers ('the AIM rules for nominated advisers').

5. LISTING SECURITIES

5.1 The Origination Team

LEARNING OBJECTIVES
2.5.1 understand the role of the Origination Team

Deciding to list (or 'float') securities on a stock exchange such as the London Stock Exchange is a significant decision for a company to take. Flotations have both pros and cons - the fact that the company can gain access to capital and enable their shares to be readily marketable are often quoted positives. The most often quoted negatives are the fact that the original owners may well lose control of the company and that the ongoing disclosure and attention paid to the company after listing is much greater than previously.

Once the decision has been made to list, the company will have to find and appoint a **sponsor**. As seen earlier in this chapter, the sponsor is likely to be an investment bank, a stockbroking firm or a professional services firm like an accountancy practice. The role of the sponsor includes assessing the company's suitability for listing, the best method of bringing the company to the market and co-ordinating the production of the 'prospectus'.

The prospectus is a detailed document about the company, including financial information that should enable prospective investors to decide on the merits of the company's shares. The sponsor is only part of the **origination team** helping the company in the flotation. In addition to the sponsor, the issuing company will appoint a variety of other advisers, such as reporting accountants, legal advisers, public relations (PR) consultants and a corporate broker.

The reporting accountants will attest to the validity of the financial information provided in the prospectus. The **legal advisers** will make sure that all relevant matters are covered in the prospectus and the statements made are justified. The combination of the reporting accountants and the legal advisers are said to be providing 'due diligence' for the prospectus – making sure the document is accurate and complies with the regulations.

A **public relations consultant** is generally appointed to optimise the positive public perception of the company and its products and services in the run up to listing.

Finally, the origination team may require a **corporate broker** to ensure that there is a market in the company's shares, to facilitate trading in those shares and to provide ongoing information about the company to interested parties. This role will probably be provided by the sponsor, if the sponsor is an investment bank or a stockbroking firm.

5.2 The Syndicate Group

LEARNING OBJECTIVES

2.5.2 understand the role of the Syndicate Group: different roles within a Syndicate; bookrunner; co-lead; co-manager; marketing and bookbuilding

For large listings, where the issuing company is planning to issue substantial quantities of shares to interested investors, the sponsor will gather together a **syndicate** of investment banks and stockbrokers to market the share issue to their clients. These clients may be a mixture of both institutional clients (such as insurance companies and asset management firms) and retail clients. The sponsor will generally act as the **lead manager** of the syndicate, appointing a host of **co-managers** to assist. Sometimes the issue may be large enough to warrant the appointment of more than one lead manager, perhaps with each **co-lead manager** taking responsibility for particular geographical areas – for example one lead manager for Europe, another for the US.

The process of finding buyers for the issuing company's shares is known as **'bookbuilding'** and the lead managers are co-ordinating the overall level of demand across the syndicate. This role is commonly referred to as that of the **'book runner'**.

During the bookbuilding, the syndicate will be gathering the willingness of investors to purchase the shares, which will be sensitive to the price at which the shares are sold. Usually, the bookbuilding begins with an indicative range of prices, the finalisation of the price will come just prior to listing. This is illustrated in the following example:

Example

Cauldron Stanley is a large investment bank. It is acting as lead-manager and sponsor for a new issue of shares for a client, Wizard Enterprises plc, that is looking to raise several billion pounds. Because of the size of the issue, Cauldron Stanley sets up a syndicate of 10 investment banks to assist in the marketing and act as co-managers.

The syndicate initially markets the shares at an indicative price range of £2 to £2.20 each. The strength of demand is strong so that, as listing approaches, the final price is set at the top of the range, at £2.20 per share.

5.3 Underwriting

> **LEARNING OBJECTIVES**
>
> 2.5.3 understand the purpose and practice of underwriting, rights and responsibilities of the underwriter: benefits to the issuing company; risks and rewards to the underwriter

In circumstances where a company is attempting to sell shares to the investing public, there is a danger that the demand is not sufficient, perhaps because of a general fall in share prices near to the flotation date. This could lead to the flotation failing, so it is usual to 'underwrite' new issues of shares. Underwriting is agreeing with financial institutions, such as banks, insurance companies and asset managers, that if the demand is insufficient, the financial institutions will buy the shares. Effectively, underwriting creates an insurance policy that the issue will happen because, in the worst case, the underwriters (the financial institutions that have agreed to underwrite the offer) will buy the shares.

In such circumstances the price at which the underwriters guarantee to buy is generally at a discount to the share price at which the shares are offered to the public. For example, shares offered to the public at £5 each might be underwritten at £4.75 each.

The benefits to the issuing company of an underwriting arrangement are obvious – the sale of the shares and minimum proceeds are guaranteed. For the underwriters, the risk is that they may end up buying shares for more than they are worth. However, in return for accepting this risk, the underwriters will be paid fees, regardless of whether there is a lack of demand for the shares from the public or not.

5.4 Stabilisation

> **LEARNING OBJECTIVES**
>
> 2.5.4 understand stabilisation and its purpose: governing principles and regulation with regard to stabilisation activity; who is involved in stabilisation; what does stabilisation achieve; benefits to the issuing company and investors

Stabilisation is the process whereby, to prevent a substantial fall in the value of securities when a large number of new securities are issued, the lead manager of the issue agrees to support the price by buying back the newly issued securities in the market if the market price falls below a certain, pre-defined level. This is done in an attempt to give the market a reasonable chance to adjust to the increased number of securities that have become available, by stabilising the price at which they are traded.

By increasing the demand for the securities in the market at the same time as more securities become available, the price should remain more stable. This will mean the issuing company's securities appear less volatile, and existing investors will be less likely to begin panic selling, creating a downward spiral in the security's price. The securities that are bought back by the lead manager of the issue will then be sold back into the market over time.

There are strict rules laid down by regulators regarding stabilisation practices. For example, the FSA restricts the stabilisation period and requires disclosure to the market that stabilisation is happening, and that the market price may not be a representative one because of the stabilisation activities.

5.5 Capital Raising Methods

LEARNING OBJECTIVES

2.5.5 know why different capital raising methods are used, the structure of such transactions and role of investment banks

When capital is raised by a company, the company has two broad choices – equity or debt. Equity could be issued by way of an IPO with all the related costs, or a private sale of shares which is likely to be more appropriate for relatively small capital raising purposes. Clearly, a company will only embark upon an equity fund raising when their shares are in demand at a suitably high price. If the equity markets are going through a bearish phase, an equity fund raising is unlikely to be selected.

Debt could be issued in the form of bonds or by bank loans, which may be syndicated. Generally, debt is more attractive than equity when interest rates are low; when interest rates are high, the impact on reported profits and cash flow implications may be too great.

As already outlined, the role of the investment bank is to act as sponsor and corporate broker on a new issue that will be listed, as well as lead managing the issue, running the syndicate of co-managers and arranging any underwriting.

5.6 IPOs

LEARNING OBJECTIVES

2.5.6 understand the use of an initial public offering: why would a company choose an IPO; structure of IPO – base deal plus greenshoe; stages of an IPO; underwritten versus best efforts

The key advantages of initial public offers (IPOs) over other capital raising methods are that IPOs can raise substantial sums of capital and create a great deal of publicity for the issuing companies.

An IPO is usually structured with a base number of shares that the company is planning to issue. However, the issuing company may also reserve the right to increase the number of shares that it issues, if significant levels of demand would remain unsatisfied if only the base number of shares were issued. The option to increase the number of shares is referred to as a **greenshoe**.

As seen, there are three broad stages to an IPO:

1. **The decision.** The issuing company (in conjunction with its advisers, particularly the investment bank) makes a decision to raise capital via an IPO. This will involve careful consideration of the pros and cons of a public offer.

2. **The preparation of the prospectus.** This is the necessary document that must accompany an IPO, involving the whole team of advisers, including the investment bank, reporting accountants and legal advisers.

3. **The sale of securities.** The investment bank will lead manage the sale and may well establish a syndicate of co-managers to assist in selling the securities to their clients.

Underwriting the offer is generally the responsibility of the investment bank(s) and they typically arrange **'firm' underwriting** where there are guarantees in place to buy the securities. The investment bank(s) may well provide part, or even all, of the underwriting. When they do this, they sometimes demand that some of their clients expressing a wish to buy shares agree to undertake **'best efforts' underwriting**. 'Best efforts' underwriting is simply stating that they will do their best to sell a certain number of shares – there is no guarantee, but they run the risk of not getting a chance to be involved in future IPOs managed by that investment bank if they are unable to fulfil the best efforts target.

5.7 Follow-on Offerings

LEARNING OBJECTIVES

2.5.7 understand the use of follow on offerings:
why would a company choose a follow-on offering;
structure of follow-on – base deal plus greenshoe;
stages of follow-on offering; underwritten versus best efforts

An already-listed company looking to raise some more capital can choose to go through a follow-on offering. A follow-on offering is alternatively referred to as a 'secondary' offer. Clearly, issuing more shares in a follow-on offering would only be considered if the equity markets were sufficiently robust – in a bear market there is unlikely to be sufficient demand for the shares at the price the issuing company is looking for.

Like an initial public offering, a follow-on offering will be structured with a base number of shares that the company is planning to issue. Again, the issuing company may also retain a greenshoe option to increase the number of shares that it issues, if significant levels of demand would otherwise remain unsatisfied.

A secondary offering will inevitably be quicker, easier and cheaper than an IPO, simply because the company has been through the stages before in its IPO. The broad stages of a follow-on offer are the same as an IPO:

1. **The decision.**

2. **The preparation of the prospectus.** This should be relatively easy, since the issuing company has prepared a prospectus before when it first became a listed entity.

3. **The sale of securities.** As in an IPO, the appointed investment bank will lead manage the sale and may well establish a syndicate of co-managers to assist in selling the securities to their clients.

As with an IPO, the follow-on offering may also be underwritten, with a potential combination of firm underwriting by the investment bank(s) and best efforts underwriting by clients such as stockbroking firms.

5.8 Rights Issues

> **LEARNING OBJECTIVES**
>
> 2.5.8 understand the use of rights issues: reasons for a rights issue; structure of rights issue; stages of rights issue; impact of a rights issue on share price; pre-emptive rights; ability to sell nil paid

Dilution occurs when new shares in a company are issued, diluting the influence and value of the existing shares.

> **Example**
>
> Suppose an investor holds 400 shares out of a total of 10,000 shares in XYZ plc, a four percent stake in the company. XYZ plc then decides to issue 10,000 further shares.
>
> That means that there are now 20,000 shares in issue. The investor's original 400 shares now represents a two percent stake rather than a four percent stake. That is dilution.

UK company law offers some protection against dilution, with most companies requiring a special resolution from shareholders for new shares to be allotted in cash to anyone other then the existing shareholders in proportion to their existing holding. This is known as the shareholders' **pre-emptive right**.

In the above example, the investor's pre-emptive right would be to be offered 400 of the further issue of 10,000 shares.

A **rights issue** is a way of avoiding the negative effects of dilution on shareholders.

When a company wishes to raise further equity capital, whether to finance expansion, develop a new product or repay existing borrowings, it can make a rights issue to its existing ordinary shareholders.

New shares are offered in proportion to each shareholder's existing shareholding, usually at a price deeply discounted to that prevailing in the market to ensure that the issue will be fully subscribed and often to reduce, or even avoid, the cost of underwriting the shares. The number of new shares issued and the price of these shares will be determined by the amount of capital to be raised.

The right to participate in such an issue is only conferred upon those shareholders who hold the issuing company's shares cum-rights. That is, those who hold the company's shares before trading in the shares is conducted on an ex-rights, or without rights, basis. The ex-rights period begins on, or shortly after, the day on which the rights issue announcement is made and runs for a further 21 days through to the acceptance date, the date by which the shareholder should have decided whether or not to take up these new shares.

Those entitled to participate in the rights issues are advised of their entitlement by means of a provisional allotment letter. As we will see, the provisional allotment letter is renouncable and transferable and it sets out the shareholder's existing shareholding, the rights allotted over the new shares and the acceptance date. The ex-rights period begins on the day after the allotment letter is posted.

As these new shares rank equally, or **pari passu**, with the existing shares in issue, once the existing shares are declared ex-rights, the market price should fall to reflect the dilution effect that the new shares will have on the prevailing share price. The price to which the shares should fall is termed the theoretical ex-rights price, and is calculated as follows:

Theoretical ex-rights price =

$$\frac{\left(\begin{array}{c}\text{No. shares held cum-rights} \\ \times \\ \text{cum-rights share price}\end{array}\right) + \left(\begin{array}{c}\text{No. rights allocated} \\ \times \\ \text{rights issue price}\end{array}\right)}{\text{Total no. shares held assuming rights exercised}}$$

Example

A rights issue is announced on a one for four basis at 200p when the cum-rights share price stood at 350p. Calculate the theoretical ex-rights price.

Solution

Number of shares	Price per share (p)	Total value of holding (p)
4 existing	350	1,400
1 new	200	200
5 post rights		1,600

The theoretical ex-rights price = 1600 / 5 = 320p.

The reason for this price being referred to as theoretical is because it ignores shareholder reaction and market sentiment towards the rights issue. Sometimes the share price will settle above this level if the shareholders believe a highly satisfactory return will be achieved on the capital raised whilst at other times a rights issue may meet with a lukewarm reception with not all shareholders wanting or being able to take up their rights in full. Therefore, the ex-rights price will fall below this theoretical level.

As noted above, shareholders have 21 days to decide how to react to the announcement following receipt of the provisional allotment letter and must choose between one of the four following courses of action:

I. Take up the rights in full by purchasing all of the shares offered. To take up the rights in full, the shareholder simply sends the company the provisional allotment letter with a cheque by the due date.

ii. Sell the rights nil paid in full. If a shareholder entitled to take up the rights issue decides not to, then they can sell the rights to these new shares nil paid. The purchaser of the nil paid rights will be able to take up the shares at the discounted price. Essentially they have a short dated option on these new shares that can only be exercised, or traded, during the three week, ex-rights period.

> **Example**
>
> Given the above example, the price of each nil paid right
>
> = ex-rights share price - price of the new shares
>
> = 320p - 200p
>
> = 120p.
>
> Obviously, it would not be rational to pay more than 120p for the right to purchase a new share for 200p when the ex-rights price of the existing shares in issue is 320p.

To sell the rights nil paid in full the shareholder must sign the form of renunciation on the reverse of the provisional allotment letter and send is to their broker by the due date.

iii. Sell sufficient rights nil paid to finance the take up of the remaining rights. This course of action would be taken by a shareholder wishing to retain their shareholding in the company but without any desire to invest any further capital at this stage.

> **Example**
>
> Using the example above, if a shareholder with, say, 2,000 shares and, therefore, a right to take up 500 shares via the rights issue, sold 313 nil paid rights at 120p, the £375.60 raised would be sufficient to take up the remaining 500 minus 313, or 187 shares at 200p,
>
> ie, £374.
>
> The number of nil paid rights to be sold is given by the equation:
>
> $$\frac{\text{issue price of new shares}}{\text{ex-rights price of existing shares}} \times \text{number of shares allotted}$$
>
> = 200 / 320 x 500 = 312.5 nil paid rights.
>
> As nil paid rights cannot be sold in fractions, this is rounded up to 313.

When selling the rights nil paid in part, the shareholder does exactly the same as when selling them in full but requests that their broker split the allotment letter in accordance with the number of rights sold and those to be taken up. One of the split allotment letters will go to the purchaser of the rights and the other to the original shareholder.

iv. Take no action. Any shareholder not taking any action by the acceptance date stipulated in the provisional allotment letter will automatically have their rights sold nil paid. The proceeds, less any expenses incurred by the company, are then distributed to all such shareholders on a pro rata basis. For the smaller shareholder not wishing to increase their shareholding in the company, this is often the most economic way to proceed.

5.9 Open Offers and Offers for Subscription

LEARNING OBJECTIVES

2.5.9 understand the use of Open offers and Offers for subscription: why would a company choose an open offer; structure of offer; stages of offer; tenders, strike price, who is involved in the offer process

As seen in the previous sections, a company applying for admission to the official list in the UK needs to have at least 25% of its ordinary shares in the hands of the public. In order to achieve this, and to raise capital through their listing, a company can have an IPO of ordinary shares by making an **offer for subscription**.

An offer for subscription involves the company sending a prospectus (including the share price) and an application form to potential investors. The company's sponsor will assist in the preparation of the prospectus, along with reporting accountants and legal advisers. Those potential investors that want to invest in the company apply for shares. The company then issues **allotment letters** to successful applicants.

Only new (not previously issued) shares may be issued in this way.

This method is rare in large IPOs mainly because issuing companies like to use the expertise of the investment banks to facilitate their IPOs, in particular their ability to price and sell shares to their substantial client base. As a result, large IPOs tend to follow the offer for sale route outlined in the next section.

Diagrammatically:

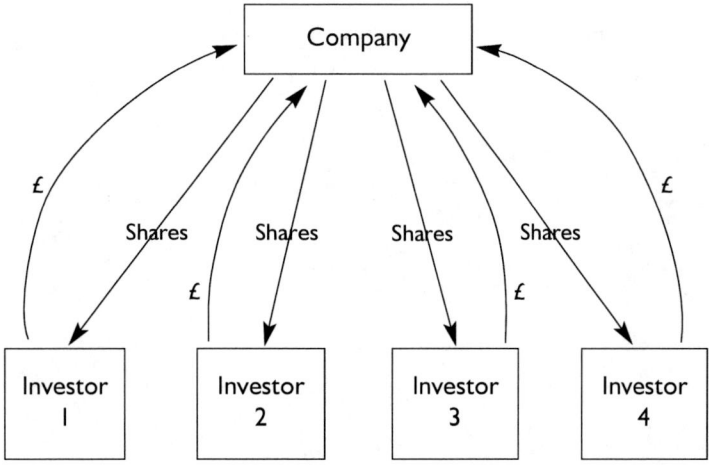

An **open offer** is similar in that it is an invitation to subscribe for new shares. However, open offers are follow-on offers that only offer the new shares to the existing shareholders, in proportion to their existing shareholding. This meets the pre-emptive rights of the shareholders, but it differs from the rights issue outlined earlier in that the rights are not able to be sold 'nil paid'. The offer is simply open for the existing shareholders to take up, or not.

5.10 Offers For Sale

LEARNING OBJECTIVES

2.5.10 understand the use of offers for sale:
why would a company choose an offer for sale; structure of a offer for sale; stages of a offer for sale; tenders, strike price, who may receive an allotment, who is involved in the offer process

Offers for sale are a much more common way of achieving a listing. The company seeking to sell the shares approaches an **issuing house** (usually an investment bank) that specialises in approaching potential shareholders and preparing the necessary documentation. The issuing company sells its shares to the issuing house (usually an investment bank) which then invites applications from the public at a slightly higher price than the issuing house has paid and on the basis of a detailed prospectus, known as the **offer document**. For a company applying for a full listing, this provides comprehensive information about the company and its directors and how the proceeds from the share issue will be applied. As seen, this document must be prepared by the company's directors and assessed by their sponsor to satisfy the UKLA of the company's suitability to obtain a full listing.

Diagrammatically:

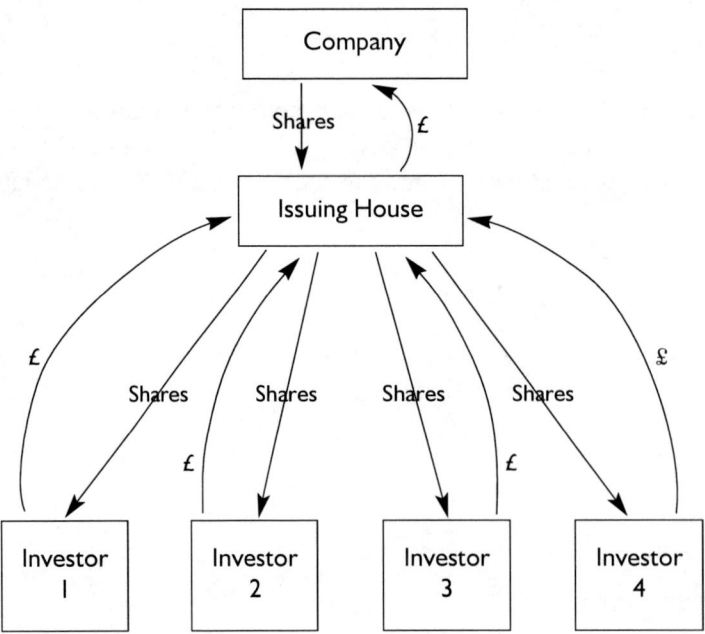

Offers for sale do not necessarily require the company to create new shares specifically for the share issue. Indeed, offers for sale are often used by a company's founders to release part, or all, of their equity stake in their company and have also been the preferred route for government privatisation programmes, where former nationalised monopolies have been sold to the public. In both cases, existing shareholdings are disposed of, rather than new shares being created, in order to obtain a listing.

An offer for sale, or an offer for subscription, can be made on either a fixed or a tender price basis:

1. Fixed price offer

When a fixed price offer is made, the price is usually fixed just below that at which it is believed the issue should be fully subscribed so as to encourage an active secondary market in the shares. Subscribers to a fixed price issue apply for the number of shares they wish to purchase at this fixed price. If the offer is oversubscribed, as it nearly always is given the favourable pricing formula, then shares are allotted either by scaling down each application or by satisfying a randomly chosen proportion of the applications in full. The precise method used will be detailed in the offer document.

2. Tender offer

Given the judgement required in setting the price at a level that does not lead to the issue being excessively oversubscribed but which leads to a successful new issue, and the fact that market sentiment can and often does change between the announcement of the IPO and the end of the offer period, offers for sale and offers for subscription can be made on a tender basis. By not stipulating a fixed price for the shares, but by inviting tenders for the issue, usually by setting a minimum tender price, investors state the number of shares they wish to purchase and state the price per share they are prepared to pay.

Once the offer is closed, a single strike price can then be determined by the issuing house or by the company, as appropriate, to satisfy all applications tendered at, or above, this price. Although this auctioning process is the more efficient way of allocating shares and maximising the proceeds from a share issue, tender offers are also more complex to administer and, as such, tend to be outnumbered by fixed price offers.

Placings

In placing its shares, a company simply markets the issue directly to a broker, an issuing house or other financial institution, which in turn places the shares to selected clients. Although the least democratic of the three IPO methods, given that the general public does not initially have access to the issue, a placing is the least expensive as the prospectus accompanying the issue is less detailed than that required for the other two methods and no underwriting is required.

A placing is often referred to as a **selective marketing**, because the intermediary is selecting the clients to whom the offer is directed.

Diagrammatically:

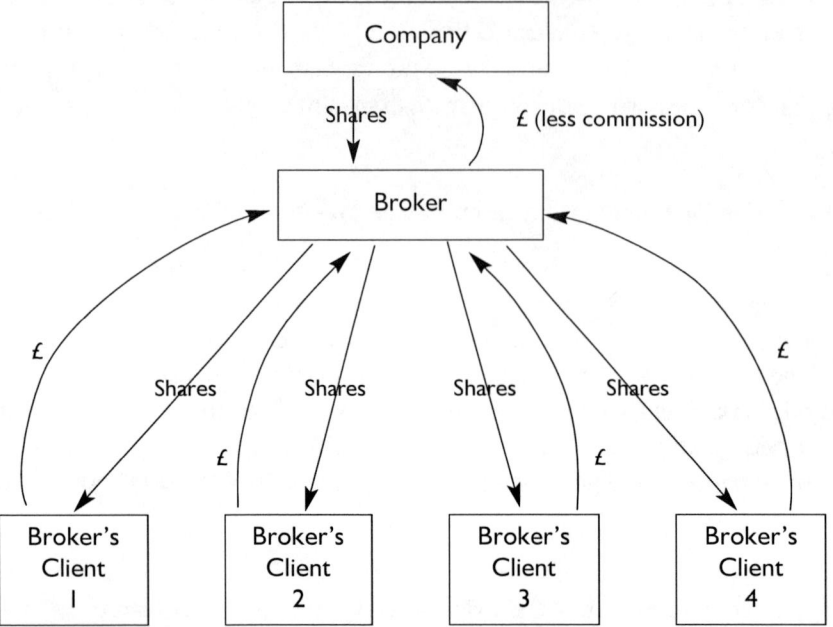

5.11 Introductions

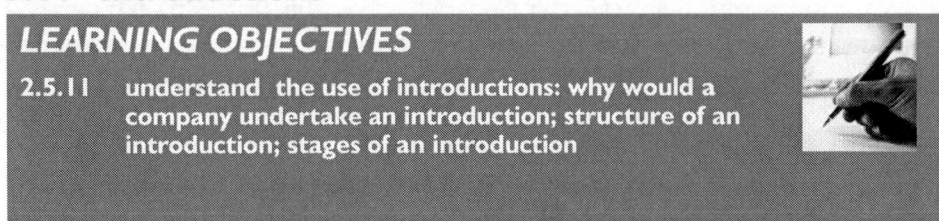

LEARNING OBJECTIVES

2.5.11 understand the use of introductions: why would a company undertake an introduction; structure of an introduction; stages of an introduction

An **introduction** is not actually an issue at all. It is used by a company that wishes to become listed (eg, on the London Stock Exchange) to gain access to the secondary market that it provides.

An introduction is unusual because most companies use listing as an opportunity to raise extra funds and some companies are forced to issue more shares to comply with the listing rules.

An introduction is used by a company that does not need to raise extra capital through share issues, but wishes to gain the extra liquidity in its shares that a listing provides. This might be a company that is already listed on another, overseas stock exchange, a new company formed from two previously listed companies that have merged or a demutualised organisation.

Because an introduction raises no funds, it is not a marketing operation in the same way as an offer for sale, offer for subscription or placing.

5.12 Exchangeable/Convertible Bond Offerings

LEARNING OBJECTIVES

2.5.12 understand the use of exchangeable/convertible bond offerings: the difference between exchangeable and convertible bonds; structure of offering – base deal plus greenshoe; stages of offering; underwritten versus best efforts

Exchangeable bonds and convertible bonds are similar instruments – they both can be described as hybrid instruments, with characteristics of both equities and bonds. A **convertible bond** is a bond, paying a coupon and with a nominal value to be repaid on maturity, that offers the holder of the bond the right to convert the bond into a set number of ordinary shares of the company that issued the bond.

> **Example**
>
> XYZ issues convertible bonds paying a 6% annual coupon and redeeming in 5 years' time. The holder of the convertible can choose to convert £100 nominal value of the bonds into 25 XYZ shares at redemption.
>
> Clearly the holder of the bonds will convert as long as the shares are trading at more than £4 each at the redemption date.

An **exchangeable bond** is again a bond that pays a coupon and has a set redemption date. However, like a convertible, it has the right to exchange the bond for a set number of shares, but these shares are not those of the bond issuer, but of another company's shares that are held by the issuer.

> **Example**
>
> XYZ plc holds ABC plc shares and issues exchangeable bonds paying a 6% annual coupon and redeeming in 5 years' time. The holder of the exchangeable can choose to convert £100 nominal value of the bonds into 20 ABC shares at redemption.
>
> Clearly the holder of the bonds will exchange as long as the shares are trading at more than £5 each at the redemption date.

The holder of either a convertible or an exchangeable bond has the safety of coupons and repayment, combined with the potential upside of equity growth. The difference between the two instruments is simply that the convertible can be converted into the issuer of the bond's shares, whereas an exchangeable can be converted into the shares of a company other than the issuer of the bonds. Both types of bond will enable the issuer to raise borrowed funds more cheaply because the bonds have the upside potential of the conversion/exchange into shares.

The structure of an offering of a convertible or exchangeable bond mirrors that of equities – the issuer will set a base amount of bonds it wishes to issue and perhaps retain a greenshoe, reserving the right to issue more if demand is strong.

The stages of the convertible/exchangeable offer are the same as an IPO:

1. **The decision.**
2. **The preparation of the prospectus.**
3. **The sale of securities.**

As with an IPO, the offer may also be underwritten, with a potential combination of firm underwriting by the investment bank(s) and best efforts underwriting by clients of the investment bank(s) such as stockbroking firms.

6. BOND OFFERINGS

6.1 Types of Issuer

LEARNING OBJECTIVES

2.6.1 know the different types of issuer: supranationals; governments; agency; municipal; corporate; financial institutions & special purpose vehicles

As we have seen, bonds are essentially 'I owe you' (IOU) instruments that specify a face value, coupon rate and redemption date. They are issued by a variety of organisations including:

- **Supranationals.** Organisations like the World Bank raise money through issuing bonds
- **Governments.** Most governments have a requirement to borrow money at some stage, and the long term borrowing is generally financed by bond issues, such as the UK gilts and the US Treasury bonds.
- **Agencies.** Agencies (often backed by the Government) issue bonds for particular purposes. These are common in the USA where examples include the Federal National Mortgage Association ('Fannie Mae') created to provide mortgage finance for the disadvantaged and the Student Loan Marketing Association ('Sallie Mae') created to finance student education.
- **Municipalities.** Municipalities in the USA issue municipal bonds to finance local borrowing. These municipal bonds are often tax efficient, particularly for investors who reside in that municipality.
- **Corporates.** Large companies often use bonds to finance borrowing needs.
- **Financial Institutions and Special Purpose Vehicles.** Like other corporates, financial institutions issue bonds to finance borrowing. These financial institutions also arrange borrowing for themselves and others by creating 'special purpose vehicles ('spv') to enable money to be raised that does not appear within the accounts of that entity. This type of finance is often described as 'off balance sheet finance', because it does not appear in the balance sheet that forms of part of the company's accounts.

6.2 Debt Seniority

LEARNING OBJECTIVES

2.6.2 understand the seniority of debt and how they rank in default: senior; subordinated; mezzanine; PIK

Debt issued by companies can come in a variety of forms including bonds and bank borrowing. When there are multiple forms of debt the issuer will have to establish some sort of order as to which debt will be serviced and repaid first in the event of the company encountering financial difficulties. In broad terms the seniority of the debt falls into three main headings:

- **Senior.** Senior debt or bonds have a claim that is above that of the more junior forms of borrowing and the equity of the issuer in the event of liquidation.

- **Subordinated.** Subordinated debt or bonds have accepted that their claim to the issuer's assets ranks below that of the senior debt in the event of a liquidation. As a result of accepting a greater risk than the senior debt, the subordinated borrowing will be entitled to a greater rate of interest than that available on the senior debt.

- **Mezzanine and PIK.** The mezzanine level of debt, if it exists at all, will be even more risky than the subordinated debt. It will rank below other forms of debt, but above the equity in a liquidation. As the most risky debt, the mezzanine debt will offer a greater rate of interest than the subordinated and senior levels of debt. Mezzanine borrowing can be raised in a variety of ways – one example is the issue of payment in kind notes (PIK notes). PIK notes are simply zero coupon bonds that are issued at a substantial discount to their face value. When they are repaid, the difference between the redemption value and the purchase cost will provide the investors return.

It should be noted that each of the three main categories can themselves contain sub-categories such as **senior secured**, **senior unsecured**, **senior subordinated** and **junior subordinated**. In practice, the various rating agencies look at debt structures in these narrower terms. Seniority can be contractual as the result of the terms of the issue, or based on the corporate structure of the issuer.

6.3 Pricing Benchmarks

LEARNING OBJECTIVES

2.6.3 understand the pricing benchmarks: spread over government bond benchmark; spread over/under LIBOR; spread over/under swap

As seen, the seniority of bonds is reflected in the returns that are available on those bonds – subordinated bonds pay a greater rate of return than the senior bonds from the same issuer. In a similar way, bonds issued by different issuers will pay different levels of return to reflect investors' perceptions of the relative risks of default by those issuers. This is measured and assessed by looking at 'spreads'. The spread is simply the difference between the rate of return (the yield) on one instrument compared to another. It is generally quoted in basis points, with each basis point representing one one-hundredth of a percentage point (ie, 0.01%).

The use of a particular pricing benchmark is generally determined by the type of debt asset class. Also, specific features of a bond can mean that pricing off a benchmark security/rate becomes more difficult eg, a 10 year corporate bond, with a put/call feature, is unlikely to price off the 10 year gilt but rather a benchmark curve as the estimate of the maturity of the corporate bond is unlikely to coincide with the specific maturity of the given gilt because of the put/call feature.

The comparison tends to be against one of three yields:

1. **Government bond yields**, such as the yield on the 10 year US Treasury Note or the yield on long-dated gilts.
2. **LIBOR** (the London Inter Bank Offer Rate), which is the rate at which funds in a particular currency and for a particular maturity are available to one bank from other banks. LIBORs are gathered and published by the British Bankers Association (BBA) in London on a daily basis.
3. **Swap rates.** There is a very active market in exchanging floating rates for fixed rates in the so-called 'swaps market'. The rates available on swaps are also used as benchmarks against which to judge yields.

The spreads on a particular instrument could be above or below benchmarks as shown in the following illustration:

> **Example**
>
> UBX Inc is a well-established and highly-rated company. It has bonds in issue that expire in approximately 10 years' time and are currently yielding 5.40%. Comparative government bonds (based on the 10 year Treasury Bond) are yielding 5.15%, and the 10 year swaps rate is 5.20%. Three month LIBOR is 5.54%.
>
> The spreads can be summarised as follows:
>
> UBX bonds spread above government bonds = 25 basis points (5.40% − 5.15%)
>
> UBX spread under LIBOR = 14 basis points (5.40% − 5.54%)
>
> UBX bonds spread over swap rates = 20 basis points (5.405 − 5.20%)

6.4 Bond Issuance

LEARNING OBJECTIVES

2.6.4 know the methods of issuance: scheduled funding programmes and opportunistic issuance (eg, MTN); auction/tender; reverse inquiry (under MTN)

Traditionally, borrowing money via a bond issue had been only sensible when large sums of money were being raised in a single capital raising transaction. The sums had to be large enough to make the costs involved in issuance worthwhile. The details of the bond would be established including its coupon and maturity and the bonds would be marketed to potential investors. The investors would either be invited to bid for the bonds in an auction type process or a tender method was adopted. Both of these are illustrated in the examples that follow in relation to UK Government bonds.

The **Debt Management Office (DMO)** is the part of the **Treasury** that oversees gilt issues. It uses a number of different issue methods, depending on the circumstances. Most commonly used is the auction method, where the DMO announces the auction, receives bids and allocates the gilts to those that bid highest, at the price they bid. Gilt Edged Market Makers (GEMMs) are expected to bid for gilts when the DMO makes a new issue, and the DMO reserves the right to take the gilts onto its own books if the auction is not fully taken up.

> **Example**
>
> Auction example:
>
> First, the DMO sets a minimum price. Applicants bid for the gilt and successful bidders pay the price at which they bid.
>
> Imagine the auction is for £1m nominal and the DMO's minimum price is £100 for £100 nominal.
>
> - A offers to buy £0.5m nominal, willing to pay £101.50 for every £100 nominal.
> - B offers to buy £0.5m nominal, willing to pay £100.75 for every £100 nominal.
> - C offers to buy £0.5m nominal, willing to pay £100.50 for every £100 nominal.
>
> A and B are awarded the gilts **for the prices that they bid** and there is nothing left for C.

Up until 1987 the tender method was standard, where all bidders paid a common strike price.

> **Example**
>
> Tender example
>
> A minimum price is set by the DMO and investors make bids. The gilts are awarded at the highest price at which they can all be sold.
>
> Imagine the tender is for £1m nominal and the minimum price is £100 for £100 nominal. The bids submitted are:
>
> - A offers to buy £0.5m nominal, paying £101.50 for every £100 nominal.
> - B offers to buy £0.5m nominal, paying £100.75 for every £100 nominal.
> - C offers to buy £0.5m nominal, paying £100.50 for every £100 nominal.
>
> In this instance, A and B are awarded the gilts, but both pay the lower price: £100.75 (the highest price at which all the gilts could be sold).

Because many issuers, particularly companies, may need to borrow money regularly in line with the developments of their business, they tended to prefer to set up scheduled programmes with their banks under which they will be able to borrow money, instead of issuing bonds. However, a US innovation has been introduced that has been subsequently adopted in many other jurisdictions that enables bond financing to be much more flexible. Traditionally, it was awkward and expensive to regularly raise bond finance because each bond issue had to be separately registered with the financial regulator (the SEC in the USA). A process known as 'shelf registration' was introduced that enabled a single registration to be used for a number of bond issues over a period of up to 2 years. This has been heavily used in the medium term note (MTN) market for bonds with generally 2 to 10 years between issue and maturity. Shelf registration introduced flexibility to the bond market, allowing companies to issue smaller batches of bonds with the coupons and maturity varying according to market demand at the time.

The process involves the bond issuer finding two or more dealers that are willing to offer their services to market the bonds to their clients on a best efforts basis. The issuer will then issue bonds as and when the money is required, with coupon rates and maturity in accordance with market demand. Indeed it is not unusual for some MTNs to be issued in response to an enquiry from clients of the dealers that want a particular maturity and coupon. These are termed 'reverse inquiries' in the USA and the issuer can decide whether to accept the terms and issue the bonds or not.

6.5 The Role of the Origination Team

> **LEARNING OBJECTIVES**
>
> 2.6.5 understand the role of the Origination team including: pitching; indicative bid; mandate announcement; credit rating; roadshow; listing; syndication

Much of the activities in originating bond issues are similar to those of originating equity issues, particularly if the bonds are going to be listed and therefore need a prospectus. In such cases there will be a whole **'origination team'** involving the issuer, its investment bank, reporting accountants, legal and PR advisors.

A typical new issue of bonds could contain any, or all of the following stages:

1. **Pitching.** The issuer of the bonds will need to decide that a bond issue is appropriate and which investment bank(s) it wants to assist in the issue. The final decision will be dependant upon an assessment of the qualities of the potential banks. A final decision is usually made on the basis of a presentation made by the banks, to the issuer. This is known as a 'pitch'.

2. **Indicative bid.** During the pitching stage, the banks will detail their views of how much finance the issuer is likely to raise given the terms of the bond issue. This is the 'indicative bid'.

3. **Mandate announcement.** Once the issuer has decided upon the bank(s) to raise the finance on its behalf, it will announce the names of the banks that have been given the mandate to arrange the issue on its behalf.

4. **Credit rating.** Vital to the amount of finance that is able to be raised will be a credit rating from one of the credit rating agencies. The details of the proposed terms and conditions of the bond will have to be provided to the agency to get a credit rating, and there may be a need for credit enhancements, such as insurance, to enable a higher rating to be achieved.

5. **Roadshow.** Once the bank running the issue has been appointed, the bank will arrange and run a series of visits to the potential buyers of the bonds. This is commonly described as the 'roadshow', because it involves travelling around a number of major financial centres to see the key investors.

6. **Listing.** As mentioned above, if the bond is to be listed it will need a prospectus to submit to the relevant listing authority.

7. **Syndication.** For larger bond issues there will be a number of banks acting for the issuer, described as a lead manager (the primary contact with the issuer) and the other co-managers that will sell into their particular client base, perhaps based on geographical regions. The total of all the banks involved is the 'syndicate'.

6.6 Takeover Financings

LEARNING OBJECTIVES

2.6.6 understand methods of raising new capital to finance takeovers: follow on offerings; rights issues; convertible bond offerings

When financing the takeover of another company, the predator can choose between raising equity – perhaps by way of a follow-on offering or a rights issue – or raising debt. A hybrid between debt and equity is also a possibility in the form of a convertible bond issue. A convertible would provide the investor with the safety of coupons and repayment, plus the possibility of a substantial gain if the resultant group of companies performs well. This could mean that the coupons payable on the bond may be less than an equivalent issue that did not have the convertible option.

7. SECONDARY ISSUES AND BUYBACKS

7.1 Share Buybacks

LEARNING OBJECTIVES

2.7.1 understand why share buybacks are undertaken: governing regulation; resolution at AGM; limits on percentage of shares and price; use of company's own money; key aspects of share buybacks – criteria to comply with; different structures regarding block trades; accelerated bookbuild – best efforts basis; accelerated bookbuild – back stop price; bought deal

Share buybacks are where a company decides to use its own money to buy back shares from existing investors. There are two obvious examples where share buybacks might be considered:

1. Where the company has reduced its activities (perhaps having sold a major part of its business) and has surplus cash to return to shareholders.

2. Where the company wants to reorganise its capital structure to include more debt and less equity. In these circumstance the company can borrow money (by issuing bonds or from banks), and use it to buyback and therefore reduce the number of shares it has in issue.

There will inevitably be restrictions on company's ability to buyback its own shares, partly to prevent shareholders from being unfairly preferred to creditors, and partly to make sure that the company has gained approval to buyback from its own shareholders. To prevent unfair prejudice against the creditors, regulation limits the amount that can be used to repurchase shares. For example, in the UK there are various accounting tests that need to be satisfied to prevent erosion of what is referred to as the 'creditors' buffer'. In simple terms the creditors buffer is the money original paid into the company as capital.

Approval from shareholders generally requires a resolution at the AGM to grant permission to buy shares back. Such permissions inevitably place limits on the percentage of shares to be purchased and the price paid to those shareholders that sell.

The actual mechanics of undertaking a share buyback once regulatory and shareholder approval has been gained can be done in a variety of ways, such as:

- **Block trades**, where an investment bank acting for the company will seek to do a small number of large trades with investors, perhaps through an exchange.
- **Accelerated bookbuild**, where the investment bank will contact a number of institutions investors in the company, seeking their willingness to sell at particular price points. If the buyback is sufficiently large to require a syndicate, some of the more junior members may only be willing to be involved on a 'best efforts' basis, and the whole syndicate will have a price at which it cannot go above (the 'back stop price').
- **Bought deal.** This is where the buyback is achieved by agreeing the terms with the investment bank(s) at the outset. The investment bank guarantees to buy back the particular number of shares, potentially for more than the company is paying if necessary.

8. ROLE AND RESPONSIBILITY OF MARKET MAKERS FOR NEW ISSUES

8.1 Stake Building

> **LEARNING OBJECTIVES**
>
> 2.7.2 understand how and why stake building is used: strategic versus acquisition; direct versus indirect; direct – outright purchase, ie, dawn raid; indirect – CFDs; disclosure thresholds, including mandatory takeover threshold

A stake is simply a shareholding, and many investors buy stakes in companies simply for the investment potential. Sometimes stakes are built in companies for reasons over and above the simple investment potential. **Strategic** stakes may be accumulated in order to prevent a company being taken over by a competitor and to influence the company concerned. This may be in order to protect supplies – the company may be a key supplier of raw materials to the strategic stakeholder, without which the strategic stakeholder may have difficulty obtaining the quantity and quality of raw materials it seeks.

A stake may be accumulated in the hope of bringing about an **acquisition**. An acquisition of another company is achieved by purchasing more than 50% of the shares, and thereby gaining 'control' of the votes and the company. It is usual to talk in terms of the acquiring company being the 'predator' or 'offeror' and the company being acquired as the 'target' or 'offeree'. As a potential predator building a stake in order to eventually acquire a target company, there are certain regulatory restrictions.

Firstly, as a stake becomes more significant, there are disclosure requirements. In the UK these disclosure requirements are contained within the FSA's Disclosure and Transparency Rules. An investor is judged to have a **notifiable interest** in a public company if he holds 3% or more of its shares. At this point he is obliged to inform the company of his holding.

Once the investor's holding is above 3%, he must also inform the company if it rises or falls through a whole percentage point.

- A stake of 3.7% rising to 4.1% would need to be reported, but a stake of 3.7% rising to 3.9% would not.
- A stake of 5.4% falling to 4.9% would need to be reported, but a stake of 5.4% falling to 5.1% would not.

An investor must also inform the company if his stake falls back to below 3%.

Why is this disclosure deemed necessary, when the company maintains a register of its shareholders? The notifiable interest rules not only include those shares held directly by the investor, but also those shares held indirectly by parties connected to them, known as **connected parties**. These would include shares held by the following:

- the investor's spouse;
- the investor's infant children (less than 18 years old);
- companies controlled by the investor. For these purposes, control is assumed if the investor holds at least one third of the voting rights of the company;
- concert parties. This is simply an agreement between two or more persons to influence the company together, such as voting together. If the combined holding reached 3% or more it would become notifiable, as if it were a single holding.

As seen above, 3% is the level at which notification starts and this information must be reported in writing to the company and the FSA within two business days.

Fund managers and operators of regulated collective investment schemes (such as authorised unit trusts and open-ended investment companies) are deemed to be non-beneficial holders and are exempt from reporting at 3%. Disclosure requirements for fund managers and the like start at 5%.

Some shareholders are completely exempted from the disclosure rules, eg, if the shares are held by:

- a market maker, or dealer in shares, for the purposes of that business;
- a custodian (that is not able to control the voting rights of the shares concerned).

The company is required to maintain a register of notifications of interests in shares and make this available at its registered office.

At the time of writing, shares acquired under contracts for differences (CFDs) are not subject to these disclosure requirements, although the FSA continues to analyse how best to deal with CFDs.

Secondly, and in addition to the rules relating to notification and disclosure of significant shareholdings, there are also rules laid down by the Panel on Takeovers and Mergers (POTAM or PTM) in the UK that apply to stakebuilding during the course of a takeover bid. Under PTM rules, a mandatory offer is required if any person either:

1. acquires shares that take their holding to 30% or more of the voting rights of the **target** company; or
2. increases their holding from a starting point of 30% or more, but less than 50%.

If a mandatory bid is required, the consideration offered must be in the form of cash, or there must be a cash alternative. The cash offer must not be less than the highest price paid by the offeror in the previous 12 months.

There are some exceptions to this rule, the main one being for additions to the offeror's stake during the course of a formal offer. In any other instances the Panel's permission would be required to acquire shares that breach the rule.

During the course of an offer, dealings in relevant securities by the offeror or the offeree company, or any associates, for their own account must be publicly disclosed. The requirement is that disclosure must be made to the Panel and a Regulatory Information Service (such as the London Stock Exchange's Regulatory News Service, or 'RNS') by noon on the business day following the transaction.

Relevant securities are the shares of the offeror and offeree, and any derivatives such as options on these shares.

Additionally, PTM rules require that anyone holding more than 1% (before or after the transaction) of the offeree or offeror company shares must disclose any further transactions (excluding acceptance of the offer itself) to the Panel and a Regulatory Information Service by noon on the next business day.

8.2 Bonus Issues

> **LEARNING OBJECTIVES**
>
> 2.7.3 understand the use of scrip (also known as bonus or capitalisation) issues: why a company will undertake a scrip issue; impact on share price; effect on earnings per share

Occasionally a company may issue new shares to its shareholders for nothing, raising no further capital, often as a public relations exercise to accompany news of a recent success or as a means to make its shares more marketable. Such issues are known as bonus, scrip or capitalisation issues.

A company quite simply converts its reserves, which may have arisen from issuing new shares in the past at a premium to their nominal value and/or from the accumulation of undistributed past profits, into new ordinary shares. These shares rank pari passu with those already in issue and are distributed to the company's ordinary shareholders in proportion to their existing shareholdings free of charge.

Although as a result of the bonus issue the nominal value of the company's share capital will increase proportionately to the number of new shares issued, the net worth or intrinsic value of the business should remain the same. However, given that the company's earnings, or profits, and dividends will now be spread over a wider share capital base, the company's earnings per share (EPS) and dividends per share (DPS) should fall proportionately with the number of new shares in issue. This should result in the market price of the shares reducing by this same proportion, thereby leaving the company's market capitalisation unchanged.

> **Example**
>
> Z plc makes a bonus issue to its shareholders on a one for four basis to coincide with the launch of its new product. Prior to the announcement of the issue, the company's ordinary shares traded at 200p per share. If the company had 1m ordinary shares, each with a nominal value of 25p in issue prior to the announcement, calculate:
>
> i. The nominal value of the company's share capital immediately before and immediately after the announcement;
>
> ii. The new theoretical market price for the shares; and
>
> iii. The market capitalisation of the company immediately before and immediately after the announcement based on the pre-existing share price and the new theoretical market price.
>
> Solution
>
> i. Nominal value of the company's share capital
>
>   a. Immediately before = 1m x 25p = £250,000
>
>   b. Immediately after = 1m x 5 / 4 x 25p = £312,500
>
> ii. Theoretical market price = 200p x 4 / 5 = 160p
>
> iii. Market capitalisation
>
>   a. Immediately before = 1m x 200p = £2m
>
>   b. Immediately after = 1m x 5 / 4 x 160p = £2m

Traditionally, once a UK company's share price starts trading well into double figures in £'s, its marketability starts to suffer as investors shy away from the shares. Therefore, a reduction in a company's share price as a result of a bonus issue usually has the affect of increasing the marketability of its shares and often raises expectations of higher future dividends. This in turn usually results in the share price settling above its new theoretical level and the company's market capitalisation increasing slightly.

Exercise 1

Try the following exercise. The answer can be found at the end of this chapter.

A company has a 1 for 1 bonus issue. What is the ex-bonus price (the price after the issue) if the cum-bonus price (the price before the issue) is £10?

Here is a blank table to help:

	Number of shares	Price per share	Total value of holding
Before			
Bonus			
After			

EXERCISE ANSWERS

Answers to Exercise 1

	Number of shares	Price per share	Total value of holding
Before	1	£10.00	£10.00
Bonus	1	£0.00	£0.00
After	2		£10.00

Ex-bonus price = $\dfrac{£10.00}{2}$ = £5.00

PRIMARY AND SECONDARY MARKETS

1.	METHODS OF TRADING AND PARTICIPANTS	83
2.	MAREKETS IN FINANCIAL INSTRUMENTS DIRECTIVE (MiFID)	85
3.	THE CAPITAL REQUIREMENT DIRECTIVE	89
4.	PRE- AND POST-TRADE TRANSPARENCY REQUIREMENTS	90
5.	TRANSACTION REPORTING	91
6.	LONDON STOCK EXCHANGE - UK EQUITIES	95
7.	LONDON STOCK EXCHANGE INTERNATIONAL EQUITY MARKET	102
8.	OTHER EQUITY MARKETS	107
9.	GOVERNMENT BONDS	108
10.	CORPORATE BOND MARKETS	114
11.	DEALING METHODS	114
12.	MARKET DATA	116
13.	REGULATORY INFORMATION AND FINANCIAL COMMUNICATIONS	117

This syllabus area will provide approximately 28 of the 100 examination questions

Certificate in Securitiesand Financial Derivatives - Part 1

1. METHODS OF TRADING AND PARTICIPANTS

1.1 Quote Driven versus Order Driven Systems

LEARNING OBJECTIVES
3.1.1 Understand the differences between quote driven and order driven markets and how they operate

Stock exchanges exist throughout the world as centralised forums for dealing in investments.

For companies offering shares and bonds, these exchanges provide a means of raising money in order to develop and expand. For investors, they provide a safe marketplace for buying and selling their investments.

The major example of a stock exchange in the UK is the London Stock Exchange (LSE). The LSE is like a club whose members are able to take advantage of the club's facilities. In the case of the LSE, the members are investment banks and stockbroking firms. The facilities that the exchange offers are its trading systems.

Trading systems provided by exchanges around the world can be classified on the basis of the type of trading they offer. Broadly, systems are either order driven or quote driven:

- **Order Driven Systems.** On order driven systems, the investors (or agents acting on their behalf) indicate how many securities they want to buy or sell, and at what price. The system then simply brings together the buyers and sellers. Order driven systems are very common in the equity markets, where the New York Stock Exchange, the Tokyo Stock Exchange and the LSE's Stock Exchange Electronic Trading Service (SETS) are all examples of order driven equity markets.
- **Quote Driven Systems.** On quote driven systems, market makers agree to buy and sell at least a set minimum number of shares at quoted prices. The buying price is the 'bid' and the selling price is the 'offer'. The prime example of a quote driven equity trading system is NASDAQ in the US.

The presence of market makers on quote driven systems provides liquidity that might be lacking on an order driven system. Market makers are required to quote two-way prices, resulting in an ability for trades to be executed. In contrast, an order driven system could lack liquidity, since transactions can only be matched against other orders - if there are insufficient orders, trades cannot be matched.

The orders that await matching are included in the so called 'order book'. The buy side of the order book lists orders to buy, and the sell side of the order book lists orders to sell. New sell orders entered into the system potentially match existing orders on the buy side. New buy orders potentially match existing sell side orders in the order book.

Increasingly trading systems are run electronically, allowing participants to trade via computer screens. However, there are notable exceptions - for example, the New York Stock Exchange still retains a physical trading floor where buyers and sellers gather to trade.

As we will see later in this chapter, some trading systems combine features of both order-driven and quote-driven systems - these are referred to as 'hybrid' systems and include the LSE's SETSqx (considered later in this chapter).

1.2 Participants

> **LEARNING OBJECTIVES**
>
> 3.1.2 Know the functions and obligations of: market makers; broker dealers; inter-dealer brokers; stock lending and borrowing intermediaries

There are two roles that firms can play on exchanges like the LSE.

First, they can act as **principals** buying shares for themselves, in the hope of the shares increasing in value before they sell them. Firms acting in this way are also described as **dealers** or in some cases **market makers**.

Second, they can act as **agents**, arranging deals for others and making money by charging a commission on the deal. This agency role is commonly described as acting as a **broker**.

Brokers arrange deals. They receive orders to buy and sell equities on behalf of their clients, and find matches for the trades that their clients want to make. In return for these services, brokers charge commission.

Dealers are exchange member firms that have chosen to trade as a principal. This simply means that they buy and sell equities for their own profit.

Dealers take risks, often by investing their own money in the markets. They take positions either by buying shares, hoping to sell them later at a profit, or by selling shares, hoping to pick them up more cheaply elsewhere.

Most exchange's members are **broker dealers**. This means they have the dual capacity to either arrange deals (acting as a **broker**), or to buy and sell shares for themselves (acting as a **dealer**). Some of these member firms have chosen to take on the special responsibilities of a **market maker**.

A **market maker** is a member firm that specialises in dealing in particular securities on the exchange's systems, such as the SETSqx system considered later in this chapter.

To become a market maker a member firm must **apply** to the stock exchange, giving details of the securities in which they have chosen to deal. They must provide prices at which they are willing to buy and sell a minimum number of their chosen shares throughout the course of the trading day.

Because some of the exchange systems rely on market makers to honour their commitments, the exchange closely vets firms before allowing them to quote prices to investors.

In return for agreeing to take on these extra responsibilities, market makers hope to enjoy the benefits of a steady stream of business, from broker dealers and from other investors.

An **inter-dealer broker (IDB)** is an exchange member firm that has registered with the exchange to act as an agent between dealers (such as market makers). When one dealer trades with another dealer, it prefers its identity to remain a secret. This is the key benefit of using an IDB. The IDB is acting as agent for the dealer, but settles any transactions as if it were principal, in order to preserve the anonymity of the dealer. An IDB is not allowed to take principal positions, and an IDB has to be separate firm, not a division of another broker dealer.

Some firms specialise by acting as **stock borrowing and lending intermediaries (SBLIs)**. These are firms that arrange for one party (perhaps a market making member firm) to borrow shares from another party (perhaps a long-term holder of shares, like a pension fund). This may arise because the market maker has sold shares it does not own - known as 'selling short'. By borrowing shares, the market maker can satisfy the need to deliver the shares. After an agreed period, the borrower will return an equivalent number of the same shares to the lender. The borrower is charged a fee for arranging the transaction (paid to the SBLI), and for borrowing the shares (paid to the lender). During the period of the loan, the lender retains all the benefits of owning the shares (such as dividends) except the voting rights.

2. MARKETS IN FINANCIAL INSTRUMENTS DIRECTIVE (MiFID)

2.1 MiFID Markets

LEARNING OBJECTIVES

3.2.1 know in what markets MiFID will be implemented

The Markets in Financial Instruments Directive (MiFID) is part of the European Union's Financial Services Action Plan that is designed to help integrate the financial markets of Europe. Once implemented, MiFID will apply across the European Economic Area (EEA), which consists of all EU member states plus Norway, Iceland and Liechtenstein.

2.2 Client Classification

LEARNING OBJECTIVES

3.2.2 know the client classifications: retail; professional; eligible counterparty

MiFID adopts two main categories of client – **retail** and **professional**. There is also an additional category of 'eligible counterparty' that can be applied in certain circumstances.

A **retail client** is simply defined as any client who is not a professional client.

A **professional client** is an entity with the experience, knowledge and expertise to make its own investment decisions and properly assess the risks that it incurs. These are assumed to include other financial services firms, national and regional governments and large undertakings meeting two out of the following three size requirements:

- Balance sheet total of 20 million euros.
- Net turnover of 40 million euros.
- Own funds of 2 million euros.

Eligible counterparties are considered to be the most sophisticated investors or market participants; they are broadly other financial services firms and governments. However, they are limited to certain types of business:

- Execution of orders.
- Dealing on an own account basis.
- Receiving and transmitting orders.
- Any directly related ancillary service to the above types of business.

2.3 Client Protection Levels

LEARNING OBJECTIVES

3.2.3 understand the level of protection that is afforded to each client classification

Under MiFID, the client classification determines the levels of regulatory protections that each client is granted. The retail client is given the full range of protections, the professional client has a lower range of protections and the eligible counterparty gets little or no protections under the regulations. In summary, there is a trade-off between knowledge and protection levels – those clients assumed to have little knowledge of the world of financial services (the retail clients) get more protections, and those clients assumed to know exactly what they are getting involved in (the eligible counterparties) get fewer protections. Obviously the professional clients get some, but not all, of the protections under the rules because they are assumed to sit somewhere between the two extremes of the retail client and the eligible counterparty.

2.4 Types of Instrument Affected by MiFID

LEARNING OBJECTIVES

3.2.4 understand the types of instruments that will be affected

The instruments covered by MiFID are broadly the following:

- Transferable securities (such as shares and bonds).
- Money market instruments (such as cheques, bills and certificates of deposit).
- Units in collective investment undertakings (such as units in unit trusts).
- A wide range of options, futures, swaps, forward rate agreements and other derivative contracts relating to securities, currencies, interest rates or yields, commodities, other derivative instruments, financial indices or financial measures which may be settled physically or in cash (including credit derivatives and financial contracts for difference).

2.5 MiFID Execution Obligations

LEARNING OBJECTIVES

3.2.5 understand what is meant by 'contractual best execution' and the 'consistent best possible result' obligation for Professional and Retail clients

Under MiFID, there is a contractual duty of best execution that is owed to both retail and professional clients. Best execution specifies that the firm has the obligation to execute orders on terms most favourable to the client. Best execution should take into account the characteristics of the following:

- Client.
- Client order.
- Financial instrument.
- Execution venues.

The **contractual best execution** duty requires the firm to provide the client with the **best possible result**. For a retail client, to get a consistent best possible result will entail getting the best price. The price is judged on the basis of total consideration paid by the client, including all the additional costs such as the firm's fees.

When the client is a professional client, the price will still be an important part of getting the best possible result, however other factors such as speed, likelihood of execution and settlement and market impact may also be significant determinants.

2.6 Pre- and Post-Trade Transparency

LEARNING OBJECTIVES

3.2.6 understand the objectives of the pre- and post-trade transparency requirements, reporting and publication

Under MiFID, there are various requirements for disclosure to the market of trading activities. These apply to regulated markets (like the London Stock Exchange) and multilateral trading facilities on a pre-trade basis, and to all firms on a post-trade basis. The aim is to improve transparency and thus help to increase competition between trade execution venues.

At the time of writing, these requirements apply only in relation to shares. However, MiFID will extend these to trades in instruments other than shares, such as bonds and derivatives, at some point in the future.

Pre-Trade Transparency

MiFID will require market operators running continuous order-matching systems to make aggregated information public on orders at each of the five best price levels on each side of the book (if there are orders at those levels). In the case of quote driven markets, the operator must publish the best bids and offers (price and volume) of all designated market makers.

Systematic Internalisers

MiFID also establishes, for the first time, a comprehensive regulatory framework governing the organised execution of investor transactions not just on exchanges, but also through other trading systems and through investment firms themselves – so-called 'systematic internalisers'. MiFID defines a systematic internaliser as "an investment firm which, on an organised, frequent and systematic basis, deals on own account by executing client orders outside a regulated market or an MTF".

Systematic internalisers will be obliged to publish firm quotes in liquid shares and maintain those quotes on a regular and continuous basis during normal business hours.

Post-Trade Transparency

The post-trade transparency provisions under MiFID will require, for the first time, all investment firms to publish the price and volume of all completed trades which they undertake in the 'over-the-counter' (OTC) market, ie, outside a regulated market or MTF. The size and price of completed trades will have to be published as close to real-time as possible, although for large risk trades there will be scope to defer announcement.

2.7 Client Consent

LEARNING OBJECTIVES

3.2.7   know what client consent is required for execution

Under MiFID, firms are required to take all reasonable steps to obtain the best possible result when executing transactions for their clients. To support this, the firm must have effective arrangements including an 'execution policy' that explains the factors that the firm will consider when executing orders and providing information about the 'execution venues' it will use. Firms also have to inform clients about its execution policy and obtain their consent. At the time of writing, the FSA has not finalised its client consent rules.

3.   THE CAPITAL REQUIREMENT DIRECTIVE

3.1 The Impact of the CRD on Settlement

LEARNING OBJECTIVES

3.3.1   know the impact of CRD on securities firms' trading books

The Capital Requirements Directive (CRD) is the EU implementation of the latest agreement from the Basel Committee on Banking Supervision, generally referred to as **Basel 2**. The original Basel Accord was agreed in 1988 and this 1988 Accord, now referred to as Basel 1, helped to strengthen the soundness and stability of the international banking system by setting minimum levels of capital that banks had to hold to reflect the risks that their business faced. Basel 2 is a revision of the existing framework which aims to make the framework more risk-sensitive and representative of modern banks' risk management practices.

For banks that run trading books – taking principal positions in transactions involving financial instruments – Basel 2 and the CRD offers some flexibility in how firms measure the risks arising from their trading books. Such firms have to quantify the risks arising from the trading book positions on an ongoing basis, incorporating all of the positions taken (both exchange-traded and over-the-counter). However, the way the risks are calculated can be determined by the firms. If the methodology is to the satisfaction of the FSA, it can be used. This provides incentives for firms to improve their risk management practices, potentially adopting more sophisticated approaches to risk management.

4. PRE- AND POST-TRADE TRANSPARENCY REQUIREMENTS

4.1 UK Equities, International Equities and Derivatives

LEARNING OBJECTIVES

3.4.1 understand the pre- and post-trade transparency requirements for UK and Continental European Equities

As seen earlier in this chapter in Section 2.6, pre- and post-trade transparency is required for shares under MiFID. These requirements apply to market operators including regulated markets, multi-lateral trading facilities and systematic internalisers.

4.2 Key Initiatives

LEARNING OBJECTIVES

3.4.2 understand key initiatives in this area (eg, Project Boat)

Traditionally, the reporting of trades has been limited to exchange transactions, and logically these trades have been reported to the exchange. However, given the MiFID requirement for pre- and post-trade transparency for both over-the-counter and on-exchange trades, the banks that regularly trade OTC are faced with three possibilities:

- Using the traditional route by reporting to the Exchange.
- Reporting to another body – information and technology providers like Reuters have attempted to sell their services in this regard.
- Setting up their own mechanism for reporting trades – for example, a small group of banks have set up a project team to create a reporting system (the project has been named 'Project Boat').

5. TRANSACTION REPORTING

5.1 Reportable Transactions

LEARNING OBJECTIVES
3.5.1 understand the definition of a reportable transaction

In order to keep track of what the various firms are doing, the regulator needs to collect data on the deals that have been done. For example, the FSA requires transactions to be reported where they involve authorised firms and involve certain designated investments that include shares, bonds and certain derivatives. They specifically do not include stock lending or borrowing transactions, repo or reverse repo transactions, asset trading transactions or syndications.

5.2 Role and Purpose of Trade and Transaction Reporting

LEARNING OBJECTIVES

3.5.2 understand the role and purpose of transaction reporting for the firm and the regulator

Transaction reporting or settlement reporting is done to facilitate settlement of the transaction and provide information to the regulator, enabling review of transactions after the fact – a measure of market completeness.

Trade reporting is a mechanism to feedback to the marketplace on market depth and liquidity – a measure of market transparency. Trade reports must include a variety of details, including the identity of the reporting member firm, the date and time of the transaction, the security traded and the type of trade. The type of trade is detailed by using a trade type indicator. Trade type indicators include the following:

B	for a broker to broker transaction
M	for a market maker to market maker transaction
X	for an agency cross trade, arranged by a member firm
K	for a block trade
PN	for a worked principal portfolio trade notification
WN	for a worked principal single se curity trade notification
NM	for a transaction that is 'not to mark' – used where there is permission not to publish the trade

5.3 Responsible Party

LEARNING OBJECTIVES

3.5.3 know which party to a transaction is responsible for reporting including transactions carried out by overseas branches

For domestic transactions on systems run by the London Stock Exchange, both parties to a transaction should report to CREST by 8.00pm on the day of the trade. For international equities the Thomson Report, an online trade confirmation service provided by an organisation called Omgeo, can be used for settlement reporting, with transactions reported by both participants by 9.00pm on the day of the trade.

5.4 Reporting Channels and Systems

LEARNING OBJECTIVES

3.5.4   know the reporting channels and systems

Order Book Transactions

Trade reporting is automatic for all those trades that are executed on the LSE's electronic order books - embracing UK equities traded on SETS, depository receipts traded on the IOB and international equities traded on the ITBB. Since the trades are executed automatically on the order books, they will generate automatic trade reports and there is no need for participants to manually report the trades.

Off Order Book Transactions on IOB and ITBB

'Off order book' transactions are trades executed by one or more member firms in IOB or ITBB securities away from the order book, often over the telephone. Such trades need to be reported by the member firm to the exchange within 3 minutes of execution.

International Retail Service (IRS)

Only one party is required to trade report and the report is required within three minutes of the trade. The report should be submitted by the more senior party to the trade, ie, the committed principal that is acting as market maker. Note that committed principal seniority is established by being a committed principal in one or more shares, not necessarily the shares in which the trade is executed. If a deal was done between committed principals, it is the selling committed principal that is responsible for reporting the trade.

Trades in gilt-edged securities need to be reported into the LSE within the same timetable as trades in equity securities (normally within three minutes of the trade) by reference to the trade reporting period.

- The trade reporting period is the period when the LSE system is able to accept trade reports. It runs from 7:15am to 5:15pm.
- If a trade is executed between 7:15am and 8:00am, the report must be submitted before 8:00 or within three minutes, if later.
- If a trade is executed within the last three minutes of the trade reporting period, it should be submitted before 5:15pm.
- If a trade is executed outside the trade reporting period, it must be submitted before 7:45am in the next trade reporting period.

As with equities, the responsibility for trade reporting rests with the more senior party to the trade, ie, the market maker member firm, followed by the broker-dealer member firm, followed by the non-member. If the two parties to the trade are of the same seniority, it is the selling member firm that trade reports.

The main details that need to be included within the trade report are as follows:

- The identity of the reporting member and their counterparty;
- Date and time;
- Whether the trade is a buy or sale;
- Trade type (for example agency or principal);
- Security and quantity traded;
- Price;
- Settlement due date;
- Any special conditions (such as ex-dividend trades).

The Exchange is then free to publish trade details as it chooses. The trades will be published on a daily basis in the **Stock Exchange Daily Official List (SEDOL)**.

Transaction reports for settlement purposes are required via CREST by a deadline on each business day of 8.00pm.

TRAX

TRAX is the post-trade, pre-settlement, trade matching and regulatory confirmation system for the OTC market. It was launched by ICMA (formerly known as ISMA) in 1989, initially to eliminate the costs and risks associated with paper-based trade confirmation. TRAX offered an electronic alternative, enabling counterparties to identify potential misunderstandings and problem trades early in the settlement cycle.

It operates as a reporting hub to multiple regulators (competent authorities) within the EU/EEA and is the primary approved reporting mechanism for bonds.

6. LONDON STOCK EXCHANGE – UK EQUITIES

6.1 Stock Exchange Electronic Trading System (SETS)

LEARNING OBJECTIVES

3.6.1 understand the rules, procedures and requirements applying to dealing through the Stock Exchange Electronic Trading System (SETS) in the listed areas

(see the syllabus learning map at the back of the book for the listed areas)

SETS is the abbreviated name for the Stock Exchange Electronic Trading System.

Basically, SETS is a computer system that automatically matches orders to buy and orders to sell equities. It is formally described as an electronic order driven system.

It operates an electronic order book into which LSE member firms submit their orders to buy and sell equities, and when there are orders that can be matched, SETS automatically brings them together. The SETS system is available to all LSE member firms and automatic trading takes place on it between 8.00am and 4.30pm each business day.

The shares traded on SETS include:

- Shares in companies within the FTSE All Share.
- Exchange-traded funds and commodities.
- The most traded AIM and Irish securities.

Example companies include BP, GlaxoSmithKline, HSBC and Marks & Spencer.

The SETS Order Book

In the **order book**, orders are given priority first by price and then by time.

The electronic screen reflecting the order book for the shares of the fictional company ABC plc might look something like this:

Company: ABC plc			
Orders to buy		Orders to sell	
Volume	Price	Price	Volume
10,000	315	316	4,000
2,000	315	317	12,000
4,000	314	318	14,000
8,000	313	318	3,000

The order priority adopted by SETS is by price, and then time. The best buy and sell prices are always at the top of the two columns of orders and will be executed first. In the case of the **buy** orders this is the **highest priced** order (315p in the above example, where the order to buy 10,000 shares must have been entered into the system before the order to buy 2,000 shares).

In the case of the **sell** orders this is the **lowest priced** order (316p in the above example). Below the best priced orders all of the other orders are displayed, giving an immediate picture of the depth of liquidity on the order book.

Essentially, the way that the SETS system works is that LSE members have access to the order book and can enter orders electronically. If a firm of brokers entered a sell order on behalf of a client for up to 12,000 shares in ABC plc at the best available price, the order would be executed by the system by matching with the best buy orders (10,000 and 2,000 shares). The matched order would proceed to settlement at 315p per share, and be immediately revealed to the market in terms of size (12,000 shares) and price (315p).

The minimum order size is a single share and there is no maximum order size.

SETS Order Types

There are six types of order that can be entered into SETS, each will be treated slightly differently by the system.

1. **Limit orders** have a price limit and a time limit. For example, a limit order may state "sell 1000 shares at 360p by next Tuesday". SETS will **attempt** to sell these shares at a price no worse than 360p by next Tuesday. Any time limit up to a maximum of 90 days can be put on these orders. If no time limit is placed on the order, it will expire at the end of the day that it is entered. Limit orders can be partially filled, and it is only limit orders that are displayed on the SETS order book.

2. **Iceberg orders** are a particular type of limit order. They enable a market participant with a particularly large order to partially hide the size of their order from the market and reduce the market impact that the large order might otherwise have. The term 'iceberg' comes from the fact that just the top part of the order is on view (the peak of the iceberg), the rest is hidden (the bulk of the iceberg is below the water). Once the top part of the order is executed, the system automatically brings the next tranche of the iceberg order onto the order book. This process continues until the whole of the iceberg order has been executed, or the time limit for the order expires.

3. **At best orders** can only be input during automatic execution (explained in more detail below) and have no specified price. The order will fill as much as possible at any available price and the remainder will be cancelled (ie, it does not wait on the order book to match against later orders).

4. **Execute and eliminate orders** can only be entered during automatic execution. As with the **at best** order, this type will execute as much of the trade as possible and cancel the rest. However, unlike an at best order, this order type has a specified price and will not execute at a price worse than that specified.

5. **Fill or Kill orders** can only be entered during automatic execution. They normally have a specified price (although they can be entered without one) and either the entire order will be immediately filled at a price at least as good as that specified, or the entire order will be cancelled (ie, if there are not enough orders at the price specified or better).

6. **A market order** can only be entered during auction call periods (explained in more detail below). This is an unpriced order with **highest priority** for execution. This order would be used if you wish to maximise your chance of trading during the auctions.

SETS Auctions

At the start of automatic execution on SETS each day there is an opening auction. Leading up to the auction, the period between 7.50am and 8.00am is known as the **opening auction call period**. In this period no trading takes place, however three types of order (limit, iceberg and market orders) can be placed on the order book to take part in the opening auction.

The auction itself does not necessarily happen at 8:00am. Instead, it is subject to a **random start** and will occur at 8.00am plus a random number of seconds between 0 and 30. The **auction** uses an **uncrossing algorithm**, through which those orders that overlap on the order book are executed at the single price that maximises the number of shares traded. Simultaneously, the opening price for the security is calculated. During the course of the uncrossing, no further orders can be added and existing orders cannot be deleted or amended.

There is a possibility of the opening auction being delayed beyond its scheduled time. The delay can be caused by either market orders not being fully satisfied, or the price arrived at by the uncrossing algorithm being extreme, or a combination of both of these. The resultant delay is termed an 'extension'.

- A **market order extension** occurs if there are unexecuted market orders on the order book following the auction. This extension is two minutes plus an additional 0-30 second random end period;
- A **price monitoring extension** occurs if the opening price is more than the price tolerance level of 5% away from the price of the last automated trade, which took place on the previous business day. The price tolerance level is a predefined percentage threshold either side of a base price set by the LSE and currently standing at 5% for the opening auction. The price monitoring extension is five minutes long, again plus an additional 0-30 second random end period.

So, there is the potential for a seven minute delay to the opening auction if both the market order and price monitoring extensions are applied.

Once the opening auction is complete, automatic execution commences. As orders are entered onto the system, SETS tries to match them. If SETS finds a buyer and seller with agreeable prices and volumes, the trade is automatically executed.

There is a possibility of an interruption to this automatic execution of orders. If the price of a trade is more than the price tolerance level away from the previous trade price, an **Automatic Execution Suspension Period (AESP)** occurs to allow investors time to react to large price changes. The price tolerance level during the continuous trading period varies from 5% to 25%, depending upon the share.

The AESP lasts for five minutes (plus a period of 0-30 seconds) and during this time no trades are executed (although orders can be entered, deleted and amended). Automatic execution then recommences after the uncrossing auction program is run.

If a SETS security is suspended from trading by the Exchange, as with an AESP, no execution takes place, although orders can be entered, deleted or amended.

After 4.30pm, when automatic execution is completed, the trading day ends with another auction. The auction call period runs from 4:30pm to 4:35pm, and at 4.35pm (plus a period of 0-30 sec) the auction uncrossing algorithm is run.

If auction matching occurs in the closing auction, then the day's closing price will be based on the closing auction price. If no execution occurs, the Volume Weighted Average Price (VWAP) of the last ten minutes of continuous trading will be used. In the event of no automatic trades in the VWAP period, the last automatically executed trade price will be used.

For the last 25 minutes until 5:00pm, SETS allows participants to delete orders. No execution takes place during this period.

Worked Principal Agreements (WPA)

A worked principal agreement is where a firm agrees to buy or sell a large number of shares for a client. Because of the size of the transaction, the LSE allows the trade to remain secret for a time.

Typically, an institutional investor, like a pension fund wishing to buy (or sell) a large quantity of shares, contacts an LSE member firm. The two parties enter into a provisional agreement - the LSE member firm agrees a limit price and size upon which the pension fund hopes the actual execution will achieve some improvement. This agreement is the Worked Principal Agreement (WPA) between the LSE member firm acting as principal and the institutional client. The terms are reported to the exchange in the form of a Worked Principal Notification (WPN), but not published.

The LSE member firm then attempts to find counterparties with whom to execute the trade at prices better than the limit agreed. If the LSE member firm is unable to find sufficient counterparties, the deal will go ahead, with the LSE member meeting the remainder of the client's requirement.

A WPA is only allowed if the number of shares involved is at least **eight times the Normal Market Size** of the shares in question (normal market size is covered in section 3.3.2 of this chapter), or it is a **portfolio transaction of 20 or more stocks** which includes at least one SETS security. The parties must execute and report the trade by the earlier of the completion of the trade or:

- the firm managing to complete 80% of the deal (for a single stock WPA), or 100% (for a portfolio WPA); or
- the market close on that business day (in relation to SETS securities, this is the end of the closing auction at 4:35pm).

Viewing the SETS Order Book

Any market participant can view the SETS order book for a particular security (by looking at a Bloomberg screen, for example). However, membership of the LSE is required to interact with the order book. It is for brokers and dealers only.

6.2 Central Counterparty

LEARNING OBJECTIVES

3.6.2 understand the operation and purpose of the LSE's Central Counterparty: LCH.Clearnet Limited; x-clear; Benefits and any limitations

SETS transactions utilise a central counterparty. The central counterparty is either the **London Clearing House (LCH.Clearnet)** or **SIS x-clear (x-clear)**. The impact of the central counterparty is best illustrated by way of a simple example:

> **Example**
>
> A trade is executed on SETS that involves A agreeing to sell some shares to B. One of the central counterparties, say LCH.Clearnet, steps in between the two parties and two new obligations replace the initial obligation of A to sell to B. The two obligations are for A to sell to LCH.Clearnet and then for LCH.Clearnet to sell to B. This transfer of obligation is known as **novation**.
>
> If either of the two parties to this transaction (A or B) were to default, it would no longer affect the other party, as they no longer have a contract with each other. It would only impact LCH.Clearnet.

The use of a central counterparty provides certain benefits to market participants, particularly:

- **Reduced counterparty risk.** The risk that the other side of the transaction will default is reduced because they are replaced by one of the central counterparties, both of which are well capitalised and have insurance policies in place lessening the risk of default. This reduces the risk of systemic collapse of the financial system;

- **Providing total anonymity.** Both sides of the trade do not discover who the original counterparty was;

- **Reduced administration.** All trades are settled with one of the two central counterparties, rather than a variety of counterparties improving operational efficiency;

- **Facilitating netting of transactions.** Because all the trades are with a central counterparty, receipts and payments for transactions in the same share that settle on the same day can be netted against each other (this is covered in more detail in Chapter 5);

- **Improved prices.** Because more participants are willing to transact anonymously, it is argued that a central counterparty results in improvements in price.

The central counterparty charges a flat fee to both parties for fulfilling its role and also requires margin payments (similar to derivatives margin) to reduce their potential loss, should one party default. Crest is the settlement system that is used to settle the transactions between the central counterparty and the member firms. Crest will be covered in more detail in Chapter 4.

6.3 Trading Halts

LEARNING OBJECTIVES

3.6.3 know the LSE's right to call for a halt in trading in any listed security: for any reason; length of trading halt

The London Stock Exchange reserves the right to prohibit any transaction from being dealt on exchange for any reason. This is referred to as a **trading halt**, and typically arises from the suspension of a security's listing.

If a security is suspended, permission is required from the exchange before a member firm can effect a transaction in that security. The length of the trading halt is at the discretion of the exchange. Trades that have occurred, but have not yet settled at the time of suspension, are settled as normal.

6.4 SETSqx

LEARNING OBJECTIVES

3.6.4 know the features and requirements of SETSqx dealing: SETSqx as an order driven trading system; order types; relative illiquidity; securities covered; Normal Market Size; Minimum number of market makers

SETSqx (Stock Exchange Electronic Trading Service – quotes and crosses) is the London Stock Exchange's trading service for less liquid securities. Less liquid securities are those domestic listed securities that are not traded on SETS or SETSmm (SETSmm is used for trading medium sized companies and is not included within the current syllabus).

SETSqx is a hybrid system, combining some of the order driven features of SETS with the potential for two-way quotes from market makers. Functionally it is similar to the SETS order book, with buy and sell orders displayed in a central order book. However, it is supplemented by one or more market makers also displaying two-way prices. Furthermore, unlike SETS, execution on the central order book is only at periodic auctions (uncrossings) that occur four times per day – at 8.00am, 11.00am, 3.00pm and 4.35pm. Like SETS, these auctions can be subject to 'price monitoring extensions'.

The order types that are accepted into the SETSqx central order book are anonymous limit orders and named orders, which detail the firm as well as the order. Any member firm has the option to phone the counterparty behind a named order and fill the order before the next uncrossing if the two parties agree.

The minimum number of market makers for securities traded on SETSqx is zero, but if there are one or more market makers they must provide continuous liquidity throughout the trading day. They must quote prices to buy or sell at least one times the normal market size (NMS).

Normal Market Size

Something used on both SETS and SETSqx is a share classification system based on a company's Normal Market Size (NMS). The London Stock Exchange sets this figure quarterly for each listed security. It is an indication of liquidity and represents the number of shares traded in an average deal for this company.

The NMS figure for each company is assigned to one of **15 bands** - based on the number of shares. They are:

100
200
500
1,000
2,000
3,000
5,000
10,000
15,000
25,000
50,000
75,000
100,000
150,000
200,000

Although you are unlikely to be required to remember all of the bands for the exam, they give you an idea of the variability of liquidity of listed company shares, and the smallest and largest levels should be remembered.

The NMS is used to derive levels for **Worked Principal Agreements** on SETS and the NMS is also the minimum quantity that market makers must be willing to buy or sell on SETSqx. It is alternatively referred to as the **Minimum Quote Size (MQS)**.

7. LONDON STOCK EXCHANGE INTERNATIONAL EQUITY MARKET

As well as providing trading mechanisms for domestic shares, the LSE is also an important centre for trading international equities. There are three trading services for international equities provided by the LSE that are included in the examination syllabus: the International Order Book (IOB), the International Bulletin Board (ITBB) and the International Retail Service (IRS).

7.1 The International Order Book (IOB)

LEARNING OBJECTIVES

3.7.1 understand the rules, procedures and requirements applying to dealing through The International Order Book (IOB) in the listed areas

(see the syllabus learning map at the back of the book for the listed areas)

The International Order Book (IOB) is an order driven trading service primarily for depository receipts of international securities. It operates in the same way as the SETS order book with one additional feature - the facility for inputting orders that are not anonymous. Such orders are commonly referred to as 'named orders' and are placed by LSE member firms dealing in a principal capacity and wanting to display their willingness to deal on the order book. The acronym that identifies the firm appears next to their order on the IOB.

Both Global Depository Receipts (GDRs) and American Depository Receipts (ADRs) are traded on the International Order Book, mostly from companies in developing countries in Central and Eastern Europe and Asia. Orders are required to be for at least 50 shares, with no restriction on the maximum order size. The International Order Book is accessible to all LSE member firms. The depository receipts are either traded on the IOB as a 'continuous trading day' security, or as an 'auction only' security.

Continuous Trading

The more liquid, actively traded depository receipts are continuously traded with the market opening with an auction at 9:00am, followed by continuous trading of matched orders until 3:30pm, with a closing auction approximately 10 minutes later. The IOB follows a similar process to SETS, with the opening and closing auctions subject to random starts and a pre-opening 10 minute period for orders to be input.

IOB: Continuous Trading Day

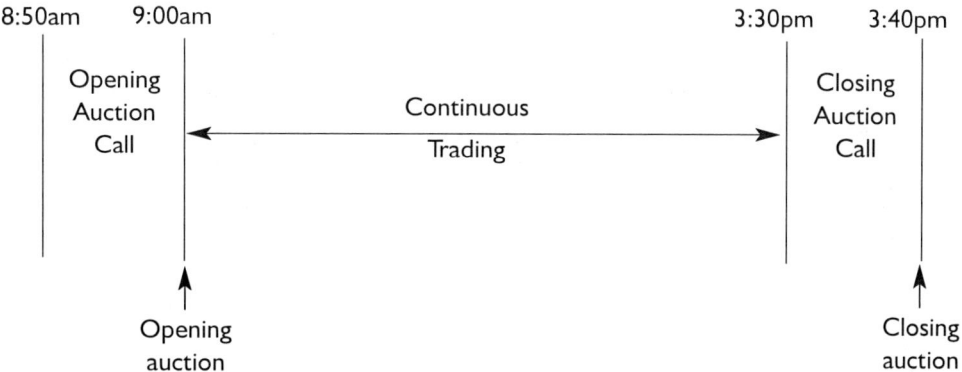

Between 8:50am and 9:00am member firms are able to enter and delete limit orders, iceberg orders, named orders and market orders. The match for these orders will not occur until a random start of between 9:00am and 30 seconds later, when the auction uncrossing algorithm is run. However, like SETS, before the trades are actually executed a price monitoring check is run. If the auction price is above or below 5% either side of the previous day's closing price, the auction call period is extended by a further 5 minutes. There is also the possibility of a two minute market order extension if there are any unexecuted market orders at the time the auction uncrossing is run.

During the continuous trading period there are price monitoring checks before execution takes place. If the price exceeds set thresholds from the previous trade, then the automatic execution will be suspended for 5 minutes and restarted with an auction match.

The closing auction call period starts at 3:30pm and 3:40pm with a random end. The closing auction match has the possibility of two price monitoring extensions, lasting 5 minutes each. The first occurs if the auction price is above or below a predetermined level compared to previous prices and the second will occur if, after the initial extension, the resultant price is still beyond the price tolerance.

Auction Only Trading

The 'auction only' model is for the less liquid depository receipts. Trades can be input in a lengthy pre-auction period, and are then only traded at one of three auctions each day.

IOB: Auction Only Trading Day

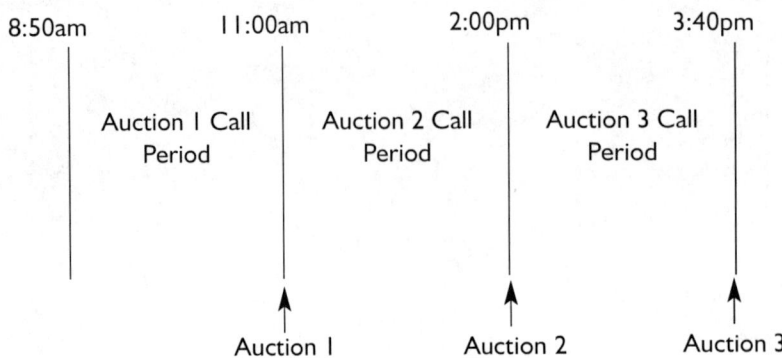

The first auction occurs with a random start of up to 60 seconds after 11:00 am, with the call period for orders starting at 8:50am and ending at 11:00am. As with the continuous trading model, there is a possibility of a market order extension of 2 minutes and a price monitoring extension of 5 minutes.

The second and third auctions occur at 2:00pm and 3:40pm, again with a random start of up to 60 seconds and the possibility of a market order extension (2 minutes) and a price monitoring extension of 5 minutes.

7.2 The International Bulletin Board (ITBB)

> **LEARNING OBJECTIVES**
>
> 3.7.2 understand the rules, procedures and requirements applying to dealing through the International Bulletin Board (ITBB) in the listed areas
>
> (see the syllabus learning map at the back of the book for the listed areas)

The International Bulletin Board (ITBB) is similar to the domestic SETSqx system. It is an order driven trading service provided by the LSE for a range of international equities - example companies include Sony Corporation from Japan, Colgate-Palmolive from the USA and Euro Disney from France. It combines an order book with electronically-executable market maker quotes, although there is no requirement for a set number of market makers for each security. Indeed, if a security attracts no market makers, the method of trading simply collapses to that of a continuous order book or auction only model as applied on the International Order Book.

The individual equities are each quoted in the currency of their home market and assigned a default place of settlement that members will use to settle order book trades. The standard trading day for the continuous order book is as follows:

ITBB: Continuous Trading Day

* Note for Japanese Securities the opening call period starts at 8:15 am with the opening auction at 8:30am.

The standard trading day for the auction only equities is as follows:

ITBB: Auction Only Trading Day

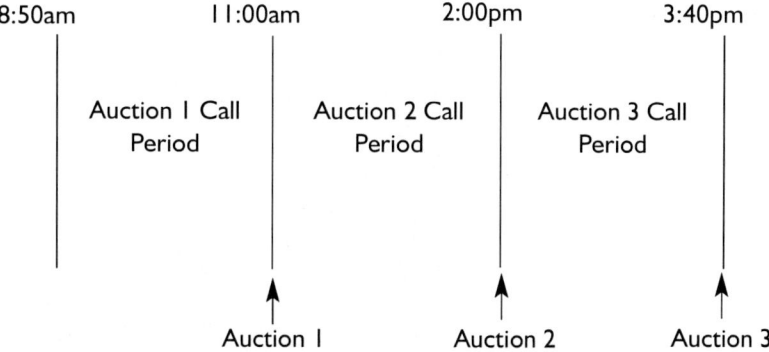

For the equities that attract one or more market makers, the market makers are obliged to quote two-way prices by entering 'committed principal' orders on each side of the order book with the quantity of securities being at least one half of the normal market size. The LSE does specify a maximum spread that the market makers are allowed to have between their buy and sell prices.

The market makers are required to post their orders within 60 seconds of the uncrossing of the opening auction, replenish their orders within 60 seconds of their execution, deletion or expiry and maintain the two orders throughout the mandatory period that starts at the uncrossing of the opening auction and ends at the end of the closing auction.

The market makers are not obliged to post orders outside the period of automatic execution, during automatic execution suspension periods nor the five minutes after the end of such auctions.

Transactions undertaken by LSE member firms in securities traded on the International Bulletin Board are defined as 'on-exchange' and need to be reported into the exchange. There are a variety of systems that can be used to transaction report international equity trades, including the LSE's Exchange Reporting System, the Thomson Report and TRAX. The transaction reporting requirement exists regardless of whether the deal is undertaken via the order book or away from the order book.

7.3 International Retail Service (IRS)

LEARNING OBJECTIVES

3.7.3 understand the purpose of and firms' obligations towards the International Retail Service (IRS): Purpose of the IRS; "Committed Principals"; Mandatory Quote Period for most European stocks; Currency of quotation

This service is aimed at UK private client brokers and their clients. It provides access to major European and US blue chip stocks, priced in £s.

Committed principals (CPs) provide two-way prices throughout a mandatory committed principal period for those securities in which they have registered. For the majority of European securities this period is 8:15am-4:00pm, and for US securities 2:45pm-5:00pm.

The two-way prices appear on the screen as buy and sell orders and the brokers can submit orders to execute against committed principal orders. If there is a single committed principal in any security, then the exchange specifies the maximum spread between bid and offer prices that they can apply.

8. OTHER EQUITY MARKETS

8.1 PLUS

LEARNING OBJECTIVES

3.8.1 understand the rules, procedures and requirements of trading securities on PLUS: Recognised Investment Exchange; securities covered; PLUS listed; PLUS quoted; PLUS traded – listed or unlisted

PLUS Markets plc (PLUS) is another stock exchange in London in addition to the London Stock Exchange (LSE). Like the LSE, it is a recognised investment exchange in the UK and provides a trading platform for securities that are on the full list, on the LSE's AIM market and other securities that are traded on its own PLUS market.

PLUS provides both a primary listing facility for those securities seeking access to the full list (referred to as PLUS listed), and has a primary listing facility for smaller, growing companies like the LSE's AIM market (referred to as PLUS quoted).

In the secondary market, so-called 'PLUS traded' securities can be purchased or sold on the trading platform and these securities embrace both listed and unlisted securities, including those that are PLUS listed and those that are PLUS quoted.

8.2 virt-x

LEARNING OBJECTIVES

3.8.2 know the functions of virt-x as an alternative exchange trading facility for listed company shares

(see the syllabus learning map at the back of the book for the full learning objective)

virt-x started life as 'Tradepoint', a computerised order-driven trading service for large UK equities. Tradepoint was set up to compete with the LSE's trading system that at the time was wholly quote driven. However, the LSE responded to the competitive threat of Tradepoint by introducing their own computerised, order driven trading service - SETS. Subsequently, Tradepoint was taken over by the Swiss Stock Exchange and renamed 'virt-x'.

Since the takeover by the Swiss Exchange, virt-x has become a pan-European market, trading the constituent shares in all the major European indices including the UK's FTSE 100, France's CAC index of 40 companies and Germany's DAX index of 30 companies. Clearly, virt-x now competes with the LSE and other major European exchanges such as Paris and Frankfurt, with its declared aim of providing cross border trading at the equivalent cost of domestic trading.

The system virt-x provides is similar to SETS, a computerised, order driven system where orders are given priority by price and then time. However, the pan-European dimension means that real-time trading is available in the constituents of the major European indices on a single, cross border exchange. In a similar fashion to the portfolio worked principal agreements encountered on SETS, virt-x offers 'portfolio trades' that benefit from delayed publication, however the virt-x portfolio is only required to consist of 10 stocks.

Like the LSE, virt-x has been granted Recognised Investment Exchange status under the Financial Services and Markets Act.

9. GOVERNMENT BONDS

9.1 Basic Characteristics

> **LEARNING OBJECTIVES**
>
> 3.9.1 understand the basic characteristics and purpose of government bond markets in the US, UK, Japan and the Eurozone: ratings and the concept of 'risk free'; currency, credit and inflation risks; inflation indexed bonds

The government bond markets are the facilities that enable investors to buy and sell bonds issued by the relevant government – such as UK gilts, issued on behalf of the UK government and US Treasury notes and bonds issued on behalf of the US government. The government bonds are important since they are the benchmark bonds on which the return provided by other bonds is based.

For example, the yield available on UK gilts is considered the risk-free rate for sterling denominated bonds – after all, it is the UK government that ultimately controls the printing of sterling, so the UK gilts are effectively credit risk-free. If a 15-year gilt was trading at a price to produce a 5% yield, a 15-year sterling denominated corporate bond would be expected to yield 5%, plus a margin to cover the increased credit risk that the corporate borrower presents.

A conventional government bond still displays two particular risks to investors: inflation risk to all investors, and currency risk if it is an overseas investor. To counter currency risks, governments can, and occasionally do, issue bonds denominated in currencies other than their home currency, for example the US government issuing a euro-denominated bond. This type of bond would remove the currency risk for a eurozone investor, but would lose an element of the risk-free status, since the US government cannot print euros.

To counter inflation risks, government bonds can be issued that pay a coupon that is linked to an inflation index – if the inflation rate increases, the investors will get a larger coupon to compensate, These bonds also link the redemption amount to an inflation index – like the coupon, the investor will get a greater amount on redemption, if inflation has been significant over the life of the bond.

9.2 Participants in the Government Bond Markets

> **LEARNING OBJECTIVES**
>
> 3.9.2 know the functions, obligations and benefits of the following in relation to government bonds: primary dealers; broker dealers; inter dealer brokers; government issuing authority such as the UK Debt Management Office

In addition to the government itself, there are three major groups of participants that facilitate deals in the government bond markets:

- Primary dealers – such as gilt-edged market makers (GEMMs) in the UK.
- Broker dealers.
- Inter-dealer brokers.

These three participants will be illustrated using the UK government bond market as an example.

Issuing Agency

The Debt Management Office (DMO) is the issuing agency for the UK government. It is an executive agency of the Treasury, making new issues of UK government securities (gilt-edged securities or gilts). Once issued, the secondary market for dealing in gilts is overseen by two bodies, the DMO and the LSE.

The DMO is the body that enables certain LSE member firms to act as primary dealers, known as gilt-edged market makers (GEMMs). It then leaves it to the LSE to prescribe rules that apply when dealing takes place.

Gilt-Edged Market Makers (GEMMs)

The GEMM, once vetted by the DMO and registered as a GEMM with the LSE, becomes a primary dealer and is required to provide two-way quotes to customers (clients known directly to them) and other member firms of the LSE throughout the normal trading day. There is no requirement to use a particular system like SEAQ for making those quotes available to clients, and GEMMs are free to choose how to disseminate their prices.

The obligations of a GEMM can be summarised as follows:

- to make effective two-way prices to customers on demand, up to a size agreed with the DMO, thereby providing liquidity for customers wishing to trade;
- to participate actively in the DMO's gilt issuance programme, broadly by bidding competitively in all auctions and achieving allocations commensurate with their secondary market share - effectively informally agreeing to underwrite gilt auctions;
- to provide information to the DMO on closing prices, market conditions and the GEMM's positions and turnover.

The privileges of GEMM status include:

- executive rights to competitive telephone bidding at gilt auctions and other DMO operations, either for the GEMM's own account or on behalf of clients;
- an exclusive facility to trade as a counterparty of the DMO in any of its secondary market operations;
- exclusive access to gilt Inter Dealer Broker (IDB) screens.

A firm can register as a GEMM to provide quotes in either:

- all gilt-edged securities; or
- gilt-edged securities excluding index linked gilts; or
- index-linked gilts only.

There are exceptions to the requirement to customers, including the members of the LSE. The obligation does not include quoting to other GEMMs, fixed interest market makers or gilt inter-dealer brokers.

Broker-Dealers

These are non-GEMM LSE member firms that are able to buy or sell gilts as principal (dealer) or as agent (broker). When acting as a broker, the broker dealer will be bound by the LSE's best execution rule, ie, to get the best available price at the time.

When seeking a quote from a GEMM, the broker-dealer must identify at the outset if the deal is a small one, defined as less than £1 million nominal.

Gilt Inter-Dealer Brokers

Gilt inter-dealer brokers arrange deals between gilt-edged market makers anonymously. They are not allowed to take principal positions and the identity of the market makers using the service remains anonymous at all times. The IDB will act as agent, but settle the transaction as if it were the principal. The IDB is only allowed to act as a broker between GEMMs, and has to be a separate company and not a division of a broker/dealer.

9.3 The Repo Market

LEARNING OBJECTIVES

3.9.3 know the basic purpose and characteristics of the repo markets: sale and repurchase at agreed price, rate and date; reverse repo – purchase and resale at agreed price and date; documentation; benefits of the repo market

A repo is a sale and repurchase agreement. It is legally binding for both buyer and seller. For example, a gilt repo is a contract in which the seller of gilts agrees to buy them back at a future specified time and price. In effect, a gilt repo is a means of borrowing, using the gilt as security. This is illustrated in the following example:

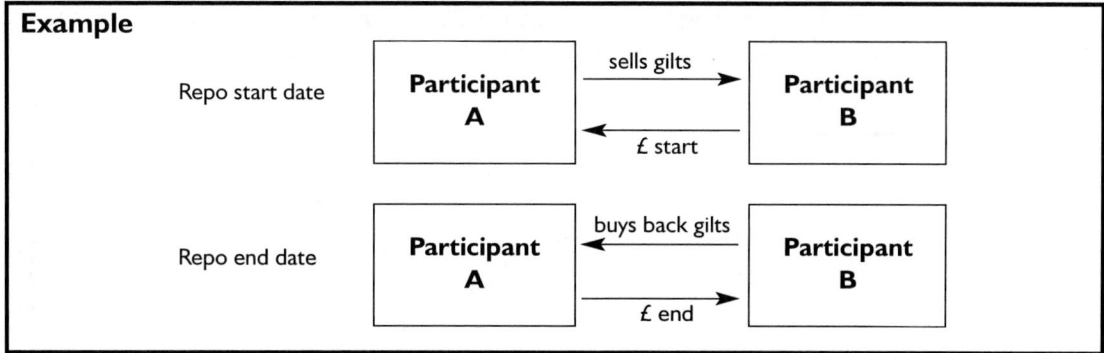

In the above example, both parts of the repo transaction are agreed between the participants at the outset. Participant A has entered into a repo transaction, Participant B has entered into a 'reverse repo' agreement.

The amount of cash paid over by Participant B at the start of the repo will be less than the amount paid over to Participant B at the end of the repo period. The difference between the two amounts, expressed as a percentage, is the effective interest rate on the repo transaction. It is usually referred to as the 'repo rate'.

The obvious benefit to Participant A in the above example is that they are able to raise finance against the security of the gilts that they hold - potentially a relatively cheap source of short term finance. If Participant B is considered a conventional bank simply providing finance, then the benefit of using the repo is the security gained by holding the gilts. However, Participant B may be a GEMM that has sold gilts that it does not hold. The repo transaction enables the GEMM to access the gilts that it requires to meet its settlement obligations. In this way, gilt repo facilitates the smooth running of the secondary market in gilts.

The smooth running of the gilts market is further assisted by the DMO's 'Standing Repo Facility'. This enables any GEMM, or other DMO counterparty to enter into a reverse repo arrangement with the DMO, perhaps to cover a short position in gilts. They must first sign the relevant documentation provided by the DMO and then are able to request any amount of a gilt above £5 million nominal. This facility is for next day settlement, and the facility can be rolled forwards for up to two weeks. The DMO does charge a slightly higher than normal repo rate for firms accessing the Standing Repo Facility.

Although the gilt market has been used as an example, it should be noted that the use of repos is an important liquidity provider for the debt markets as a whole.

9.4 STRIPS

LEARNING OBJECTIVES

3.9.4   know the basic purpose and characteristics of the strip market: result of stripping a bond; number of securities possible from a strippable bond; zero coupon securities

STRIPS is an acronym of Separate Trading of Registered Interest and Principal of Securities. Stripping a bond involves trading the interest (each individual coupon) and the principal (the nominal value) separately. Each strip forms the equivalent of a zero-coupon bond. It will trade at a discount to its face value, with the size of the discount being determined by prevailing interest rates and time. For example:

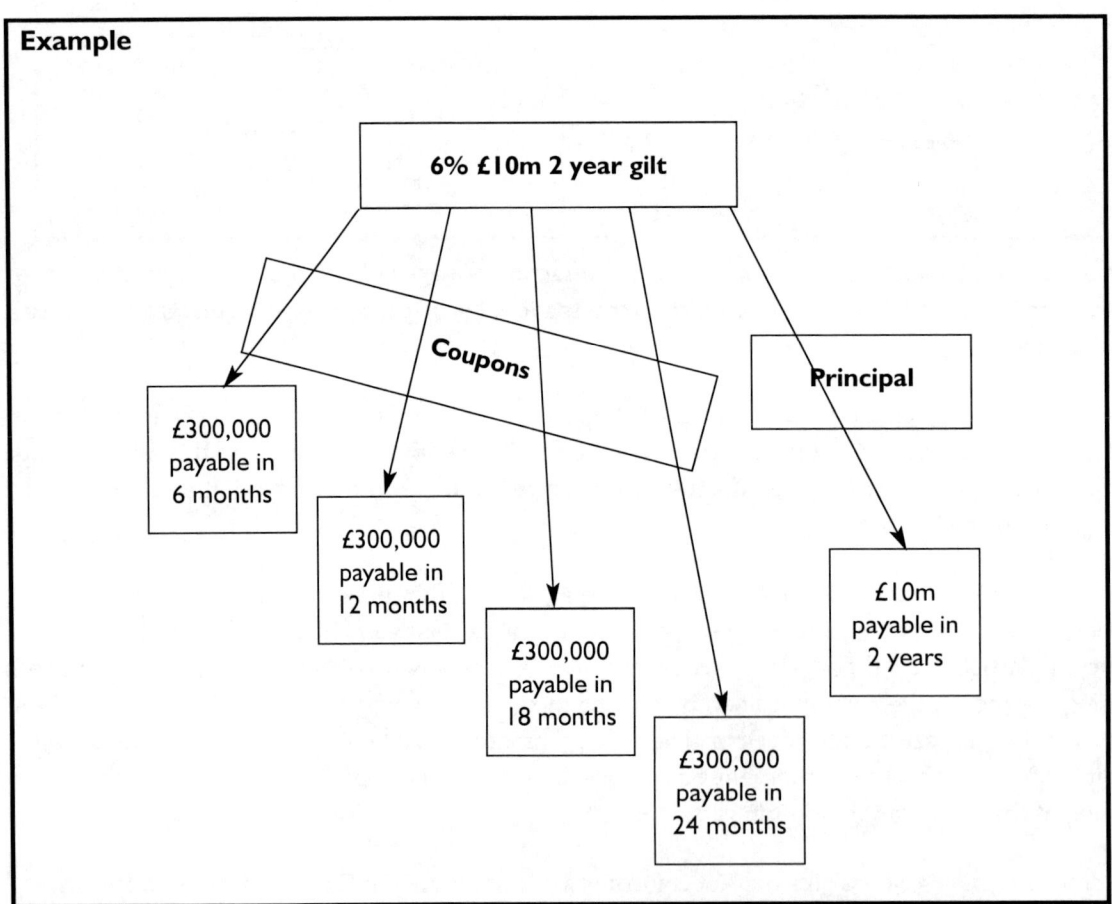

A STRIPS market has been developed in the UK within the gilts market. Only those gilts that have been designated by the DMO as 'strippable' are eligible for the STRIPS market, not all gilts. Those gilts that are stripped have separate registered entries for each of the individual cash flows that enable different owners to hold each individual strip, and facilitates the trading of the individual strips. Only GEMMs, the Bank of England or the Treasury are able to 'strip' gilts.

The key benefits of strips are that investors can precisely match their liabilities, removing any reinvestment risk.

> **Example**
>
> For example, an investor wants to fund the repayment of the principal on a £1m mortgage, due to be paid in 5 years' time. Using gilts, there are three major choices:
>
> 1) He could buy a £5m nominal coupon paying gilt, but the coupons on this would mean that it would generate more than £5m.
>
> 2) He could buy less than £5m nominal, attempting to arrive at £5m in 5 years. However, he would have to estimate how the coupons over the life of the bond could be reinvested and what rate of return they would provide - his estimate could well be wrong.
>
> 3) He could buy a £5m strip. This would precisely meet his need.

As seen in the above example, strips can precisely meet the liabilities of the investor, removing any 'reinvestment risk' that is normally faced when covering liabilities with coupon paying bonds. Furthermore, investors in gilt strips need not worry about the risk that the issuer of the bonds will default - gilt edged securities are considered to be free of any default risk (also known as credit risk).

9.5 Bond Prices and Bond Futures

LEARNING OBJECTIVES

3.9.5 understand the broad mechanisms by which bond prices are driven by bond future prices

We have seen how the price of a bond is driven by a number of factors, such as credit rating and required yields. Clearly, the required yield will itself be driven by expected **future** interest rates. A key indicator of the markets collective expectation of future interest rates is implicit within derivatives of bonds, such as bond futures. As a result, the prevailing price of bonds are to an extent, driven by the price at which derivatives of those bonds are trading, such as bond futures.

10. CORPORATE BOND MARKETS

10.1 Characteristics

LEARNING OBJECTIVES

3.10.1 understand the characteristics of corporate bond markets: decentralised dealer markets and dealer provision of liquidity; the impact of default risk on prices; the differences between bond and equity markets; dealers rather than market makers; bond pools of liquidity versus centralised equity exchange

As we have seen, the price of a corporate bond is based on the equivalent government bond, less a discount to represent the risk that the corporate may default compared to the default risk-free nature of the government bond. Unlike the market for equities, the method of dealing in corporate bonds tends to be away from the major exchanges in what is commonly described as a **decentralised dealer market**. The dealers provide liquidity by being willing to buy or sell the bonds. As we will see below, the systems that the dealers use to display their willingness to deal are numerous, with each being described as a separate 'pool' of liquidity.

11. DEALING METHODS

11.1 Trading Methods for Bonds

LEARNING OBJECTIVES

3.11.1 know the different trading methods for bonds

(see the syllabus learning map at the back of the book for the full learning objective)

Bond trading including both corporate and government bonds is either conducted between dealers, some of which is arranged by inter-dealer brokers, or between dealers and their customers, like asset managers.

Dealer-to-dealer trading can occur in three ways:

- Direct telephone contact.
- Indirect via an inter-dealer broker voice broking the deal.
- Via an electronic market, known as an electronic trading platform, such as MTS or Brokertec.

Dealer-to-customer trading is done either by voice trading between the two parties, or via an electronic platform, such as TradeWeb, BondVision or proprietary single dealer systems developed by some of the larger banks.

A relatively small proportion of corporate bond dealing takes place via the exchanges, like the London Stock Exchange.

11.2 Trends in Trading Methods

LEARNING OBJECTIVES

3.11.2 understand the different trends between trading methods

(see the syllabus learning map at the back of the book for the full learning objective)

The trading methods in the corporate and government bond markets are essentially driven by the liquidity of the instruments. Instruments issued in high volumes by developed country governments tend to be increasingly traded electronically, sometimes via inter-dealer brokers. This is also true of liquid agency bonds and corporate bonds.

However, where the deals involve lower liquidity instruments, high volatility bonds or trades of unusually large size, the over-the-counter trading is often via a 'request for quote' (RFQ) from the customer to the dealer. For deals between dealers, less commoditised bonds that are traded OTC include those bonds that are high yield, many asset-backed securities and bonds issued from the emerging markets.

11.3 Trends in Trading Methods

LEARNING OBJECTIVES

3.11.3 know the factors that influence bond pricing

(see the syllabus learning map at the back of the book for the full learning objective)

Broadly, the factors that influence the prices of bonds can be sub-divided into two: issuer factors, and market factors. As seen in earlier chapters, the characteristics of a particular issue and the quality of the issuer encompass the following:

- Issuer's current credit rating (which itself will reflect the issuer's specific prospects) and highlight the issuer's default risk.

- The structure and seniority of the particular issue, for example the bonds may be high or low priority in the event of default by the issuer and may be structured in a way that gives the bonds particular priority in relation to particular assets (such as mortgage-backed bonds).

- The above aspects, combined with prevailing yields available on other benchmark bonds (such as government issues in the same currency, with similar redemption dates), will determine the required yield to maturity and, therefore, the appropriate price.

Additionally, market factors will include the following:

- Liquidity – the more liquid bonds tend to be more expensive, encompassing a liquidity premium and having lower bid/offer spreads.

- Method of trading – some bonds attract firm quotes whilst others are traded with indicative quotes only, the precise price will only be arrived at by negotiation.

- Ability to borrow – bonds with active repo markets, and the ability to short positions relatively easily, will inevitably react more quickly to underlying interest rate changes and, therefore, yield changes.

11.4 Quotation Methods

LEARNING OBJECTIVES

3.11.4 know the different quotation methods (ie, yield, spread, price) and the circumstances in which they are used

There are two major elements of a quote for a bond – the **price** and, as a result of the price, the **yield**. Most traders will be looking for particular yields and then adjust the price to achieve that yield.

When dealing in corporate bonds, or across different bond markets (such as different countries' government bonds), traders and researchers will also be looking at the yield **spreads** that are available and anticipating changes in those spreads. For example, assessing whether the additional yield that is currently available for a BBB-rated sterling-denominated corporate bond over a gilt with similar maturity is likely to increase or decrease.

12. MARKET DATA

12.1 Inflation and Interest Rate Expectations

LEARNING OBJECTIVES

3.12.1 understand the relationship between inflation and interest rate expectations

As we have seen, a major driver of bond prices is the prevailing interest rate and expectations of interest rates to come. Yields required by bond investors are a reflection of their interest rate expectations. For example, if interest rates were expected to rise, bond prices would fall to bring the yields up to appropriate levels to reflect the interest rate increases. To remain competitive, equities prices would also suffer.

The interest rate itself is heavily impacted by inflationary expectations. Simplistically, if inflation was expected to be at 4% per annum, the interest rate would have to be greater than this in order to provide the investor with any real return. The interest rate might stand at 7% per annum.

If economic news suggested that inflation was likely to increase further, to say 6%, then the interest rate would increase too, perhaps up to 9%.

The reverse would be true if inflation was expected to fall.

Technically, the interest rate referred to in the preceding paragraphs is the **nominal interest rate**. The nominal rate is the interest rate including inflation. The interest rate excluding inflation is generally referred to as the **real interest rate**.

12.2 Interest Rates and Securities Prices

LEARNING OBJECTIVES

3.12.2 understand how interest rates impact securities pricing

As explained above, when interest rates rise, or are expected to rise, securities prices tend to fall. Bonds fall in price to bring about a more competitive yield and equity prices fall to remain competitive with bonds and because companies may now face increased costs on their borrowing, reducing profits. Consumers are also likely to reduce expenditure because of increased costs on their borrowing (such as mortgages) which will adversely impact company sales.

In contrast, when interest rates fall, or are expected to fall, securities prices tend to rise. Bonds rise in price to reduce the yield in line with the fall in interest rates that is expected. Other investments, such as equities, will also rise in price since cheaper interest rates will reduce the costs of borrowing for companies and, therefore, likely increase their profits.

13. REGULATORY INFORMATION AND FINANCIAL COMMUNICATIONS

13.1 Main Sources

LEARNING OBJECTIVES

3.13.1 know the main sources of regulatory information and financial communications within UK equity: RNS, PIPS & SIPS; Bloomberg, Reuters; Analyst research Live); Web Sites: FSA, LSE, EU (Europa, CESR)

As we have seen, companies that have their shares traded on the LSE need to keep market participants posted on any price sensitive information that might have arisen. For example, if a company has won a new, significant contract or simply announced its most recent set of results, it needs to inform the market participants in an orderly manner. This is achieved by notifying one of the FSA's 'Regulatory Information Services'.

Regulatory Information Services are also referred to as Primary Information Providers or PIPs. PIPs simply offer a service that receives regulatory information from listed companies, process that information and disseminate it by circulating it to Secondary Information Providers (or SIPs).

The SIPs then disseminate the information to the wider financial community such as stockbrokers and research analysts.

The PIPs include the LSE's own Regulatory News Service (RNS) as well as others such as PR Newswire and Newslink. The SIPs include well known information providers like Reuters, Bloomberg and Thomson Financial. The information that reaches the financial community via the PIPs and SIPs is used to inform and update research reports written by research analysts that comments on the likely future movements in the companies' share prices.

Obviously, this is not the only source of information that may impact securities' prices and trading generally. Regulatory websites, such as the FSA, LSE and European Union sites like Europa and CESR (the Committee of Securities Regulators), will be of interest to financial services firms and investors alike.

SETTLEMENT

1.	INTRODUCTION	121
2.	REGISTERED TITLE	123
3.	DESIGNATED VERSUS POOLED NOMINEE	124
4.	STAMP DUTY AND STAMPY DUTY RESERVE TAX (SDRT)	125
5.	SECURITIES EXEMPT FROM STAMP DUTY	126
6.	CUM- AND EX-DIVIDEND	127
7.	CONTINUOUS LINKED SETTLEMENT	129

This syllabus area will provide approximately 6 of the 100 examination questions

1. INTRODUCTION

LEARNING OBJECTIVES

4.1.1 know the principal details of settlement in UK, EU, US and Japan: trade confirmation; settlement periods; instruments settled; settlement systems: Euroclear UK & Ireland; LCH.Clearnet; Clearstream; DTCC; Jasdec

Settlement occurs after a deal has been executed. It is simply the transfer of ownership from the seller of the investment to the buyer, combined with the transfer of the cash consideration from the buyer to the seller. However, the process actually consists of several key stages, collectively described as **clearing and settlement**:

- **Confirmation** of the terms of the deal by the participants.
- **Clearance** - the calculation of the obligations of the deal participants, the money to be paid and the securities to be transferred.
- **Settlement** - the final transfer of the securities (**delivery**) in exchange for the final transfer of funds (**payment**).

There are two basic elements to the settlement of trades that can differ across different instruments and/or markets.

- **Timing of settlement:** this is normally based on a set number of business days after the trade is executed, known as **rolling settlement**.
- **Settlement system:** there are a variety of settlement systems that are used in particular markets, for example the majority of transactions in UK equities are settled via an electronic settlement facility called CREST.

CREST is a computer system that settles transactions in shares, gilts and corporate bonds, primarily on behalf of the LSE. It is owned and operated by a company that is part of the Euroclear group of companies, called **Euroclear UK & Ireland**. CREST has the status of a Recognised Clearing House (RCH) and, as such, it is regulated by the FSA.

The financial instruments settled by CREST are **dematerialised**. Paper share certificates are replaced by an electronic entry in the underlying company's register of members. This allows shares transactions to be settled electronically.

CREST **clears** the trade by matching the settlement details provided by the buyer and the seller. The transaction is then **settled** when CREST updates the register of the relevant company to transfer the shares to the buyer, and at the same time CREST instructs the buyer's bank to transfer the appropriate amount of money to the seller's bank account.

In summary, to complete the settlement of a trade, CREST simultaneously:

- **updates the register of shareholders:** CREST maintains the so-called 'operator register' for UK companies' dematerialised shareholdings;
- **issues a payment obligation:** CREST sends an instruction to the buyer's payment bank to pay for the shares;
- **issues a receipt notification:** CREST notifies the seller's payment bank to expect payment.

If a trading system provides a central counterparty to the trades (such as LCH.Clearnet for trades on SETS), it is the central counterparty that assumes responsibility for settling the transaction with each counterparty. The buyer and seller remain anonymous to each other.

For SETS trades, CREST gives the option to LSE member firms to settle with LCH.Clearnet on a gross basis or on a net basis. If a firm has 20 orders executed in the same security through SETS, they can either settle 20 trades with LCH.Clearnet (settling gross), or choose to have all 20 trades netted so that the firm just settles a single transaction with LCH.Clearnet.

The settlement period (the time between the trade and the transfer of money and registration) for UK equities is **normally on a T + 3 basis**, where **T** is the trade date and 3 is the number of business days after the trade date that the cash changes hands and the shares' registered title changes. In other words, if a trade is executed on a Tuesday, the cash and registered title will change three business days later, on the Friday. So, if the trade were executed on a Wednesday, it will be the following Monday that settlement will occur. This is referred to by the LSE as **standard settlement**. Standard settlement applies to all deals automatically executed on an LSE trading system, such as SETS.

The following table provides an overview of the settlement systems in the UK, EU, the US and Japan:

Country/Region	Instruments settled	Settlement period	System name
UK	Listed equities and corporate bonds	T+3	CREST
	Government bonds (gilts)	T+1	CREST
EU (particularly Germany)	Listed German equities	T+2	Clearstream
	International bonds	T+3	Clearstream/Euroclear
US	Listed equities	T+3	Depository Trust Clearing Corporation (DTCC)
	Government bonds	T+1	DTCC
Japan	Listed equities and convertible bonds	T+3	Japan Securities Depositary Center (JASDEC)

2. REGISTERED TITLE

LEARNING OBJECTIVES

4.1.2 understand the implications of registered title: registered title versus unregistered (bearer); legal title; beneficial interest; voting rights; right to participate in corporate actions

When settling a trade involving UK shares, settlement must involve communicating the change in ownership to the company registrar. This is because the issuing company maintains a register listing all of its shareholders. Whenever shares are bought or sold, a mechanism is required to make the company registrar aware of the change required to the register.

If there were no register, the shares would be described as unregistered or **bearer shares** and physically handing over the shares would be a valid transfer of ownership.

In any situation, the seller is unlikely to be willing to hand over legal title unless he is sure that the cash is flowing in the opposite direction, known as **delivery versus payment (DVP)**. Similarly, the buyer is unlikely to be willing to hand over the cash without being sure that the legal ownership is passing in the other direction, known as **cash against delivery (CAD)**.

So, **registered title** simply means ownership that is backed by registration. In terms of share ownership, registered title gives shareholders the right to vote on important company matters, to claim dividends on their shares and to participate in other corporate actions such as rights issues.

When shares are bought and sold, it is the **company registrar** who is responsible for updating the **register of members** and giving the new owner registered title.

Busy shareholders often want to avoid the administrative tasks connected with registered title, so they choose to appoint their stockbroker, or another professional, to act as a **nominee**.

The nominee takes the registered title to the shares and all the responsibilities that go with it, but the nominee's client retains **beneficial ownership** - it is the client that ultimately receives all of the cashflows generated by the shares. The nominee is referred to as the **legal owner** of the shares and the client retaining the benefits of ownership, mainly the dividends and capital growth, is known as the **beneficial owner**.

3. DESIGNATED VERSUS POOLED NOMINEE

LEARNING OBJECTIVES

4.1.3 understand the effect of designated and pooled nominee accounts on shareholder rights

The nominee structure provided by a stockbroker to its clients could take the form of a **designated nominee,** or a **pooled nominee**.

A **designated nominee** is where there is a single nominee account for the individual investor. This enables the investor to maintain a separate identity from other nominees on the register. So, if for example the nominee for the firm of stockbrokers was ABC Nominees, the register would contain multiple entries like ABC Nominees Account 0001, 0002 etc. This enables the issuing company to forward separate dividend payments for each investor.

In contrast, a **pooled nominee** is where all the clients' individual holdings are grouped within the same nominee account. For a pooled nominee there will only be a single entry in the issuing company's register. It is the nominee that has to break the single dividend payment from the company into multiple, smaller payments for each of the clients.

Some companies offer their shareholders certain perks, such as discounts on their products. By using a nominee (either a designated or a pooled structure), the shareholder perks may not be available to the individual investor. This is simply because the stockbrokers may be unwilling to undertake the necessary administration to facilitate the provision of these perks.

A corporate nominee (alternatively referred to as a **corporate sponsored nominee**) is where the issuing company itself provides a facility for its smaller shareholders to hold their shares within a single **corporate nominee**.

The corporate nominee is a halfway house between the pooled and the designated nominee structures offered by stockbrokers. It will result in a single entry for all the shareholders together in the company's register (like the pooled nominee) but beneath this the issuing company (or its registrar) will be aware of the individual holdings that make up the nominee. In a similar way to the designated nominee structure, the company will be able to forward separate dividend payments to each of the individual shareholders, as well as voting rights and other potential shareholder perks. Shares held within a corporate nominee in dematerialised form enable quick and easy transfer through CREST.

4. STAMP DUTY AND STAMP DUTY RESERVE TAX (SDRT)

LEARNING OBJECTIVES

4.1.4   know which securities may be subject to UK stamp duty/SDRT

Stamp duty is a tax payable on documents that transfer certain kinds of property by the purchaser of that property. If property can be handed over, eg, furniture, there is no charge to stamp duty, because there is no document executed on which to charge the duty. Some property, such as houses, land and shares in a company, can only be transferred in a prescribed legal form and the legislation requires that documents liable to stamp duty may not be registered or used unless they have been duly stamped. Since owners want to be able to demonstrate their title to property, they are effectively required to have their document stamped if they want it to be recognised as their own.

There are different rates of stamp duty for shares and for other property. Stamp duty on share transfers is **charged to the purchaser at 0.5%** of the price (excluding any commissions payable to the stockbroker), with no threshold. Normally there is no charge on the issue, as distinct from the transfer of shares. The duty is rounded to the next £5, so that a transfer of shares priced at £800 would be charged at £5, and a transfer priced at £1,240 would be charged at £10.

However, there is a charge of **1.5% made on the creation of a bearer share, or the transfer of shares into a depositary receipt** (eg, ADR), because subsequent transfers will not attract stamp duty.

In summary:

Rate:	0.5% of the consideration value of the purchase (rounded up to the next £5)
Paid by:	the buyer
Trigger:	transfer to new ownership (not primary issue)
Example:	UK equity transfers

Stamp duty depends upon there being a document to stamp. It cannot be used for paperless transactions. Stamp Duty Reserve Tax (SDRT) was, therefore, introduced to cater for the paperless transfer of shares through CREST. The SDRT regulations impose an obligation on the operator of CREST (Euroclear UK & Ireland) to collect SDRT on transfers going through the system.

SDRT applies in place of stamp duty in cases where the agreement is not completed by an instrument of transfer (ie, a document, the stock transfer form). The tax is **charged at 0.5% on the consideration** given for the transfer, payable by the purchaser. Unlike stamp duty, there is no rounding to the next £5, and it is charged to the penny.

The following is a summary of the major instances where SDRT is charged:

Situation	Why can't we charge stamp duty?	Rate of SDRT	Levied When?
Transfer of nominee holdings	No change of name on certificate but beneficial owner has changed	½%	On each transfer
CREST transactions	No paper certificate to stamp	½%	On each transfer

5. SECURITIES EXEMPT FROM STAMP DUTY

LEARNING OBJECTIVES

4.1.5   know which transactions are exempt UK stamp duty

Gilts and bonds are not liable to stamp duty unless they are equity-related, for example, convertible into equity. Gifts are not liable to stamp duty since there is no consideration paid on the transactions.

Securities that are exempt from stamp duty, such as gilts and non-convertible bonds, are also exempt from SDRT. For both stamp duty and SDRT there are also exemptions for purchases by registered charities, on-exchange stock lending transactions, gifts and purchases by LSE member firms (who are granted 'intermediary' status) and the clearing house.

6. CUM- AND EX-DIVIDEND

LEARNING OBJECTIVES

4.1.6 understand the concepts, requirements, benefits and disadvantages of deals executed cum, ex, special cum and special ex: timetable; effect of deals on the underlying right; effect on the share price before and after a dividend; the meaning of 'books closed', 'ex-div' and 'cum div', cum and ex rights effect of late registration; benefits that may be achieved; disadvantages/risks; when dealing is permitted

Normally, a company's shares are quoted **cum-dividend**. This means that buyers of the shares have the right to the next dividend paid by the company. However, there are brief periods when the share becomes **ex-dividend**, meaning that it is sold without the right to receive the next dividend payment. The **ex-dividend** period occurs around the time of a dividend payment.

The sequence of events leading up to the dividend payment is as follows.

1. Dividend declared:

    On this date the company announces its intention to pay a specified dividend on a specified future date. The declaration must occur at least three clear business days before the ex-dividend date.

2. Ex-dividend date

    The ex-dividend date is invariably a Wednesday, the first Wednesday that falls at least three clear business days after the day that the dividend was declared.

3. Record or books-closed date:

    The record, or **books-closed** date is the date on which a copy of the shareholders' register is taken. The people on the share register at the end of this day will be paid the next dividend. The books-closed date is the second business day after the ex-dividend date. Because the ex-dividend date is a Wednesday, the books-closed date is usually a Friday, except where the Friday is a public holiday, in which case the books-closed date is the next available business day.

4. Dividend paid:

    The dividend is paid to those shareholders who were on the register on the record/books-closed date.

5. Ex-dividend period:

    The period from the ex-dividend date up to the dividend payment date is the ex-dividend period. Throughout this period the shares trade **without** entitlement to the next dividend.

The relationship between the ex-dividend date and the books-closed date is easily explained. Since the equity settlement process takes three business days, for a new shareholder to appear on the register on the Friday they would have to buy the shares by Tuesday at the latest. Tuesday is the last day when the shares trade cum-dividend, because new shareholders will be reflected in the register before the end of the books-closed date. A new shareholder buying their shares on the Wednesday will not be entered into the register until the following week - too late for the books-closed date and therefore ex-dividend.

On the Wednesday when the shares first trade without the dividend (ex-dividend), the share price will fall to reflect the fact that if an investor buys the share he will not be entitled to the impending dividend.

At all times other than during ex-dividend periods, shares trade cum-dividend, ie, if an investor purchases shares at this time, he will be entitled to all of the future dividends paid by the company for as long as he keeps the share.

During the ex-dividend period, it is possible to arrange a **special cum-trade**. That is where, by special arrangement, the buyer of the share during the ex-dividend period **does** receive the next dividend. These trades can be done up to and including the day before the dividend payment date, but not on or after the dividend payment date.

In a similar manner to a special cum-trade, an investor can also arrange a **special ex-trade**. This is only possible in the 10 business days before the ex-date. If an investor buys a share during the cum-dividend period, but buys it special ex, he will not receive the next dividend.

Using special cum or special ex transactions enables the sellers or buyers to avoid the receipt of a dividend - essentially deciding whether or not they want to collect their right to the dividend. During the period when the LSE allows such trading, it effectively allows the right to the dividend to be traded. The motivation for investors buying or selling with or without the dividend entitlement tends to be related to tax. Dividend income is normally subject to income tax, so selling the right to the dividend might avoid some income tax.

The inherent disadvantage of special cum trades and special ex trades is that they will, potentially, result in dividends from the company being paid to the wrong person. Equally a trade that settles later than usual could mean that the correct owner is not reflected in the shareholders' register on the books-closed date - and the dividend is paid by the company to the wrong person. In such situations, it is the broker acting for the buyers (or seller, as appropriate) that will need to make a claim for the dividend.

7. CONTINUOUS LINKED SETTLEMENT

LEARNING OBJECTIVES

4.1.7   know what Continuous Linked Settlement (CLS) is and its purpose: the sale of currencies across time zones; receiving and matching trades

As international trade and investment has increased, so has the foreign exchange market. Indeed the average daily turnover in the global foreign exchange market has grown rapidly and is now around $1,900 billion. However, while transaction volumes were increasing, the way in which they were settled was not changing. Traditionally, foreign exchange transactions were settled by each side of a trade making separate payments. The risks implicit in this approach became clear in 1974, when the German banking regulators withdrew the banking licence of Bankhaus Herstatt, putting it into liquidation at the close of business on June 26.

Bankhaus Herstatt had been active in the foreign exchange markets and had received currency from counterparties during the day, but had not yet made any payments when its licence was withdrawn and it was declared bankrupt. Several banks had irrevocably paid over deutschmarks to Herstatt during the day, but had not received the anticipated currency in exchange. In addition, banks had entered into forward trades that were not yet due for settlement, and some lost money replacing the contracts. In short, there were serious repercussions in the foreign exchange market after the Bankhaus Herstatt default and the intra-day settlement risk highlighted has subsequently been termed 'Herstatt risk'.

The result was the impetus to set up a more robust and reliable system that ensured payment from one party was only made where there was a payment coming in the opposite direction to fulfil the other side of the foreign exchange deal - payment versus payment or PVP. Continuous linked settlement, or CLS, was the result that solved the PVP problem, despite the counterparties potentially being in different parts of the world and time zones.

The initiative for the CLS system came from reports commissioned by the Bank for International Settlement. CLS is only available through a unique relationship set up between CLS Bank, the central banks in whose currencies CLS settles, and the members of CLS Bank. CLS Bank is owned by nearly 70 of the world's largest financial groups - between them they are responsible for more than 50% of the value transferred in the global foreign exchange market. Each shareholder has an exclusive right to become a CLS Bank Settlement Member with direct access to the CLS system. They are also able to sponsor other 'User Members', such as smaller banks, to enable them to use CLS. Both Settlement Members and User Members can act on behalf of other third parties to enable CLS to be used to settle their foreign exchange deals.

The CLS settlement process is focused on a five-hour window each business day from 7.00am to 12 midday in Central European Time (CET). This window was created to provide an overlap across the business days in all parts of the world and facilitate global trading.

By 6:30am CET the settlement members must submit their settlement instructions for transactions to settle that day. At 6:30am each settlement member receives a schedule of what monies need to be paid in that day. From 7:00am the Settlement Members pay in the net funds that are due to settle in each currency to their central banks, and CLS will then begin to attempt to settle deals. In the event that CLS Bank's strict settlement criteria are not met for each side of a trade, then no funds are exchanged. This achieves the payment versus payment system that removes the so-called 'Herstatt risk'. Those trades that can be settled are settled and money is paid out via the central banks.

As outlined above, the payments made to CLS Bank are made via the central banks. In the UK, both sterling and euro payments are made via CHAPS (the Clearing House Automated Payment System). CHAPS is the electronic transfer system for sending payments between banks that operates in partnership with the Bank of England.

In Europe, the Trans-european Automated Real-time Gross settlement Express Transfer system (TARGET) is used. TARGET is an electronic transfer system for sending euro-denominated payments between banks, operating in partnership with the European Central Bank (ECB). UK banks link to TARGET via CHAPS euro payments.

SPECIAL REGULATORY REQUIREMENTS

1.	EU TAKEOVER DIRECTIVE	133
2.	UK TAKEOVER CODE	134
3.	DISCLOSURE OF INTERESTS	136
4.	SPECIFIC REGULATIONS IN THE US, CANADA AND JAPAN	139

This syllabus area will provide approximately 5 of the 100 examination questions

1. EU TAKEOVER DIRECTIVE

LEARNING OBJECTIVES

5.1.1 know the implications of the EU Takeover Directive

(see the syllabus learning map at the back of the book for the full learning objective)

A **takeover** occurs if one company buys a majority of the shares of another company; it gains control over the other company and is, therefore, termed the parent company, whilst the other company is its subsidiary. A **merger** is the term used when the two companies are of a similar size and come together to form a larger, merged entity.

The Takeover Directive is (like MiFID) one of the measures adopted under the European Union's Financial Services Action Plan. It aims to contribute to the creation of a single market in financial services by facilitating cross-border mergers and acquisitions and standardising protections for minority shareholders. The way that the Directive has been constructed is to require member states to implement certain minimum requirements, but to allow the member states to incorporate more stringent requirements if they wish.

The Takeover Directive applies to takeover bids for the securities of an EU company, where all or some of those securities are admitted to trading on a regulated market, such as a stock exchange, in one or more member states.

Under the Directive, member states are required to designate the authority (or authorities) competent for the purpose of supervising any bids, to ensure they meet the appropriate rules. Since the precise rules can vary across member states because of the minimum requirements approach taken by the Directive, there are requirements to determine which member state's rules apply and, therefore, the designated supervisory authority. It is the designated supervisory authority of the:

- member state in which the company subject to the offer (the offeree) has its registered office, where the offeree's securities are traded on a regulated market in that member state;
- member state in which the offeree's securities are traded, where the offeree's securities are traded on a regulated market in an EU country that is not the country in which it has its registered office.

Due to the possibility of cross-border takeovers involving an offeror in one member state and an offeree in another, the Directive also includes a requirement that supervisory authorities co-operate and supply each other with information when necessary.

The Takeover Directive's minimum requirements include six general principles that are covered in Section 2 below, and the requirement to launch a mandatory bid in certain circumstances. The mandatory bid provision states that where a natural or legal person, as a result of an acquisition by him or in concert with him, reaches a specified percentage to gain control, he is required to make a mandatory bid for the remaining shares at an equitable price. The equitable price is the highest price paid by the offeror for the same securities over a period of between six and twelve months prior to the bid.

The Directive also requires information about any takeover bid to be made public. The Directive states that the decision to make a bid is made public without delay, and that the supervisory authority is informed of the bid. Furthermore, the offeror is required to draw up and make public, in good time, an offer document containing the information necessary to enable the holders of securities in the offeree to reach a properly informed decision on the bid.

2. UK TAKEOVER CODE

LEARNING OBJECTIVES

5.1.2 know the legal nature and purpose of the UK Takeover Code (section 2 of the Introduction); the six General Principles; the definitions of "acting in concert", "dealings", "interest in shares" and "relevant securities"

The UK supervisory authority that carries out the regulatory functions required under the EU Takeover Directive is the **Panel on Takeovers and Mergers** (the **Panel** or **POTAM**). The Panel's requirements are set out in a Code that consists of six General Principles, and a number of detailed rules.

The Code is designed principally to ensure that shareholders are treated fairly and are not denied an opportunity to decide on the merits of a takeover. Furthermore, the Code ensures that shareholders of the same class are afforded equivalent treatment by an offeror. In short, the Code provides an orderly framework within which takeovers are conducted, and is designed to assist in promoting the integrity of the financial markets.

The Code is not concerned with the financial or commercial advantages or disadvantages of a takeover. These are matters for the company and its shareholders. Nor is the Code concerned with competition policy, which is the responsibility of government and other bodies.

Each of the six general principles are reproduced in full below. Although the detail of each principle is probably outside the syllabus, it is useful to be able to review the principles to fully appreciate the spirit of the Code. At its broadest, the Code simply requires fair play between all interested parties.

1. All holders of the securities of an offeree company of the same class must be afforded equivalent treatment; moreover, if a person acquires control of a company, the other holders of securities must be protected.

2. The holders of the securities of an offeree company must have sufficient time and information to enable them to reach a properly informed decision on the bid; where it advises the holders of securities, the board of the offeree company must give its views on the effects of implementation of the bid on employment, conditions of employment and the locations of the company's places of business.

3. The board of an offeree company must act in the best interests of the company as a whole and must not deny the holders of securities the opportunity to decide on the merits of the bid.

4. False markets must not be created in the securities of the offeree company, or the offeror company or of any other company concerned by the bid in such a way that the rise or fall of the prices of the securities becomes artificial and the normal functioning of the markets is distorted.

5. An offeror must announce a bid only after ensuring that he/she can fulfil in full any cash consideration, if such is offered, and after taking all reasonable measures to secure the implementation of any other type of consideration.

6. An offeree company must not be hindered in the conduct of its affairs for longer than is reasonable by a bid for its securities.

It is also important to be aware of the following terms that are used in the Code:

- Acting in concert - persons actively co-operating through the acquisition of shares to obtain or consolidate control of a company. The Code presumes that the following will be acting in concert:

    a. a company and other group companies (parent company, subsidiaries and associated companies);

    b. a company and its directors (including the directors' close relatives and related trusts);

    c. a company and its pension fund;

    d. a fund manager and investment vehicles which the manager manages with discretion;

    e. a client and its professional advisors.

- Dealings - these include the straightforward acquisition or disposal of securities, as well as involvement in derivative contracts on, or referenced to, the securities and any other action that may result in an increase or decrease in the number of securities a person is interested in.

- Interests in shares - a person is treated as having an interest in shares if he owns the shares, has a right to exercise or direct the voting rights on them, or is otherwise interested in those shares through derivatives. A person with only a short position does not have an interest in those shares.

- Relevant securities - these include the following:

    a. securities of the offeree company which are being offered for, or which carry, voting rights;

    b. equity share capital of the offeree company and an offeror;

    c. securities of an offeror which carry substantially the same rights as any to be issued as consideration for the offer; and

    d. securities of the offeree company and an offeror carrying conversion or subscription rights into any of the foregoing.

3. DISCLOSURE OF INTERESTS

3.1 Principles behind the disclosure rules

> **LEARNING OBJECTIVES**
>
> 5.2.1 understand the principles behind disclosure of interest rules and why they are required

In developed equity markets with a substantial number of listed companies, it is felt appropriate that when investors purchase (or sell) shares to bring about (or remove) a significant stake in a company, such information should be made available to the investing public. This will let others judge the likely impact on the price.

As we will see, the level at which a shareholding is deemed significant is set at 3% in the UK; for example, if a corporate raider built up a stake of 3% or more in a listed UK company, it would be disclosed to the market. This would enable other existing and potential investors to assess the company in full knowledge that there is a new significant shareholding.

3.2 Disclosure rules

> **LEARNING OBJECTIVES**
>
> 5.2.2 know the named disclosure of interest rules
>
> (see the syllabus learning map at the back of the book for the full learning objective)

The disclosure rules vary in different jurisdictions. In this section we will consider three jurisdictions – the EU generally, more specifically the UK, and the US.

The EU has harmonised disclosure rules via the implementation of the **Transparency Directive**. The Transparency Directive establishes disclosure requirements on an ongoing basis for issuers who have securities admitted to trading on a regulated market situated or operated within the EU. Included within the Directive's requirements are notification requirements of both issuers and investors in relation to the acquisition and disposal of significant shareholdings in companies.

The notification requirement is triggered when the size of holdings reach, exceed, or move below certain thresholds. In the Directive these thresholds are set at 5%, 10%, 15%, 20%, 25%, 30%, 50% and 75%. The shareholder reaching or breaching the threshold is required to inform the issuer, and the issuer will then inform the market.

In the US, the Securities and Exchange Commission (SEC) requires disclosures by any person who directly or indirectly acquires a beneficial interest of 5% or more of any class of shares of a registered (and, therefore, listed) entity. The acquirer is required to issue a statement to both the SEC and the company within 10 days of acquisition.

Despite being an EU member state, the regulations relating to disclosure of shareholdings can (and do) vary from country to country. This is because, if they wish, EU member states are able to exceed the requirements of the Directive – a process known as 'super-equivalence'. On implementation of the Directive, the UK chose to retain its thresholds at 3% and each percentage point above that level.

So, under UK regulation, an investor is judged to have a **notifiable interest** in a public company if he holds 3% or more of its shares. At this point he is obliged to inform the company of his holding.

Furthermore, once the investor's holding is above 3%, he must also inform the company if it rises or falls through a whole percentage point.

- A stake of 3.7% rising to 4.1% would need to be reported, but a stake of 3.7% rising to 3.9% would not.
- A stake of 5.4% falling to 4.9% would need to be reported, but a stake of 5.4% falling to 5.1% would not.

An investor must also inform the company if his stake falls back to below 3%.

The reason that this disclosure is deemed necessary, despite the fact that the company maintains a register of its shareholders, is that these notifiable interest rules not only include those shares held directly by the investor, but also those shares held by parties connected to them, known as **connected parties**. These would include shares held by the following:

- the investor's spouse;
- the investor's infant children (less than 18 years old);
- companies controlled by the investor. For these purposes, control is assumed if the investor holds at least one third of the voting rights of the company;
- concert parties. This is simply an agreement between two or more persons to influence the company together, such as voting together. If the combined holding reached 3% or more it would become notifiable, as if it were a single holding.

As seen above, 3% is the level at which notification starts and this information must be reported in writing to the company within **two business days**. If the company is listed, it must then report the same information to a primary information provider, such as the London Stock Exchange (LSE), by **the end of the following business day**.

Fund managers and operators of regulated collective investment schemes (such as authorised unit trusts and open-ended investment companies) are deemed to be non-beneficial holders and are exempt from reporting under the notifiable interest (3%) rule. Disclosure requirements for fund managers and the like start at 5%.

Some shareholders are completely exempted from the disclosure rules, eg, if the shares are held by:

- a market maker, or dealer in shares, for the purposes of that business;
- a custodian (that is not able to control the voting rights of the shares concerned).

The company is required to maintain a register of notifications of interests in shares and make this available at its registered office.

Companies Act Section 793 Letter

Under Section 793 of the Companies Act 2006, a UK public company is able to send a written notice to any person that the company knows or suspects to be a shareholder and ask them to confirm whether they are holding any shares. The notice requests details of that shareholder's total interest in the company.

The notice can also request details of past shareholdings held at anytime in the last three years and, where the interest is a past interest, to give details of the identity of the person to whom the shares were sold if that is known.

However, it is rare for such a notice to be sent by the company registrar to an individual shareholder. These letters are usually sent to the **nominee companies** that appear on the register. A nominee company is the legal owner of shares on behalf of another beneficial owner.

The letter is sent to the **company secretary** of the **nominee company** requesting details of the true beneficial owner of the securities. This enables the registrar to identify when someone is using the nominee company to hide his identity and accumulate a substantial holding without anyone being aware of the fact.

Notices under Section 793 require a written response from the recipient within a reasonable time as may be specified in the letter. If requests are persistently ignored, the company could apply to court to have the shares held **frozen**. This would mean the shareholders would lose their rights to vote on those shares, lose their entitlement to dividends and be unable to sell them.

The company is required to keep a record of the Section 793 letters that have been sent, and the information received, in a separate part of its register of shareholders.

4. SPECIFIC REGULATIONS IN THE US, CANADA AND JAPAN

4.1 Restrictions

LEARNING OBJECTIVES

5.3.1 know that these markets restrict the promotion and sale of foreign equity

The United States, Canada and Japan all have rules and regulations in place to ensure that domestic investors do not have foreign equities sold and promoted to them, unless such equities have met, or exceeded, certain regulatory hurdles. Broadly, these regulatory hurdles aim to make sure that the company concerned is sufficiently well established and reputable to be held by domestic investors.

4.2 Registration

LEARNING OBJECTIVES

5.3.2 know that foreign broker-dealers must be registered with the local regulator in these markets before they can disseminate research

For similar reasons to the restrictions outlined in the previous section, the United States, Canada and Japan all have requirements relating to foreign broker-dealers. To ensure the regulatory standards of protection cannot be compromised, foreign broker-dealers are required to be registered with the local regulator before they are able to disseminate research to domestic investors.

ACCOUNTING ANALYSIS

1.	INTRODUCTION	143
2.	COMPANY BALANCE SHEETS	146
3.	THE INCOME STATEMENT	153
4.	THE CASH FLOW STATEMENT	156
5.	FINANCIAL STATEMENT ANALYSIS	160

This syllabus area will provide approximately 13 of the 100 examination questions

Certificate in Securities and Financial Derivatives - Part 1

1. INTRODUCTION

1.1 The Purpose of Financial Statements

LEARNING OBJECTIVES

6.1.1 understand the purpose of financial statements

Accounting can be defined as the recording, measuring and reporting of economic events, or activities, to interested parties in a useable form. It is about providing information relating to the financial and economic activities of a business in the form of a set of accounts. This set of accounts is alternatively referred to as the financial statements of the business. The need for accounting information in the form of financial statements was stimulated by the emergence of the limited liability company in the 19th Century and the resulting separation of ownership and control. The financial statements provided information to the owners about the business that may have been managed by someone else.

However, although companies initially provided accounting information to satisfy the informational needs of their shareholders, the form this information now takes, and the way in which it is communicated, must also meet the disparate needs of other parties with a legitimate interest in the company's activities, performance and financial position. These other users include creditors, prospective investors, employees, financial analysts, institutional investors, as well as government, consumers and environmental groups.

The directors of a company are required to prepare financial statements and make other disclosures within an annual report and accounts. These set out the results of the company's activities during its most recent accounting period and its financial position as at the end of the period. The accounting period typically spans a 12 month period.

Broadly, these financial statements comprise three major statements:

1. **A balance sheet.** This provides a snapshot of the company's financial position as at the company's accounting year end by summarising the assets it owns and how they are financed at this one point in time.

2. **An income statement.** This statement summarises income (or revenue) that has been earned by the company over the accounting period. Broadly it is a summary of the trading activities of the company over the year - if income exceeds costs, the company has made a profit; if costs exceed income then the company has made a loss.

   The income statement links the company's previous balance sheet with its current one. This relationship is depicted below:

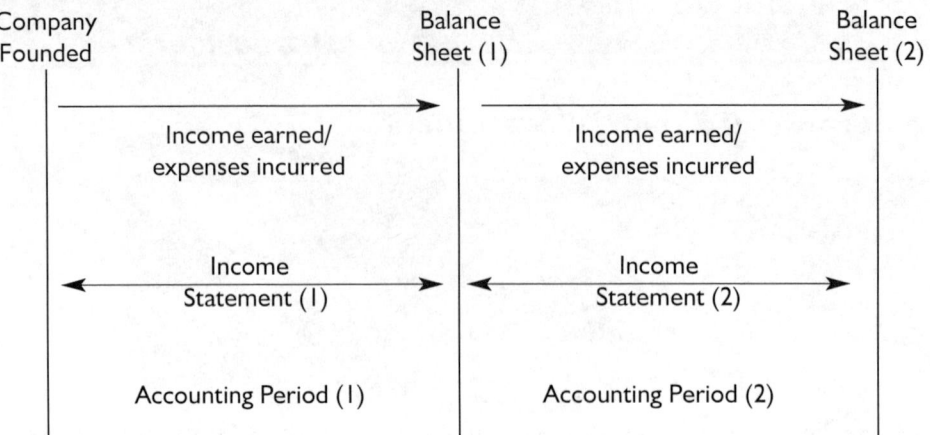

3. **A cash flow statement.** Companies must also publish a cash flow statement within their annual report and accounts. This financial statement identifies how much cash the company generated over the accounting period and how much cash has been spent.

The financial statements also include certain additional disclosures such as the comparative figures from the previous year's financial statements, explanatory notes to accompany certain individual balance sheet and profit and loss account items and disclosure of the company's accounting policies. The accounting policies are the basis on which the accounts have been prepared.

The information contained in the company's report and accounts is also required to be independently verified, or audited. An audit is an independent assessment of the company's accounts that have been prepared by the directors. This audit is concluded with an auditor's report to the members, or shareholders, of the company confirming whether or not the accounts give a true and fair view of the company's activities and financial position and whether they have been prepared in accordance with the law and other regulations. If so, then an unqualified audit report is issued. If not, then the auditor must issue a qualified report and state the reason for this qualification.

1.2 Accounting Regulations

> **LEARNING OBJECTIVES**
>
> 6.1.2 understand the requirements for companies and groups to prepare accounts in accordance with applicable accounting standards: Accounting principles; International Financial Reporting Standards (IFRS); IAS

The form and content of all company financial statements and their respective disclosures are prescribed by the law and mandatory accounting standards set by the accountancy profession. Accounting standards are authoritative statements of how particular types of transaction and other events should be reflected in financial statements. The combination of accounting regulations is often referred to as the 'generally accepted accounting principles' or GAAP. Each country's GAAP varies to a lesser or greater extent and there are efforts being made to harmonise GAAP throughout the world, spearheaded by the International Accounting Standards Board (IASB).

The IASB is an independent, privately-funded accounting standard-setter based in London. The Board members come from nine countries and have a variety of functional backgrounds. The IASB is committed to developing, in the public interest, a single set of high quality, understandable and enforceable global accounting standards that require transparent and comparable information in general purpose financial statements. In addition, the IASB co-operates with national accounting standard-setters to achieve convergence in accounting standards around the world.

Standards issued by the International Accounting Standards Board are designated International Financial Reporting Standards (IFRSs). There were standards issued by the IASB's predecessor (the International Accounting Standards Committee) that continue to be designated International Accounting Standards (IASs). The IASB has retained the IASs and also issues IFRSs.

1.3 Group versus company accounts

LEARNING OBJECTIVES

6.1.3 understand the differences between group accounts and company accounts and why companies are required to prepare group accounts. (Candidates should understand the concept of goodwill and minority interests but will not be required to calculate these).

If a company invests in another company, all that appears in the accounts of the investing company is the original cost of the investment (in the balance sheet), and the dividends received (if there are any) appears in the investing company's income statement. This treatment is fine where the investment is a small, minority shareholding in another company. However, in instances where the investment is so significant that the investing company controls the other company, another accounting treatment is required – the preparation of **group** financial statements (known as group accounts). The investing company is described as the 'parent' and the company or companies that the parent company controls are described as subsidiaries. As long as a parent/subsidiary relationship exists, then the parent company should prepare and present a set of group accounts in addition to their individual company financial statements.

These group accounts present the financial statements as if the parent and the subsidiaries were a single entity, rather than distinct individual companies. This entails the addition of the assets of the parent plus all of the subsidiaries' assets to arrive at the group assets, and similar additions to arrive at the group's liabilities, revenues, expenses and cash flows.

Two particular issues can crop up when amalgamating the figures for the parent company and its subsidiaries:

1. **Goodwill.** When presenting the group accounts as a single entity, the assets and liabilities of the subsidiaries are added to those of the parent company. This replaces the original cost of investment in the group balance sheet. If the cost of investment exceeded the net assets (assets less liabilities) of the subsidiary, the excess is described as 'goodwill' and appears as an asset in the group accounts.

2. **Minority interests.** In circumstances where the parent company owns a majority of the shares in a subsidiary, but not all of the shares, there will be minority interests. For example, if a parent owned 75% of the shares of a subsidiary, the minority interest would be 25%; if it owned 51% of the shares the minority would be 49%. Because the presentation of the group accounts adds together all of the assets and liabilities of the subsidiaries, it includes some net assets that belong to the minority interests. These are reflected by including net assets and net income that belongs to the minority interests in the group balance sheet and income statement.

2. COMPANY BALANCE SHEETS

2.1 Balance sheet purpose, format and main contents

LEARNING OBJECTIVES

6.2.1 know the purpose of the balance sheet, its format and main contents, (including on and off balance sheet items)

The balance sheet is a snapshot of a company's financial position at a particular moment. It is split into two halves that must always balance each other exactly, hence the name. The key information it provides to shareholders, customers and other interested parties is what the company owns (its assets), what the company owes others (its liabilities, or creditors) and the extent to which shareholders are providing finance to the company (the equity).

The balance sheet should reflect all of the reporting company's assets and liabilities, but over the years companies and their advisors often developed creative structures to enable items to remain 'off balance sheet' rather than 'on balance sheet'. The IASB and the adoption of its accounting standards should ensure that everything that should appear on the balance sheet is categorised as 'on balance sheet', and those items that are legitimately not assets or liabilities of the company should remain 'off balance sheet'.

The typical format of the balance sheet, with example figures, is provided below, followed by an explanation of each of the headings:

A plc Balance Sheet as at 31 December 2006	
£'000	2006
Assets	
Non-current assets	
Property, plant and equipment	8900
Intangible assets	2100
Investments	300
	11300
Current assets	
Inventories	3600
Trade and other receivables	2600
Prepayments	120
Cash	860
	7180
Total assets	18480
Equity and liabilities	
Capital and reserves	
Share capital - 10m 50p ordinary shares	5000
Share capital - preference shares	100
Share premium account	120
Revaluation reserve	180
Retained earnings	6880
Total equity	12280
Non-current liabilities	
Bank loans	2000
Provisions	
	2000
Current liabilities	
Trade and other payables	4200
	4200
Total liabilities	6200
Total equity and liabilities	18480

Assets

An asset is anything that is owned and controlled by the company and confers the right to future economic benefits. Balance sheet assets are categorised as either non-current assets or current assets.

Non-Current Assets

Non-current assets are those in long-term, continuing use by the company. They represent the major investments from which the company hopes to make money. Non-current assets are categorised as:

1. Tangible.
2. Intangible.
3. Investments.

Tangible Non-Current Assets

A company's tangible non-current assets are those that have physical substance, such as land and buildings and plant and machinery. Tangible non-current assets are initially recorded in the balance sheet at their actual cost, or book value. However, in order to reflect the fact that the asset will generate benefits for the company over several accounting periods, not just in the accounting period in which it is purchased, all tangible non-current assets with a limited economic life are required to be depreciated. The concept of depreciation will be covered in more detail in the Section 2.2 below.

Intangible non-current assets

Intangible non-current assets are those assets that, although without physical substance, can be separately identified and are capable of being sold. Ownership of an intangible non-current asset confers rights known as intellectual property. These rights give a company a competitive advantage over its peers and commonly include brand names, patents, trade marks, capitalised development costs and purchased goodwill.

As seen earlier, purchased goodwill arises when the consideration, or price, paid by the acquiring company for the target exceeds the fair value of the target's separable, or individually identifiable, net assets. This is not necessarily the same as the book, or balance sheet, value of these net assets:

purchased goodwill = (price paid for company - fair value of separable net tangible and intangible assets)

Purchased goodwill is capitalised and included in the balance sheet.

Purchased goodwill, once capitalised, cannot be revalued.

Investments

Non-current asset investments are long-term investments held in other companies. These investments might be equity investments or investments in debt instruments. They are recorded in the balance sheet at cost less any impairment to their value.

Current Assets

Current assets are those assets purchased with the intention of resale or conversion into cash, usually within a 12 month period. They include stocks (or inventories) of finished goods and work in progress, the debtor balances that arise from the company providing its customers with credit (trade receivables) and any short term investments held. Current assets also include cash balances held by the company and prepayments. Prepayments are simply where the company has prepaid an expense, as illustrated by the following example:

> **Example**
>
> XYZ plc draws up its balance sheet on 31 December each year. Just prior to the year end XYZ pays £25,000 to its landlord for the next three months' rental on its offices (to the end of March in the next calendar year).
>
> This £25,000 is not an expense for the current year - it represents a prepayment towards the following year's expenses and is, therefore, shown as a prepayment within current assets in XYZ's balance sheet.

Current assets are listed in the balance sheet in ascending order of liquidity and appear in the balance sheet at the lower of cost or net realisable value (NRV).

2.2 Depreciation and Amortisation

LEARNING OBJECTIVES

6.2.2 understand the concept of depreciation and amortisation

Depreciation is applied to tangible, non-current assets such as plant and machinery. An annual depreciation charge is made in the year's income statement. The depreciation charge allocates the fall in the book value of the asset over its useful economic life. This requirement does not, however, apply to freehold land and non-current asset investments which, by not having a limited economic life, are not usually depreciated.

To calculate the annual depreciation charge to be applied to a tangible asset, the difference between its cost and estimated disposal value, termed the depreciable amount, must first be established. This value is then written off over the asset's useful economic life by employing the most appropriate depreciation method. The most common depreciation method is the straight line method.

The straight line method simply spreads the depreciable amount equally over the economic life of the asset. The straight line method is given by the following formula:

$$\text{Straight line depreciation} = \frac{\text{(cost - disposal value)}}{\text{useful economic life in years}}$$

One thing to recognise about the annual depreciation charge is that it is an accounting book entry, or a non-cash charge. That is, no cash flows from the business as a result of making the charge: it is simply an accounting entry made against the income statement to reflect the estimated cost of resources used over an accounting period. The balance sheet value of the asset is given by its cost, less the accumulated depreciation to date, and is termed the net book value (NBV). This NBV does not necessarily equal the market value of the asset.

Depreciation Example

A machine purchased for £25,000 has an estimated useful economic life of six years and an estimated disposal value after six years of £1,000. Calculate the depreciation that should be charged to this asset and its NBV in years one to six, using the straight line depreciation method.

Solution

Straight depreciation

$$\text{Straight line depreciation} = \frac{(\text{cost} - \text{disposal value})}{\text{useful economic life (years)}}$$

$$= \frac{(£25,000 - £1,000)}{6} = £4,000 \text{ per annum}$$

Year	Opening net book value	Depreciation	Closing net book value
1	25,000	4,000	21,000
2	21,000	4,000	17,000
3	17,000	4,000	13,000
4	13,000	4,000	9,000
5	9,000	4,000	5,000
6	5,000	4,000	1,000

By reducing the book value of tangible non-current assets over their useful economic lives, depreciation matches the cost of the asset against the periods from which the company benefits from its use.

On occasion, tangible assets, such as land, are not depreciated but periodically revalued. This is done on the basis of providing the user of the accounts with a truer and fairer view of the assets, or capital, employed by the company. To preserve the accounting equation, (total assets = equity and liabilities), the increase in the asset's value arising on revaluation is transferred to a revaluation reserve, which forms part of the equity.

Closely linked to the idea of depreciating the value of a tangible asset over its useful economic life is the potential need for intangible assets to be amortised over their useful economic lives. Amortisation, like depreciation, is simply a book entry whose impact is felt in the company's reported income and financial position but does not impact its cash position.

2.3 Equity

> **LEARNING OBJECTIVES**
>
> 6.2.3 understand the difference between authorised and issued share capital, capital reserves and revenue reserves

Equity is referred to in a number of ways, such as shareholders' funds, owners' equity or capital. Equity usually consists of three sub-elements: **share capital**, **capital reserves** and **revenue reserves**. Additionally, when group accounts are presented, there may be 'minority interests' within the group equity figure.

- **Share Capital**

    This is the nominal value of equity and preference share capital the company has in issue and has called up. This may differ from the amount of share capital the company is authorised to issue as contained in its constitutional documents - the company may have only called up some of its share capital and may not have issued all of the share capital that is authorised.

- **Capital Reserves**

    Capital reserves include revaluation reserves and the share premium account. The revaluation reserve arises from the upward revaluation of non-current assets, and the share premium reserve arises when the company issues shares at a price above their nominal value. Capital reserves are not distributable to the company's shareholders in the form of dividends as they form part of the company's capital base, although they can be converted into a bonus issue of ordinary shares.

- **Revenue Reserves**

    The major revenue reserve is the accumulated retained earnings of the company - this represents the accumulation of the company's distributable profits that have not been paid to the company's shareholders as dividends, but have been retained in the business. The retained earnings should not be confused with the amount of cash the company holds or with the income statement that shows how the retained, or undistributed, profit in a single accounting period was arrived at.

- **Minority Interests**

    As covered earlier in this chapter, minority interests arise when a parent company controls one or more subsidiary companies, but does not own all of the share capital. The equity attributable to the remaining shareholders is the minority interests and this is reflected in the balance sheet within the equity section.

In total, equity is the sum of the called up share capital, all of the capital reserves and the revenue reserves:

$$\text{Equity} = \text{share capital} + \text{reserves}$$

2.4 Liabilities

LEARNING OBJECTIVES

6.2.4 know how loans and indebtedness are included within a balance sheet

A liability is an obligation to transfer future economic benefits as a result of past transactions or events; more simply, it could be described as money owed to someone else. Liabilities are categorised according to whether they are to be paid within, or after more than, one year:

1. Non-current liabilities. This comprises the company's borrowing not repayable within the next 12 months. This could include bond issues as well as longer term bank borrowing.

   In addition, there is a separate sub-heading for those liabilities that have resulted from past events or transactions and for which there is an obligation to make a payment, but the exact amount or timing of the expenditure has yet to be established. These are commonly referred to as 'provisions', as such provisions may arise as a result of the company undergoing a restructuring for example. Given the uncertainty surrounding the extent of such liabilities, companies are required to create a realistic and prudent estimate of the monetary amount of the obligation once it is committed to taking a certain course of action.

2. Current liabilities. This includes the amount the company owes to its suppliers, or trade payables, as a result of buying goods and/or services on credit, any bank overdraft and any other payables such as tax, that are due within 12 months of the balance sheet date.

3. THE INCOME STATEMENT

3.1 Purpose and contents

> **LEARNING OBJECTIVES**
>
> 6.3.1 know the purpose of the income statement, its format and main contents

The income statement summarises the company's income earned and expenditure incurred over the accounting period. The function of this financial statement is to detail how much profit has been earned and how the company's reported profit (or loss) was arrived at.

The amount of profit earned over the accounting period will impact the company's ability to pay dividends and how much can be retained to finance the growth of the business from internal resources.

Like the balance sheet, the format of the income statement is governed by the law and underpinned by the requirements of various accounting standards. The income statement of A plc is shown below. In reality, comparative numbers for the previous year and explanatory notes would be provided as well.

A plc Income Statement for the year end 31 December 2006	Notes	2006	2005
		£'000	£'000
Revenue		9,500	8,750
Cost of sales		(7,000)	(6,600)
Gross profit		2,500	2,150
Distribution costs		(110)	(90)
Administrative expenses		(30)	(20)
Loss on disposal of plant		(260)	
Operating profit		2,100	2,040
Finance costs		(230)	(250)
Finance income		120	112
Profit before taxation		1,990	1,902
Taxation		(555)	(548)
Net income		1,435	1,354
Earnings per share (pence)		16.1p	15.9p

Revenue

The income statement starts with one of the most important things in any company's accounts: its sales revenues. In accounts, sales revenues are generally referred to as revenue, or sometimes turnover - it is simply everything that the company has sold during the year, regardless of whether it has received the cash or not. For a manufacturer, revenue would be the sales of the products that it has made. For a company in the service industry, it would be the consulting fees earned, or perhaps commissions earned on financial transactions.

Costs of Sales

The costs of sales are the costs to the company of generating the sales made in the financial year. They typically include the costs of the raw materials used to make a product and the costs of converting those raw materials into their finished state, including the wages of the staff making the products.

Gross Profit

Total sales, less the costs of those sales, results in the gross profit for the year.

Operating Profit

Operating profit is also referred to as 'profit on operating activities'. It is the gross profit, less other operating expenses, that the company has incurred. These other operating expenses might include cost incurred distributing products (distribution costs) and administrative expenses such as management salaries, auditors' fees and legal fees. Administrative expenses would also include depreciation and amortisation charges. Additional items may be separately disclosed before arriving at operating profit, such as the profit or loss made on selling a non-current asset. When a non-current asset, such as an item of machinery, is disposed of at a price significantly different from its balance sheet value, the profit or loss when compared to this net book value (NBV) should be separately disclosed if material to the information conveyed by the accounts.

Operating profit is the profit before considering finance costs (interest) and any tax payable – so it can be described as **profit before interest and tax (pbit)**.

Finance costs/finance income

Finance costs are generally the interest that the company has incurred on its borrowings - that may be in the form of bonds or may be bank loans and overdrafts. Finance income is typically the interest earned on surplus funds, such as from deposit accounts.

Profit before Tax

This is the profit made by the company in the period, before considering any tax that might be payable on that profit.

Corporation Tax Payable

This is simply the corporation tax charge that the company has incurred for the period.

Net Income

Now that tax and financing costs have been deducted we have a vital figure: net income. It reflects all the income earned during the period, less all of the expenditures incurred. This net income is also the profit attributable to the shareholders of the company because, in theory, it could all be distributed to shareholders as dividends.

Earnings per Share (EPS)

This is an important figure for readers of the financial statements and is always reflected at the bottom of the income statement, in pence. EPS is the amount of profit after tax that has been earned per ordinary share. EPS is calculated as follows:

EPS = net income for the financial year
      number of ordinary shares in issue

Dividends

Some, or all, of the profit for the financial year can be distributed as dividends. Dividends to any preference shareholders are paid out first, followed by dividends to ordinary shareholders at an amount set by the board and expressed as a number of pence per share. The dividends for most listed companies are paid in two installments: an interim dividend paid after the half-year stage, and a final proposed dividend to be paid after the accounts have been approved. The dividends are shown in the accounts in a note that reconciles the movement in equity from one balance sheet to another.

A plc Statement of changes in equity for the year ended 31 December 2006						
	Ord Share Capital	Pref Share Capital	Share premium account	Revaluation Reserve	Retained earnings	Total
As at 1 January 2006	4,470	100		100	5,880	10,550
Gain on revaluation				80		80
Issue of shares	530		120			650
Net income for the year					1,435	1,435
Preference dividends paid					(5)	(5)
Ordinary dividends paid					(430)	(430)
As at 31 December 2006	5,000	100	120	180	6,880	12,280

3.2 Capital versus Revenue Expenditure

> **LEARNING OBJECTIVES**
> 6.3.2 understand the difference between capital and revenue expenditure

Money spent by a company will usually fall into one of two possible forms: **capital** expenditure or **revenue** expenditure.

Capital expenditure is money spent to buy non-current assets, such as plant, property and equipment. It is reflected on the balance sheet.

Revenue expenditure is money spent that immediately impacts the income statement. Examples of revenue expenditure include wages paid to staff, rent paid on property and professional fees, like audit fees.

4. THE CASH FLOW STATEMENT

4.1 Purpose of the Cash Flow Statement

> **LEARNING OBJECTIVES**
> 6.4.1 know the purpose of the cash flow statement, its format as set out in IAS 7

The cash flow statement is basically a summary of all the payments and receipts that have occurred over the course of the year, the total reflecting the inflow (or outflow) of cash over the year.

A cash flow statement is required by accounting standard IAS7 Cash Flow Statements particularly.

The logic of adding a cash flow statement to a set of financial statements is that it enables the readers of the accounts to clearly see how cash has been generated and/or used over the course of the year. This is felt to provide easily understood information to the users of the accounts that supplements the performance figures provided by the income statement, and the statement of financial position given by the balance sheet.

IAS7 Cash Flow Statements require a company's cash flows to be broken down into particular headings, as illustrated in the following example:

A plc Cash Flow Statement for the year ended 31 December 2006	
	2006
Operating activities	
Cash receipts from customers	4528
Cash paid to suppliers and employees	-2001
Cash generated from operations	2527
Tax paid	-440
Interest paid	-150
Net cash from operating activities	4464
Investing activities	
Interest received	80
Dividends received	40
Purchase of fixed assets	-1890
Proceeds on sale of investments	120
Net cash used in investing activities	-1650
Financing activities	
Dividends paid	-435
Repayments of borrowings	-200
Proceeds on issue of shares	650
Net cash generated from financing activities	15
Net increase in cash and cash equivalents	2829
Cash and cash equivalents at the beginning of the year	425
Cash and cash equivalents at the end of the year	3254

Looking at the key cash flow statement headings in turn:

- **Operating activities** is the cash that has been generated from the trading activities of the company, excluding financing cost (interest);

- **Investing activities** details the investment income (dividends and interest) that has been received in the form of cash during the year and the cash paid to purchase new non-current assets less the cash received from the sale of non-current assets during the year;

- **Financing activities** includes the cash spent during the year on paying dividends to shareholders the cash raised from issuing shares or borrowing on a long-term basis, less the cash spent repaying debt or buying back shares.

The resultant total should explain the changes in cash (and cash equivalents) between the balance sheets. Many short-term investments are classified as cash equivalents, such as Treasury bills.

4.2 Profit versus Cash

LEARNING OBJECTIVES

6.4.2 understand the difference between profit and cash and their impact on the long term future of the business

Profit appears in the income statement and is the excess of revenues earned over the period, over the expenses incurred in that same period. Obviously, generating profits is necessary for the long-term survival of any business, although companies can (and many do) exhibit losses for a number of years. Without a profitable business, that business is unlikely to survive indefinitely.

The extent to which a company has generated (or used up) cash is detailed in the cash flow statement. Cash is generated when cash received exceeds cash paid out, and cash is used up when the cash paid out exceeds the cash received. Cash is often described as the 'lifeblood of the company' – without it the company will not survive. If a company does not have the cash to pay a liability when it is due, there is a possibility of the company being forced to close down.

When comparing profit against cash, there are some key differences. Because profit is based on revenues earned, not cash received, there is a possibility that the two figures for a company could be very different. For example, a company might make sales on credit and, therefore, recognise the revenues at the point of sale in the income statement. The cash received for those sales could be significantly later.

Similarly, profit is based on expenditure incurred, not cash paid and there can be significant differences between the two. A key example of the potential for difference is in the different treatments of the purchase of a non-current tangible asset, like a machine. In the income statement, the impact will be a gradual expense incurred each year for the depreciation of the machine. In the cash flow statement, the full cost will be paid in cash at the time of purchase.

4.3 Free Cash Flow

> **LEARNING OBJECTIVES**
>
> 6.4.3 understand the purpose of Free Cash Flow and the difference between Enterprise Cash Flow and Equity Cash Flow

There is no single definition of 'free cash flow'. Logically, it perhaps should be drawn from the cash flow statement and represent the amount of cash that has been generated and that the company can choose what to do with. This might be the operating cash flow less the extent to which the company has to spend cash to maintain the operating capacity of the business. It is the latter figure that is difficult to isolate, and is likely to be a subjective judgement by the user of the accounts. The resultant figure might be adjusted further depending on whether the calculation is for free cash flow to the firm (enterprise cash flow), or just free cash flow to the shareholders (equity cash flow). This will be explored in more detail below.

Because of the difficulty is arriving at free cash flow from the cash flow statement, many users calculate a free cash flow figure from the income statement. This is generally arrived at by taking the net income from the income statement, adding back the charges for depreciation and amortisation and deducting capital expenditure. The capital expenditure will again be a judgement of the capital spend required to maintain the operating capacity of the business, with the use of income statement figures for operating cash flow presenting a smoother, potentially more representative figure for cash generation by removing the inconsistencies payments in advance or in arrears can create.

As well as there being two potentially different sources for free cash flow (the cash flow statement or the income statement), there are further adjustments that might be made depending on whether the free cash flow is being calculated for the whole enterprise (the enterprise cash flow) or is being calculated for the equity holders only (the equity cash flow).

The enterprise cash flow is the free cash flow before considering payments made to any of the providers of finance to the firm. The providers of finance to the firm are both the lenders and the equity holders. The enterprise cash flow will, therefore, be the free cash flow before considering any financing costs.

In contrast the equity cash flow is the free cash flow to the shareholders, so it will be after any financing costs to the lenders, but before any dividend payments to the shareholders.

5. FINANCIAL STATEMENT ANALYSIS

The three principal financial statements and associated explanatory notes published by companies in their report and accounts furnish the user with a considerable amount of information. However, the needs of the user can be met more precisely by employing ratio analysis as key relationships can be established and trends identified by consolidating this information into a more readily useable form. Ratios are commonly employed by analysts to assess the prospects for a particular company and, therefore, the investment potential of the shares of that company, as well as assisting other interested parties in assessing the company such as the Board, suppliers, competitors and employees.

The purpose of ratio analysis is three-fold:

1. To assist in assessing business performance by identifying meaningful relationships between numbers contained within company financial statements that may not be immediately apparent. Although there are no statutory rules as to how ratios should be calculated, there should be logic in the numbers being related to each other.
2. To summarise financial information into an easily understandable form.
3. To identify trends, strengths and weaknesses by comparing the ratios to those of the same company in prior periods, other similar companies, sector averages and market averages.

However, ratio analysis does have its limitations:

1. As financial statements contain historic data, ratios are not predictive, indeed occasionally historic figures can be restated in later periods, making comparison difficult.
2. Because there is no regulatory method of calculation for most ratios, comparison must only be made when the calculation methods do not differ.

The ratios required for the examination follow, first an explanation of key subsets of the ratios to meet the examiner's requirement that the candidate 'understands' the ratios, followed by the formulae so that the candidate can also 'calculate' the specified ratios.

5.1 ROCE and profitability ratios explained

> **LEARNING OBJECTIVES**
>
> 6.5.1 understand the following key ratios:
> Profitability ratios (Gross profit and Operating profit margins); Return on Capital Employed

Return on Capital Employed (ROCE) is widely seen as the best ratio for measuring overall management performance, in relation to the capital that has been paid into the business.

It looks at the amount of return (profit) that is being generated as a percentage of the finance put into the business (the capital employed). The amount of capital employed is the equity plus the long term debt. This is the money that the company holds from shareholders and debt providers, and it from this money that the management should be able to generate profits.

Profitability ratios look at the percentage return that the company generates relative to its revenues. The **gross profit** looks at the percentage of revenues that the company earns after considering just the costs of sales. The **operating profit margin** looks at the percentage of revenues that the company earns after considering costs of sales and other operating costs (such as distribution costs and administrative expenses). Clearly, all other things being equal, a greater profit margin is preferable to a lesser profit margin.

5.2 ROCE and profitability ratios calculations

LEARNING OBJECTIVES

6.5.2 be able to calculate the following key ratios: Gross profit; Operating profit margins; Return on Capital Employed

Effectively, the ROCE gives a yield for the entire company. It compares the money invested in the company with the generated return. This annual return can then be compared to other companies, or less risky investments.

The formula is:

$$\text{ROCE (\%)} = \frac{\text{operating profit}}{\text{capital employed}} \times 100$$

where operating profit is the profit before financing and tax on the income statement, and capital employed is the total for equity on the balance sheet plus the total for non-current liabilities from the balance sheet.

Using the example accounts for A plc encountered earlier:

ROCE = 2100/(12,280 + 2000) x 100 = 14.7%

The figures for the profitability ratios are drawn from the income statement. The formulae for the profitability ratios are:

Gross Profit Margin (%) = (Gross Profit / Revenues) x 100

Operating Profit Margin (%) = (Operating Profit/Revenues) x 100

Using the example from A plc earlier:

Gross Profit Margin (%) = (2500 / 9500) x 100 = 26.3%

Operating Profit Margin (%) = (2100/9500) x 100 = 22%

5.3 Financial Gearing Ratios Explained

LEARNING OBJECTIVES

6.5.3 understand the following financial gearing ratios: Investors' Debt to Equity Ratio; Net Debt to Equity Ratio; Interest Cover

Financial gearing assesses the degree to which a company is funded by borrowing (debt) compared to shareholders' funds (equity).

Gearing is a measure of **risk** within a company. It is determined by examining the amount of a company's financing that comes from debt, and the amount that comes from equity - the debt to equity ratio.

The higher the proportion of debt finance, the higher the risk that the company will not be able to meet its financing commitments. This is because interest on debt must be paid every year and the debt must be repaid at some point, whereas dividends on shares need only be paid in profitable years and share capital never has to be repaid. It is the inability to service and repay debt that brings about company failure. However, high levels of borrowing can be positive for the shareholders because debt interest is fixed and what is left after paying debt interest is the entitlement of the equity holders so, in years where the firm earns substantial returns, all of the excess belongs to the equity holders.

Whether debt levels are excessive is a matter of judgement, but gearing ratios tend to look at the total debt compared to equity. Sometimes this ratio may be less useful because, as well as holding substantial amounts of debt, the company also holds substantial cash and short-term investments that could be used to repay the debt – it is in these circumstances where **net debt to equity** is used.

Another way that can be used to assess whether debt levels are excessive is to look at the extent to which profits are being made to cover the interest burden on that debt – the **interest cover**.

5.4 Financial Gearing Ratio Calculations

LEARNING OBJECTIVES

6.5.4 be able to calculate the following financial gearing ratios: Investors' Debt to Equity Ratio; Net Debt to Equity Ratio; Interest Cover

Debt to Equity = Debt/Equity

Both figures are drawn from the balance sheet. All non-current liabilities are generally considered to be **debt**, and the total of the equity portion of the balance sheet is considered to be equity. The ratio is either stated as a simple proportion, for example debt to equity is 0.6, or as a percentage, for example debt is 60% of the equity.

Using the example of A plc from earlier in the chapter:

Debt to Equity = 2000/12280 = 0.163 or 16.3%

Net Debt to Equity = (Debt less cash and short-term investments)/Equity

For net debt to equity the figures are all drawn from the balance sheet, net debt is simply the debt as in the debt to equity ratio, less the cash and short-term investments that are within the current assets on the balance sheet.

Using the example of A plc from earlier in the chapter:

Net Debt to Equity = (2000 − 860)/12280 = 0.093 or 9.3%

Interest cover = Operating profit/Interest Costs

Interest cover figures are drawn from the income statement. The operating profit is simply divided by the interest costs (the financing costs line on the income statement).

Using the example of A plc from earlier in the chapter:

Interest cover = 2100/230 = 9.13 times

5.5 Investors' ratios explained

> **LEARNING OBJECTIVES**
> 6.5.5 understand the following investors' ratios:
> Earnings per share; Diluted earnings per share; Price
> Earnings Ratio (both historic and prospective);
> Enterprise value to EBIT; Enterprise value to EBITDA;
> Net dividend yield; Net dividend cover

Existing and potential investors look at a variety of ratios to assess whether or not a company is likely to be a good investment. These ratios look to establish:

- how expensive the shares are, in order to reach a conclusion on the likelihood of capital growth; and
- how much in dividends the shares pay, and how easily the company is able to bear the payment of those dividends, to reach a conclusion on the income those shares are likely to generate.

Earnings per share and the P/E ratio

As seen earlier in this chapter, the **earnings per share** (or **eps**) is expressed in pence and reveals how much profit was made during the year that is available to be paid out to each share. As a figure for 'profit per share' it can be divided into the current share price to assess how many times the profit per share must be paid to buy a share – in effect, how expensive (or cheap) those shares are. This is the **price/earning ratio**.

The figure for earnings per share that is used in the price/earning ratio is potentially misleading in instances where the company has substantial quantities of instruments in issue that are convertible into shares. These may be convertible bonds or share options issued to the senior management of the company. The danger is that if the earnings per share is calculated in the usual way by simply dividing the number of issued shares into the net income for the year, the users of the accounts are not incorporating the impact that the convertible instruments might have – in particular their dilutive impact on the earnings per share. More shares will mean a lower earnings per share. As a result, for companies with significant convertible instruments in issue, an adjusted earnings per share is required to be disclosed that takes this into account. This ratio is called the **diluted earnings per share**.

Furthermore, investors are particularly interested in the earnings each share will generate in the future, rather than generated in the past. As a result, stockbrokers' research departments will endeavour to anticipate what the earnings per share will be, the **prospective earnings per share**, rather than what the earnings per share were in the last reported set of results, the **historic earnings per share**.

Enterprise value multiples

Price earnings ratios provide a measure of the expensiveness, or cheapness, of a particular company's shares. Enterprise value multiples look at the whole company, incorporating both the equity and the debt. The enterprise value is the total market value of all the issued shares plus the total market value of the debt. It is used in comparison with figures from the income statement such as operating profit (that is also called **earnings before interest and tax** or **EBIT**) or even operating profit without the potential distortions of depreciation and amortisation charges (often referred to as **earnings before interest, tax, depreciation and amortisation** or **EBITDA**. Simplistically, the smaller the enterprise value to the earnings, the cheaper the company is, which could highlight a buying opportunity for investors.

Dividend yield and cover

The **net dividend yield** expresses the total dividends per share paid out over the last year as a percentage of the current share price.

A high yield may indicate that the share price is relatively low in comparison with the return it offers. This suggests that the market does not have confidence that the dividends paid in the past will continue to be paid in the future. Conversely, a low dividend yield indicates high market confidence in the company's ability to increase dividends.

The **dividend cover** can be used to assess how well a company covered their dividend payout with the profits they made. In other words, how easy was it for the company to pay these dividends?

Dividend cover compares the earnings of the company (net income in relation to the year's activity) with the dividends paid in the year. This also reveals the proportion of profits that were reinvested in the company - if dividend cover was 2 times, then half of the profits are paid out to shareholders and half are retained.

A dividend cover of less than one is known as **uncovered dividend**, meaning the year's profits were not enough to cover the dividend.

5.6 Calculating investors ratios

> **LEARNING OBJECTIVES**
>
> 6.5.6 be able to calculate the following investors' ratios:
> Earnings per share; Diluted earnings per share;
> Price Earnings Ratio (both historic and prospective);
> Net dividend yield; Net dividend cover; Corporation tax

Earnings per share

To calculate EPS simply divide the earnings (which is the net income for the financial year) by the number of ordinary shares in issue.

$$\text{EPS} = \frac{\text{earnings}}{\text{number of ordinary shares in issue}}$$

Note that if the company has preference shares in issue, the earnings are after the preference shareholders' dividend, but before the ordinary shareholders' dividend. For a group of companies preparing **consolidated accounts**, the earning line would also be after any **minority interests**. Minority interests are the profits that belong to shareholders of the subsidiary company/ies, that are not shareholders in the holding company.

For companies with significant convertibles or options, a diluted earnings per share will be calculated by adjusting both the earnings figure (for the impact that conversion/exercise would have on the net income) and the number of shares. The number of shares will be increased by the theoretical increase that would have occurred if the convertibles had been converted and the options had been exercised. Both eps and, if required, diluted eps are disclosed on the face of the income statement within a company's financial statements.

P/E ratio

The **price/earnings ratio**, or **P/E**, is calculated by dividing the current market price of a share by the earnings per share.

$$P/E = \frac{\text{current market price of a share}}{\text{earnings per share}}$$

Historic P/E ratios use the last published earnings per share from the financial statements, whereas prospective P/E ratios use forecasts of the next earnings per share that the company is likely to deliver.

Assuming that A plc's shares are currently trading at £1.60 each, and a forecast eps of 17p, the P/E ratios for A plc would be:

Historic P/E = 160/16.1 = 9.94

Prospective P/E = 160/17 = 9.41

Net dividend yield

To calculate net dividend yield, simply divide the net dividend per share by the current share price and multiply it by 100.

$$\textbf{Net dividend yield} = \frac{\text{net dividend}}{\text{current share price}} \times 100$$

For A plc, the net dividend per share must be £430,000 divided by 10m shares = 4.3p

The net dividend yield would be:

$$\textbf{Net dividend yield} = \frac{4.3}{160} \times 100 = 2.7\%$$

Dividend cover

To calculate dividend cover, take the company's earnings per share and divide it by the net dividends per share.

$$\text{Dividend cover} = \frac{\text{eps}}{\text{net dividends per share}}$$

For A plc:

$$\text{Dividend cover} = \frac{16.1}{4.3} = 3.74 \text{ times}$$

Corporation tax – effective tax rate

It would be logical to expect the tax authorities to simply tax the company on its income before taxation as presented in the Income Statement. However, the reality is not quite so simple. For example, the UK's tax authority, Her Majesty's Revenue & Customs (HMRC) has detailed requirements designed to prevent a company from evading tax by artificially reducing its taxable profits.

Normal expenses such as wages and bills are accepted as deductions from income to arrive at taxable profits. However, costs such as entertainment costs are not deemed deductible; they are termed disallowed expenses.

Depreciation cannot be counted as an allowable expenditure for tax purposes because the company may be tempted to set artificially high rates of depreciation to reduce taxable profits. Instead of using depreciation to account for the using up of an asset, the company can make a standard deduction, determined by HMRC rules, called a capital allowance.

The result is that the tax charge in the income statement is not necessarily the percentage of income that the tax rate would suggest. The effective tax rate is commonly calculated to ascertain how effective a company is at planning and controlling the tax they pay.

Effective tax rate = (tax charge from the income statement/income before tax) x 100

For the example A plc encountered earlier:

Effective tax rate = (555/1990) x 100 = 27.9%

RISK AND REWARD

1. INVESTMENT MANAGEMENT 171
2. INSTITUTIONAL INVESTMENT ADVICE 177

This syllabus area will provide approximately 8 of the 100 examination questions

1. INVESTMENT MANAGEMENT

1.1 Equities

LEARNING OBJECTIVES

7.1.1 understand the risk and reward of investment in equities: medium to high risk/reward profile; effect of longer term; can offer income and capital appreciation

Equities are shares in companies that give the investor an ownership stake in the company alongside the attraction of limited liability. If the issuing company collapses, the shareholders loss is simply the amount paid for the shares. As a part owner of the company, the investor has the opportunity to share in the company's profits and vote at general meetings. Indeed, most investors are attracted to equities in the hope of the value of the shares increases (**capital appreciation**), and this may be combined with income in the form of regular, and perhaps increasing, dividends.

Equity investments are generally considered to be risky, relative to other investments, such as bonds and money market instruments. Medium levels of risk are attached to larger, well-established company shares, and high levels of risk attached to smaller company shares and start-up company shares. However, equity investments offer the potential to deliver high returns if held long-term.

1.2 Money Market Instruments

LEARNING OBJECTIVES

7.1.2 understand the risk and reward of investment in money market instruments: lower risk; use as short term investment

For investment horizons that are very short (for example, the next six months rather than the next 20 years), there is the potential for investors to keep their funds in cash and place them on interest earning deposit, or to invest in short-term money market instruments, like Treasury bills. These investments are low risk, relatively secure and deliver income, but provide little scope for capital growth. For investors that do not want their money tied-up for long periods, the predictable value and liquidity of these short-term investments is important.

1.3 Debt Instruments

> **LEARNING OBJECTIVES**
>
> 7.1.3 understand the risk/reward profile of investment in debt (fixed interest, floating rate and index linked): lower than equities; effect of holding to maturity; can combine low risk and certain return; can provide a fixed income

Bonds are fixed-interest loan instruments, predominantly issued by companies, governments, government agencies and supranationals like the World Bank, providing the issuer with debt finance. Their attractiveness to investors is driven by the fixed-income that they offer from regular, pre-determined coupons, combined with the relative certainty of the principal amount to be repaid at redemption.

The coupons can be fixed (at a percentage of nominal value), they can float depending upon a published interest rate such as the London Inter-Bank Offered Rate (LIBOR) or they can be tied to inflation by being index linked (for example to the Consumer Price Index). The principal amount paid at maturity is generally the par or nominal value, although with index linked bonds it will be uplifted for inflation. They are generally less risky than equities, but offer less potential for substantial returns. Indeed, for highly rated bonds like gilts where the risk of default is low, investors can be virtually certain of the yield that their investment will deliver as long as they hold their bonds to maturity. If the bonds are sold before they reach maturity, there is a danger that their market value may be below their nominal value, bringing about a capital loss and the potential to adversely impact the investor's yield.

1.4 Risks in Investing in Debt Instruments

> **LEARNING OBJECTIVES**
>
> 7.1.4 understand the risk associated with investment in debt (fixed interest, floating rate and index linked): inflation risk; interest rate risk; default risk

Investors in bonds potentially face three types of risk: **interest rate risk**, **inflation risk** and **default risk**.

Interest rate risk is the risk that an interest rate movement brings about an adverse movement in the value of an investment. It is particularly acute when the investment is a fixed-interest bond and the interest rate rises. Because of the inverse relationship between bonds and interest rates, the value of the bond will fall. Interest rate risk is largely removed if the bond is floating rate, since the coupon will be reset in line with the higher market interest rate.

Inflation risk arises when inflation is more substantial than the investor expected, the value of the investments held may fall. Generally, bonds will suffer because the fixed cash payments that they deliver are less valuable. Floating rate bonds will suffer less because the higher inflation will bring about a higher interest rate, but the real value of the principal at redemption will fall. Index-linked bonds will not suffer. The coupon and the principal are linked to a measure of inflation (increases in the Retail Price Index) so the investor will not lose out.

In contrast to debt instruments, equities and property cope reasonably well with unexpected inflation. Companies are able to increase their prices and deliver larger dividends, and the property market as a whole tends to reflect the inflationary increases.

Investors in bonds face **default risk**. This is the probability of the issuer defaulting on their payment obligations. Default risk (often referred to as **credit risk**) can be assessed by reference to the independent credit rating agencies, mainly Standard and Poor's, Moody's and Fitch IBCA.

The rating agencies split bonds into two distinct classes: **investment grade** (alternatively referred to as prime) and **sub-investment grade** (alternatively referred to as **speculative**, non-prime or even **junk**).

The three rating agencies apply similar criteria to assess whether the borrower will be able to service the required payments on the bonds. Then the bonds are categorised according to their reliability. **Triple A** tends to be the best and the next best is **double A** (although the rating agencies can have lesser notches such as pluses and minuses). The categorisation is broadly as follows:

	Standard & Poor's	**Moody's**	**Fitch IBCA**
Investment grade	AAA to BBB-	Aaa – Baa	AAA – BBB
Sub-investment grade	Up to and including BB+	Up to and including Ba1	Up to and including BB

Very few organisations, except western governments and supranational agencies, have **triple A** ratings, but most large companies boast an investment grade rating. Issues of bonds categorised as sub-investment grade are alternatively known as 'junk bonds' because of the high levels of credit risk.

If the rating agencies **downgrade** the issuer of a bond, potential investors will look to compensate for the increased risk by demanding a greater yield on the issuer's bonds. This will inevitably **result in a lower price for the bond**. Some issuers of bonds utilise 'credit enhancements' to enable their bonds to be rated more highly by the credit rating agencies. Examples of credit enhancements would be bonds guaranteed by another group company, or bonds with a fixed charge over particular assets.

1.5 Property

LEARNING OBJECTIVES

7.1.5 understand the risk/reward profile of investment in property: dependant on the property; normally a longer term investment; can offer income and capital appreciation

This could take the form of residential property, commercial property, farmland or woodland. It is generally viewed as an alternative to the more conventional forms of investments (equities and bonds) that has the possibility of delivering regular and predictable income (through rent) plus capital appreciation. Like equities, the property market can go through bull and bear phases and is typically viewed as a longer term investment.

Furthermore, high quality, well located property can be a relatively low risk (and return) investment. The major disadvantages of property are that each property is unique, making it relatively illiquid and expensive to buy or sell and there is little regulation to protect the investor compared to other forms of investment, such as shares or bonds.

1.6 Overseas Equities and Bonds

LEARNING OBJECTIVES

7.1.6 understand risk/reward profile of investment in overseas shares and debt: different domestic investments; exchange rate risk; diversification overseas

To lessen the risk that a particular company, or issuer of a bond, delivers poor returns due to problems in the domestic economy, investors can invest in overseas companies' equities, or overseas bond issues. Like domestic equities and bonds, these overseas investments may offer the possibilities of income and capital appreciation.

However, the investor may be less knowledgeable about the overseas company/issuer and there may be particular idiosyncrasies in some overseas markets, for example, local custodians may not be required to give the holder access to corporate actions. These overseas investments are also higher risk than their domestic equivalents because of the additional risk that is created by the possibility of exchange rates moving against the investor.

1.7 Diversification

LEARNING OBJECTIVES

7.1.7 understand how to optimise the risk/reward relationship through the use of: correlation; diversification

Investors generally choose to avoid unnecessary risk in their portfolios by holding appropriate proportions of each class of investment. The more conservative investor will hold a greater proportion of low risk bonds and money market instruments. These lower risk investments are likely to give rise to lower, but more predictable, returns. The more adventurous investor will hold a greater proportion of medium and high-risk equity investments, because higher risk means greater potential for higher returns. Essentially, the choice of investments is driven by the investor's attitude to risk and the fact that there is a trade off between risk and return. However, diversification can remove some of the general investment risk without having to remove all high-risk investments from a portfolio.

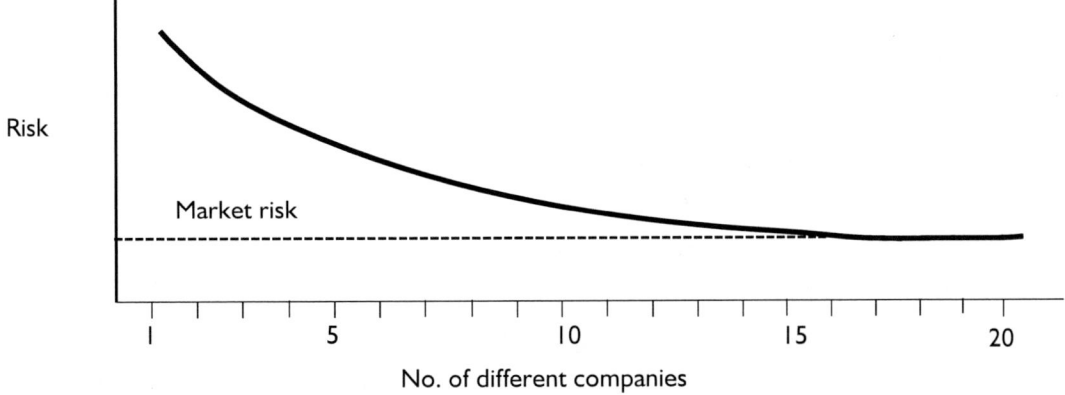

For example, an investor's portfolio might contain high risk equity investments but as the portfolio diversifies, ie, as the investor includes a wider range of companies' shares, risk diminishes, because unexpected losses made on one investment are offset by unexpected gains on another.

Diversification benefits are maximised by holding investments with **uncorrelated returns** (where the returns do not tend to move in the same direction and to the same degree). It is not necessary for the investments to be negatively correlated, with combinations of investments that are positively correlated still providing diversification benefits. It is only a combination of investments that are perfectly positively correlated that will offer no diversification benefits. However, diversification cannot remove all of the risk. There are certain things, such as economic news, that tend to impact the whole market. The risk that can be removed is known as the **specific or unsystematic risk** and the risk that cannot be diversified away is the **market or systematic risk**.

1.8 Types of risk

LEARNING OBJECTIVES

7.1.8 understand the risks facing the investor: specific/unsystematic; market/systematic; currency

Risk can be categorised in a number of different ways, but the over-riding rule for investment is that the potential for spectacular return can only arise if the investor takes a large amount of risk: the **risk-return relationship**.

Market (or Systematic) Risk

As seen above, this is the risk that the whole market moves in a particular direction. It is typically applied to equities and brought about by economic and political factors. It cannot be diversified away. For example, political crises or general recessions will tend to bring about falls in the market value of all shares, although they may affect different company shares to different degrees.

Specific (or Unsystematic) Risk

As seen earlier, this is the risk that something adverse impacts the value of a particular investment, but the adverse impact is not market-wide. An obvious example is a company's management making some sort of error – perhaps producing a defective product with resultant impact on profits and customer goodwill. Specific risk can be diversified away by holding many investments.

Currency (or Exchange Rate) Risk

For investments that are denominated in a currency other than £ sterling, an adverse exchange rate movement will create an adverse movement in the value of the investment. Clearly, this is particularly relevant for overseas investments. It can also be problematic if the investment is in a UK company that has substantial overseas business interests.

1.9 Hedging

LEARNING OBJECTIVES
7.1.9 know the role of hedging in the management of investment risk

The risks that are inevitable when investing in shares, bonds and money market instruments can be largely removed by entering into **hedging**. Unfortunately, the hedging strategies will have a cost that inevitably impacts investment performance.

Hedging is usually achieved by using derivatives, for example options, futures and forwards. Buying put options on investments held will enable the investor to remove the risk of a fall in value, but the investor will have to pay a premium to buy the options.

Futures, such as stock index futures, can be used to hedge against equity prices falling – but the future will remove any upside as well as downside.

Forwards, such as currency forwards, could be used to eliminate exchange rate risk – but, like futures, the upside potential will be lost in order to hedge against the downside risk.

2. INSTITUTIONAL INVESTMENT ADVICE

2.1 Institutional Client Profiles

LEARNING OBJECTIVES
7.2.1 know the differences between institutional client profiles including: pension funds; life and general insurance funds; hedge funds; ethical funds; banks

There are a number of institutional investors, including pension funds, the providers of life assurance, the providers of general insurance and banks.

Pension Funds are set up with the aim of providing retirement funds for the beneficiaries. They may be sponsored by an employer, be solely dependant on contributions from the workforce, or a combination of the two. Pension funds tend to be approved by tax authorities (such as HMRC in the UK), and can then accumulate income and capital gains tax-free. The money in the fund is invested by fund managers and, because pension funds have a relatively long investment horizon, they can take risks and have tended to invest heavily in equities.

Pension funds can be divided into two broad classes, those that define the benefits they will pay out (**defined benefit schemes** or **final salary schemes**), and those where the benefit is driven by the contributions made and the investment performance (**defined contribution scheme**s).

Life assurance business. Life assurance arises from insurance contracts written by an insurance company on the life of an individual. They mainly comprise:

i. term assurance policies which, in exchange for a regular premium, only pay out if the individual dies before the end of a set policy term;

ii. whole of life policies simply pay out on death in exchange for regular premiums;

iii. endowment policies are term assurance policies with a significant investment element that depends on the performance of the insurance company's fund;

iv. single premium life assurance bonds are single premium endowments; again they have a significant investment element.

Like pension funds, because of the long-term nature of life assurance business, the funds tend to be willing to invest in higher risk investments involving a heavy weighting in equity investments. Unlike pension funds, the income and the gains made within life assurance funds are subject to tax.

General insurance is where insurance is written by an insurance company against short-term personal and commercial risks, such as car or household contents insurance. Because of the short-term nature of the liabilities, the funds from the premiums tend to be invested in low-risk, liquid, short-term assets such as money market instruments. Like life assurance funds, general insurance funds are subject to tax on the income and gains within the fund.

Banks: if banks hold surplus cash at the end of each business day, they will place the funds on deposit with other banks (in the inter-bank market) and invest in eligible money market instruments (such as treasury bills and commercial paper) - relatively risk-free investments to cover the short-term nature of the banks' liabilities to depositors. An eligible money market instrument means that the Bank of England will accept it as collateral against loans. As with insurance companies, banks are taxed on income and gains they generate from their investments.

The following table provides a summary of the key distinctions and similarities across the institutional investors:

Institution	Investment horizon	Proportion of equity investments	Proportion of money market investments	Relative risk profile
Pension fund	Long-term	High	Low	High
Life assurance fund	Long-term	High	Low	High
General insurance fund	Short-term	Low	High	Low
Bank	Short-term	Low	High	Low

Collective Investment Funds

We have seen that diversification of shareholdings reduces risk, but for a private client with a relatively modest amount to invest, this would be prohibitively expensive. One way of avoiding the high cost of investing in many different companies is to invest in a pooled fund where a fund manager handles the money of a group of investors. As a result, the portfolio is conveniently and cheaply diversified. There are four major vehicles that enable individuals to diversify collectively with others. They are unit trusts, investment trusts, open-ended investment companies and exchange traded funds (ETFs).

Questions on collective investment vehicles will refer to some schemes as being **regulated** and others as being **unregulated**. This refers to authorisation by the regulator - such as the FSA in the UK. Regulated schemes can be **freely marketed**; unregulated schemes cannot be freely marketed.

Certain schemes are also granted UCITS (Undertaking for Collective Investment in Transferable Securities) status. UCITS status allows the scheme to be marketed across the **EU**.

An unauthorised collective investment scheme can still be marketed but with restrictions, eg, only to relatively large customers, more sophisticated investors or those who already hold such an investment.

Hedge Funds

Hedge funds are **unauthorised** investment vehicles that are free to invest in **high risk** strategies, including highly-geared **derivatives** and **arbitrage**, such as going long in some investments and short in others (a **long/short** strategy). Most hedge funds are offshore investments, with the fund domiciled in the most tax-efficient location. Unlike most of the conventional collective investment vehicles (such as unit trusts, investment trusts, OEICs and ETFs) that are restricted to a 'long only' investment strategy, hedge funds can be more flexible and take substantial short positions. The term 'hedge' fund comes from the fact that the unconventional nature of their investments means they can produce positive returns when the general market is suffering. For example, a long/short strategy will potentially generate positive returns regardless of the general market - it is described as a 'market-neutral strategy'.

Because of their unauthorised nature, nothing prevents hedge funds from borrowing money and 'gearing up' the returns for their shareholders. Indeed, many hedge funds have substantial amounts of borrowed funds and are highly geared.

Because they are not authorised, they cannot be freely marketed. This, combined with the requirement to invest substantial minimum amounts, means that hedge funds tend to be accessible only to institutional investors and high net worth individuals.

Ethical Funds

Ethical funds are collective vehicles designed for those that want to invest with a conscience. Increasing numbers are taking the moral high ground on a wide range of issues, from weapons development to tobacco production to nuclear energy.

Ethical (or socially responsible) investment is influenced by social, environmental or political issues. Ethical funds typically either look for companies that are actively pursuing ways of improving the environment, international relations or the economy, or avoid companies that they consider have a potentially negative effect on the way we live.

The range of funds includes some that avoid companies that, say, manufacture weapons, develop nuclear power stations or produce cigarettes and alcohol. Others invest in companies that are actively looking to better the environment by developing renewable energy techniques, recycling or helping poorer economies. There are also funds that invest in 'vegan' companies, which avoid anything to do with meat or meat products.

Most funds have their own ethical committees to decide the criteria. The fund's objectives are usually set at launch and do not vary. Some committees have the power to veto every stock, while others will take a more advisory role.

There are different levels of screening. A 'positive' approach means that the fund manager will only invest in companies that are actively working to improve the world in some way. These invest in the so-called 'industries of the future'. 'Negative' screening excludes those companies that are deemed to have a bad influence on the environment, or on our health.

ABBREVIATIONS

The following list, arranged in alphabetical order, contains abbreviations that appear in this workbook.

ADR	American Depository Receipt
AESP	Automatic Execution Suspension Period
AGM	Annual General Meeting
AIM	Alternative Investment Market
ASB	Accounting Standards Board
ASC	Accounting Standards Committee
BBA	British Bankers' Association
CAD	Cash Against Document
CAT	Charges, Access, Terms
CBO	Collateralised Bond Obligation
CC	Competition Commission
CCSS	CREST Courier and Sorting Service
CDI	CREST Depositary Interest
CDO	Collateralised Debt Obligation
CGT	Capital Gains Tax
CLO	Collateralised Loan Obligation
CLS	Continuous Linked Settlement
COB	Conduct of Business
CP	Committed Principals
CSD	Central Securities Depository
CTF	Child Trust Fund
DBV	Delivery By Value
DIE	Designated Investment Exchange
DMO	Debt Management Office
DPS	Dividends Per Share
DTCC	Depository Trust Clearing Corporation
DTI	Department of Trade and Industry
DVP	Delivery Versus Payment
ECN	Electronic Communication Network
EDGAR	Electronic Data Gathering And Retrival system

Abbreviation	Meaning
EGM	Extraordinary General Meeting
EPS	Earnings Per Share
ETF	Exchange-Traded Fund
EVA	Economic Value Added
FIFO	First In, First Out
FRS	Financial Reporting Standard
FSA	Financial Services Authority
FSMA	Financial Services and Markets Act
GDP	Gross Domestic Product
GEMM	Gilt-Edged Market Maker
GRY	Gross Redemption Yield
GUI	Graphical User Interface
HMRC	Her Majesty's Revenue & Customs
ICVC	Investment Company with Variable Capital
ICMA	International Capital Market Association (formally known as the International Securities Market Association (ISMA))
IDB	Inter-Dealer Broker
IHT	Inheritance Tax
IPA	Individual Pension Account
IPO	Initial Public Offering
IRS	International Retail Service
ISA	Individual Savings Account
IV	Intrinsic Value
JGB	Japanese Government Bond
KFI	Key Features Information
LCH	London Clearing House
LIBOR	London Interbank Offered Rate
LIFO	Last In, First Out
LSE	London Stock Exchange
MQP	Mandatory Quote Period
MQS	Minimum Quote Size
NASDAQ	National Association of Securities Dealers Automated Quotations
NMS	Normal Market Size
NRV	Net Realisable Value
NRY	Net Redemption Yield

NYSE	New York Stock Exchange
OEIC	Open Ended Investment Company
OFT	Office of Fair Trading
OTC	Over-The-Counter
P&L	Profit and Loss
P/E	Price/Earnings Ratio
PAT	Profit After Tax
PAYE	Pay As You Earn
PBIT	Profit Before Interest and Tax
PEP	Personal Equity Plan
PM	Premium
POTAM/PTM	Panel On Takeovers And Mergers
PSBR	Public Sector Borrowing Requirement
PSNCR	Public Sector Net Cash Requirement
PVP	Payment Versus Payment
RCH	Recognised Clearing House
RIE	Recognised Investment Exchange
ROCE	Return On Capital Employed
RPI	Retail Price Index
RPIX	RPI, excluding mortgage interest payments
RUR	Register Update Request
SAR	Substantial Acquisition Rule
SBLI	Stock Borrowing and Lending Intermediary
SDRT	Stamp Duty Reserve Tax
SEAQ	Stock Exchange Automated Quotation system
SEATS plus	Stock Exchange Alternative Trading Service
SEC	Securities and Exchange Commission
SEDOL	Stock Exchange Daily Official List
SETS	Stock Exchange Electronic Trading Service
SIPP	Self-Invested Personal Pension scheme
SPV	Special Purpose Vehicle
SRO	Self Regulating Organisation
SSAP	Statement of Standard Accounting Practice
STI	Statutory Total Income
STRIPS	Separate Trading of Registered Interest and Principal of Securities

SVA	Shareholder Value Added
TV	Time Value
UCITS	Undertaking for Collective Investment in Transferable Securities
UKLA	United Kingdom Listing Authority
WACC	Weighted Average Cost of Capital
WPA	Worked Principal Agreement

NOTES

NOTES

NOTES

NOTES

NOTES

NOTES

NOTES

NOTES

NOTES

NOTES

NOTES

NOTES

NOTES

Syllabus Learning Map
Certificate in Securities and Financial Derivatives
Part 1: Securities
Workbook Edition 4 Comparison

ELEMENT/LEARNING OBJECTIVES	WORKBOOK CHAPTER/SECTION
ELEMENT 1 SECURITIES	
1.1 Shares	
On completion, the candidate should:	
1.1.1 *know* the principal features and characteristics of ordinary shares and nonvoting shares:	Ch 1, Section 1.1
- 'A' ordinary shares	
- preference shares	
- bearer shares	
- partly paid shares and calls	
- ranking for dividends	
- ranking in a liquidation	
- voting rights	
- purpose of non-voting shares	
1.1.2 *understand* the differences and principal characteristics of the following classes of preference shares	Ch 1, Section 1.2
- cumulative	
- participating	
- redeemable	
- convertible	
1.1.3 *know* the broad composition and geographical scope and use of the following stock indices:	Ch 1, Section 1.3
- DJ STOXX	
- FTSE Eurofirst 300	
- MSCI World	
- FTSE 100	
- Dow Jones Industrial Average	
- Nikkei Stock 225	
- Hang Seng	
1.1.4 *understand* the use of a tax credit on a dividend	Ch 1, Section 1.4
1.2 Debt instruments	
On completion, the candidate should:	
1.2.1 *know* the principal features and characteristics of debt instruments	Ch 1, Section 2.1
1.2.2 *understand* the uses and limitations of the following:	Ch 1, Section 2.2
- flat yield	
- gross redemption yield (using internal rate of return)	
- net redemption yield	
- modified duration	
- calculation of price change	
- convexity	
1.2.3 *be able to calculate* simple interest income on corporate debt and conversion premiums on convertible bonds	Ch 1, Section 2.3
1.2.4 *understand* the concept of spreads and be able to convert spread over a Government benchmark to a LIBOR-based spread	Ch 1, Section 2.4
1.2.5 *understand* the role of the yield curve and the relationship between price and yield with reference to the yield curve (normal and inverted)	Ch 1, Section 2.5
1.2.6 *be able to calculate* the present value of a bond (maximum 2 years) with annual coupon and interest income	Ch 1, Section 2.6
1.3 Government Debt	
On completion, the candidate should:	
1.3.1 *know* the principal features and characteristics of the following classes of Government debt:	Ch 1, Section 3.1
- short-, medium-, long-dated	
- dual-dated	
- undated	
1.3.2 *understand* the following features and characteristics of Government debt:	Ch 1, Section 3.2

Syllabus Learning Map

Certificate in Securities and Financial Derivatives

Part 1: Securities

Workbook Edition 4 Comparison

- redemption price	
- interest payable	
- accrued interest	
- effect of changes in interest rates	
1.3.3 *understand* the following features and characteristics of index-linked debt:	Ch 1, Section 3.3
- index-linking	
- the retail price index and index-linking	
- effect of the index on price, interest and redemption	
- return during a period of zero inflation	
1.3.4 *understand* the features and characteristics of Treasury bills:	Ch 1, Section 3.4
- issuer	
- purpose of issue	
- minimum denomination	
- normal life	
- no coupon and redemption at par	
- redemption	
1.3.5 *know* the features and characteristics of international bonds:	Ch 1, Section 3.5
- settlement periods	
- coupons	
- terms and maturities	
1.4 Corporate Debt	
On completion, the candidate should:	
1.4.1 *know* the principal features and uses of secured debt:	Ch 1, Section 4.1
- fixed charges and floating charges	
- asset backed securities	
- mortgage backed securities	
1.4.2 *understand* the principal features and uses of unsecured debt:	Ch 1, Section 4.2
- subordinated	
- guaranteed	
- convertible bonds	
1.4.3 *understand* the principal features and uses of credit ratings:	Ch 1, Section 4.3
- rating agencies	
- impact on price	
- use of credit enhancements	
- difference between investment grade and sub-investment grade bonds	
1.4.4 *know* the principal features and uses of Commercial Paper	Ch 1, Section 4.4
- issuers	
- investors	
- discount security	
- unsecured	
- rating	
- normal life	
1.5 Eurobonds	
On completion, the candidate should:	
1.5.1 *understand* the principal features and uses of eurobonds	Ch 1, Section 5.1
- issued through syndicates of international banks	
- concept of continuous pure bearer	
- immobilised in depositories	
- ex-interest date	
- accrued interest	
- interest payments	
1.6 Other securities	
On completion, the candidate should:	
1.6.1 *know* the principal features and characteristics of depositary receipts:	Ch 1, Section 6.1

Syllabus Learning Map

Certificate in Securities and Financial Derivatives

Part 1: Securities

Workbook Edition 4 Comparison

- American Depositary Receipts	
- Global Depositary Receipts	
- transferability	
- means of creation including pre-release facility	
- how registered	
- rights attached	
- dividends	
- transfer to underlying shares	
1.6.2 *know* the rights, uses and differences between warrants and covered warrants	Ch 1, Section 6.2
- benefit to the issuing company and purpose	
- issue by a third party	
- right to subscribe for capital	
- affect on price of maturity and the underlying security	
- detachability	
- exercise and expiry	
- the calculation of the conversion premium (discount) on a warrant (warrant price + exercise price minus the share price)	
1.7 Foreign Exchange	
On completion, the candidate should:	
1.7.1 *know* the principal features and uses of spot, forward and cross rates:	Ch 1, Section 7.1
- quotation as bid-offer spreads	
- forwards quoted as bid-offer margins against the spot	
- quotation of cross rates	
1.7.2 *be able to calculate* spot and forward settlement prices	Ch 1, Section 7.2
1.8 Prime brokerage and equity finance	
On completion, the candidate should:	
1.8.1 *know* the main services provided by an Equity and Fixed Income prime broker, including:	Ch 1, Section 8.1
- securities lending and borrowing	
- leverage trade execution	
- cash management	
- core settlement	
- custody	
1.8.2 *know* the use of the main sources of equity financing:	Ch 1, Section 8.2
- stock borrowing and lending	
- repurchase agreements	
- collaterised borrowing	
- rehypothecation (tri-party repos)	
- synthetic financing	
ELEMENT 2 NEW ISSUES	
2.1 The Primary and Secondary markets	
On completion the candidate should:	
2.1.1 *know* the principal characteristics of, and the differences between, the primary and secondary markets. In particular:	Ch 2, Section 1.1
- the role of the listing authority	
- users of the primary market and why	
- users of the secondary market and why	
2.2 Stock Exchanges	
On completion the candidate should:	
2.2.1 *know* the purpose, role and main features of the major stock exchanges. In particular:	Ch 2, Section 2.1
- scope	
- provision of liquidity	
- price formation	
- brokers versus dealers	
- different types of stock exchanges	

Syllabus Learning Map
Certificate in Securities and Financial Derivatives
Part 1: Securities
Workbook Edition 4 Comparison

- electronic	
- 'open outcry'	
- major exchanges	
- Deutsche Börse	
- London Stock Exchange	
- NASDAQ	
- NYSE Euronext	
- Tokyo Stock Exchange	
2.2.2 *understand* the different types of securities listed and why	Ch 2, Section 2.2
- Ordinary shares	
- Preference shares	
- Global Depository Receipts	
- Corporate bonds	
- Government bonds	
2.2.3 *know* the role of advisors	Ch 2, Section 2.3
- Listing Agent	
- Corporate Broker	
2.2.4 *know* the Issuer's obligations	Ch 2, Section 2.4
- Corporate governance	
- Reporting	
2.3 London Stock Exchange	
2.3.1 *know* the regulatory framework for the LSE	Ch 2, Section 3.1
- Companies Act	
- FSA	
- Exchange Rule Book	
2.3.2 *know* the admissions criteria for listing	Ch 2, Section 3.2
- trading record	
- amount raised	
- percentage in public hands	
- market capitalisation	
- payment of a fee	
2.4 AIM	
On completion, candidate should:	
2.4.1 *understand* the different types of securities listed and why	Ch 2, Section 4.1
- Ordinary shares	
- Preference shares	
2.4.2 *know* the admissions criteria	Ch 2, Section 4.2
- appointment and role of a nominated advisor	
- appointment and role of a broker	
- transferability of shares	
- no minimum shares in public hands	
- no trading record required	
- no shareholder approval needed	
- no minimum market capitalisation	
2.4.3 *know* the issuer's obligations	Ch 2, Section 4.3
- Corporate governance	
- Reporting	
2.4.4 *know* the regulatory framework for AIM	Ch 2, Section 4.4
- London Stock Exchange	
- AIM Rules	
- Companies Act	
- FSA	
2.5 Listing Securities	
On completion, candidate should:	

Syllabus Learning Map
Certificate in Securities and Financial Derivatives
Part 1: Securities
Workbook Edition 4 Comparison

2.5.1 *understand* the role of the Origination Team	Ch 2, Section 5.1
2.5.2 *understand* the role of the Syndicate Group	Ch 2, Section 5.2
- different roles within a Syndicate	
- bookrunner	
- co-lead	
- co-manager	
- marketing and bookbuilding	
2.5.3 *understand* the purpose and practice of underwriting, rights and responsibilities of the underwriter	Ch 2, Section 5.3
- benefits to the issuing company	
- risks and rewards to the underwriter	
2.5.4 *understand* stabilisation and its purpose:	Ch 2, Section 5.4
- governing principles and regulation with regard to stabilisation activity	
- who is involved in stabilisation	
- what does stabilisation achieve	
- benefits to the issuing company and investors	
2.5.5 *know* why different capital raising methods are used, the structure of such transactions and role of investment banks	Ch 2, Section 5.5
2.5.6 *understand* the use of an initial public offering	Ch 2, Section 5.6
- Why would a company choose an IPO	
- Structure of IPO – base deal plus greenshoe	
- Stages of an IPO	
- Underwritten Versus Best Efforts	
2.5.7 *understand* the use of follow on offerings	Ch 2, Section 5.7
- Why would a company choose a follow on offering	
- Structure of follow on – base deal plus greenshoe	
- Stages of follow on offering	
- Underwritten Versus Best Efforts	
2.5.8 *understand* the use of rights issues	Ch 2, Section 5.8
- reasons for a rights issue	
- Structure of rights issue	
- Stages of rights issue	
- Impact of a rights issue on share price	
- Pre-emptive rights	
- Ability to sell nil paid	
2.5.9 *understand* the use of Open offers and Offers for subscription	Ch 2, Section 5.9
- Why would a company choose an open offer	
- Structure of offer	
- Stages of offer	
- Tenders, strike price, who is involved in the offer process	
2.5.10 *understand* the use of Offers for sale	Ch 2, Section 5.10
- Why would a company choose a offer for sale	
- Structure of a offer for sale	
- Stages of a offer for sale	
- Tenders, strike price, who may receive an allotment, who is involved in the offer process	
2.5.11 *understand* the use of Introductions	Ch 2, Section 5.11
- Why would a company undertake an Introduction	
- Structure of a introduction	
- Stages of a introduction	
2.5.12 *understand* the use of Exchangeable/Convertible bond offerings	Ch 2, Section 5.12
- The difference between Exchangeable and Convertible Bonds	
- Structure of offering – base deal plus greenshoe	
- Stages of offering	
- Underwritten Versus Best Efforts	

Syllabus Learning Map
Certificate in Securities and Financial Derivatives
Part 1: Securities
Workbook Edition 4 Comparison

2.6 Bond offerings	
On completion, the candidate should:	
2.6.1 *know* the different types of issuer:	Ch 2, Section 6.1
- Supranationals	
- Governments	
- Agency	
- Municipal	
- Corporate	
- Financial institutions & special purpose vehicles	
2.6.2 *understand* the seniority of debt and how they rank in default:	Ch 2, Section 6.2
- Senior	
- Subordinated	
- Mezzanine	
- PIK	
2.6.3 *understand* the pricing benchmarks:	Ch 2, Section 6.3
- spread over government bond benchmark	
- spread over/under LIBOR	
- spread over/under swap	
2.6.4 *know* the methods of issuance:	Ch 2, Section 6.4
- Scheduled funding programmes and opportunistic issuance (eg, MTN)	
- Auction/tender	
- Reverse inquiry (under MTN)	
2.6.5 *understand* the role of the Origination team including:	Ch 2, Section 6.5
- Pitching	
- Indicative bid	
- Mandate announcement	
- Credit rating	
- Roadshow	
- Listing	
- Syndication	
2.6.6 *understand* methods of raising new capital to finance takeovers:	Ch 2, Section 6.6
- follow on offerings	
- rights issues	
- convertible bond offerings	
2.7 Share capital and changes to share ownership	
On completion, the candidate should:	
2.7.1 *understand* why are share buybacks undertaken:	Ch 2, Section 7.1
- Governing regulation	
- resolution at AGM	
- limits on percentage of shares and price	
- use of company's own money	
- Key aspects of share buybacks – criteria to comply with	
- Different structures regarding block trades	
- Accelerated Bookbuild – Best Efforts basis	
- Accelerated Bookbuild – Back Stop price	
- Bought deal	
2.7.2 *understand* how and why stake building is used:	Ch 2, Section 8.1
- Strategic versus Acquisition	
- Direct versus indirect	
- Direct – outright purchase, ie, dawn raid	
- Indirect – CFDs	
- Disclosure thresholds, including mandatory takeover threshold	
2.7.3 *understand* the use of scrip (also known as bonus or capitalisation) issues	Ch 2, Section 8.2
- Why a company will undertake a scrip issue	

Syllabus Learning Map

Certificate in Securities and Financial Derivatives

Part 1: Securities

Workbook Edition 4 Comparison

- Impact on share price	
- Effect on earnings per share	
ELEMENT 3 PRIMARY & SECONDARY MARKETS	
3.1 Methods of Trading and Participants	
On completion, the candidate should:	
3.1.1 *understand* the differences between quote driven and order driven markets and how they operate	Ch 3, Section 1.1
3.1.2 *know* the functions and obligations of:	Ch 3, Section 1.2
- market makers	
- broker dealers	
- inter-dealer brokers	
- stock lending and borrowing intermediaries	
3.2 Markets in Financial Instruments Directive	
On completion, the candidate should:	
3.2.1 *know* in what markets MiFID will be implemented	Ch 3, Section 2.1
3.2.2 *know* the client classifications:	Ch 3, Section 2.2
- Retail	
- Professional	
- Eligible Counterparty	
3.2.3 *understand* the level of protection that is afforded to each client classification	Ch 3, Section 2.3
3.2.4 *understand* the types of instruments that will be affected	Ch 3, Section 2.4
3.2.5 *understand* what is meant by 'contractual best execution' and the 'consistent best possible result' obligation for Professional and Retail clients	Ch 3, Section 2.5
3.2.6 *understand* the objectives of the pre- and post-trade transparency requirements, reporting and publication	Ch 3, Section 2.6
3.2.7 *know* what client consent is required for execution	Ch 3, Section 2.7
3.3 Capital Requirements Directive (CRD)	
On completion, the candidate should:	
3.3.1 *know* the impact of CRD on securities firms' trading books	Ch 3, Section 3.1
3.4 Pre and post trade transparency requirements	
On completion, the candidate should:	
3.4.1 *understand* the pre- and post-trade transparency requirements for UK and Continental European equities	Ch 3, Section 4.1
3.4.2 *understand* key initiatives in this area (eg, Project Boat)	Ch 3, Section 4.2
3.5 Transaction Reporting	
On completion, the candidate should:	
3.5.1 *understand* the definition of a reportable transaction	Ch 3, Section 5.1
3.5.2 *understand* the role and purpose of transaction reporting for the firm and the regulator	Ch 3, Section 5.2
3.5.3 *know* which party to a transaction is responsible for reporting including transactions carried out by overseas branches	Ch 3, Section 5.3
3.5.4 *know* the reporting channels and systems	Ch 3, Section 5.4
3.6 London Stock Exchange (LSE) – UK Equity	
On completion, the candidate should:	
3.6.1 *understand* the rules, procedures and requirements applying to dealing through the Stock Exchange Electronic Trading Syetem (SETS) in the following areas:	Ch 3, Section 6.1
- order book features	
- opening the market and uncrossing	
- order types and their differences	
• limit	
• at best	
• fill or kill	
• execute and eliminate	
• iceberg	
- market close	

Syllabus Learning Map
Certificate in Securities and Financial Derivatives
Part 1: Securities
Workbook Edition 4 Comparison

- order management	
- multiple fills	
- interruptions to trading	
- worked principal agreements	
- securities covered	
- limitations and benefits of trading through SETS	
- trading hours	
- minimum and maximum trading sizes	
- who can access SETS	
- depth of liquidity	
- the auction process	
3.6.2 *understand* the operation and purpose of the LSE's Central Counterparty	Ch 3, Section 6.2
- LCH.Clearnet Limited	
- x-clear	
- Benefits and any limitations	
3.6.3 *know* the LSE's right to call for a halt in trading in any listed security	Ch 3, Section 6.3
- for any reason	
- length of trading halt	
3.6.4 *know* the features and requirements of SETSqx dealing	Ch 3 Section 6.4
- SETSqx as an order driven trading system	
- order types	
- relative illiquidity	
- securities covered	
- Normal Market Size	
- Minimum number of market makers	
3.7 London Stock Exchange International Equity Market	
On completion, the candidate should:	
3.7.1 *understand* the rules, procedures and requirements applying to dealing through the International Order Book (IOB) in the following areas:	Ch 3, Section 7.1
- Securities covered	
- Trading hours	
• Enter trade reports	
• Enter orders	
• Trades executed	
- Minimum and maximum trading sizes	
- Who can access the IOB	
- Daily auction process and timings	
3.7.2 *understand* the rules, procedures and requirements applying to dealing through the International Bulletin Board (ITBB) in the following areas:	Ch 3, Section 7.2
- Market makers' obligations	
- When to enter two way prices	
- Price quotes during and outside the Mandatory Quote Period	
- Trading hours	
• Market open	
• Opening auction	
• Continuous trading	
• Closing auction	
- Who can access the ITBB	
3.7.3 *understand* the purpose of and firms' obligations towards the International Retail Service (IRS):	Ch 3, Section 7.3
- Purpose of the IRS	
- 'Committed Principals'	
- Mandatory Quote Period for most European stocks	
- Currency of quotation	
3.8 Other Equity Markets	

Syllabus Learning Map
Certificate in Securities and Financial Derivatives
Part 1: Securities
Workbook Edition 4 Comparison

On completion, the candidate should:	
3.8.1 *understand* the rules, procedures and requirements of trading securities on PLUS:	Ch 3 Section 8.1
- Recognised Investment Exchange	
- securities covered	
• PLUS listed	
• PLUS quoted	
• PLUS traded – listed or unlisted	
3.8.2 *know* the functions of virt-x as an alternative exchange trading facility for listed company shares	Ch 3 Section 8.2
- how trading on virt-x compares with trading on the LSE	
- order priority	
- portfolio trades	
- cross border trading	
- real time trading in major European indices	
- competitors	
- the trading system used	
3.9 Government Bonds	
On completion, the candidate should:	
3.9.1 *understand* the basic characteristics and purpose of government bond markets in the US, UK, Japan and the Eurozone:	Ch 3, Section 9.1
- ratings and the concept of 'risk free'	
- currency, credit and inflation risks	
- inflation indexed bonds	
3.9.2 *know* the functions, obligations and benefits of the following in relation to government bonds:	Ch 3, Section 9.2
- primary dealers	
- broker dealers	
- inter dealer brokers	
- Government issuing authority such as the UK Debt Management Office	
3.9.3 *know* the basic purpose and characteristics of the repo markets	Ch 3, Section 9.3
- sale and repurchase at agreed price, rate and date	
- reverse repo – purchase and resale at agreed price and date	
- documentation	
- benefits of the repo market	
3.9.4 *know* the basic purpose and characteristics of the strip market	Ch 3, Section 9.4
- result of stripping a bond	
- number of securities possible from a strippable bond	
- zero coupon securities	
3.9.5 *understand* the broad mechanisms by which bond prices are driven by bond future prices	Ch 3, Section 9.5
3.10 Corporate Bond Markets	
On completion, the candidate should:	
3.10.1 *understand* the characteristics of corporate bond markets:	Ch 3, Section 10.1
- decentralised dealer markets and dealer provision of liquidity	
- the impact of default risk on prices	
- the differences between bond and equity markets	
- dealers rather than market makers	
- bond pools of liquidity versus centralised equity exchange	
3.11 Dealing Methods	
On completion, the candidate should:	
3.11.1 *know* the different trading methods for bonds:	Ch 3, Section 11.1
- bond trading has moved from voice trading (ie by telephone) to etrading using systems such as:	
- OTC inter-dealer voice trading (eg, direct dealer to dealer, dealer to dealer via voice broker)	
- inter-dealer (B2B) electronic market (eg, Electronic Trading Platforms (ETPs) such as MTS,	

Syllabus Learning Map

Certificate in Securities and Financial Derivatives
Part 1: Securities

Workbook Edition 4 Comparison

Brokertec)	
- OTC customer to dealer voice trading	
- customer to dealer (B2C) electronic market (e.g. ETPs such as TradeWeb, BondVision, proprietary Single Dealer Platform (SDP))	
- On Exchange trading	
3.11.2 *understand* the different trends between trading methods:	Ch 3, Section 11.2
- electronic methods characterised by the efficient trading of high liquidity and/or commoditised assets:	
- Government and Agency	
- debt and liquid Corporate debt	
- Price driven via Inter-dealer brokers (IDB) – dealer to dealer	
- Request for Quote (RFQ) –customer to dealer	
- OTC methods characterised by trading in lower liquidity or higher volatility classes, or trades of unusual size:	
- High Yield	
- ABS	
- Emerging Markets	
3.11.3 *know* the factors that influence bond pricing:	Ch 3, Section 11.3
- Issuer factors	
- yield to maturity	
- seniority	
- structure	
- technical factors	
- credit rating	
- specific issuer prospects	
- default risk	
- liquidity	
- benchmark bonds	
- market factors	
- benchmark bonds	
- liquidity premiums for highly-traded bond issues	
- indicative pricing versus firm two-way quotes	
- bid/offer spreads	
- availability of a liquid repo market and the difficulty in offering illiquid bonds	
- inability to borrow or cover shorts	
- impact of interest rates	
3.11.4 *know* the different quotation methods (ie, yield, spread, price) and the circumstances in which they are used	Ch 3, Section 11.4
3.12 Market Data	
On completion, the candidate should:	
3.12.1 *understand* the relationship between inflation and interest rate expectations	Ch 3, Section 12.1
3.12.2 *understand* how interest rates impact securities pricing	Ch 3, Section 12.2
3.13 Regulatory Information and Financial Communications	
On completion, the candidate should:	
3.13.1 *know* the main sources of regulatory information and financial communications within UK equity:	Ch 3, Section 13.1
- RNS, PIPS & SIPS	
- Bloomberg, Reuters	
- Analyst research	
- Web Sites: FSA, LSE, EU (Europa, CESR)	
ELEMENT 4 SETTLEMENT	
4.1 Settlement	
On completion, the candidate should:	
4.1.1 *know* the principal details of settlement in UK, EU, USA and Japan	Ch 4, Section 1

Syllabus Learning Map
Certificate in Securities and Financial Derivatives
Part 1: Securities
Workbook Edition 4 Comparison

- trade confirmation	
- settlement periods	
- instruments settled	
- settlement systems	
- Euroclear UK & Ireland	
- LCH.Clearnet	
- Clearstream	
- DTCC	
- Jasdec	
4.1.2 *understand* the implications of registered title	Ch 4, Section 2
- registered title versus unregistered (bearer)	
- legal title	
- beneficial interest	
- voting rights	
- right to participate in corporate actions	
4.1.3 *understand* the effect of designated and pooled nominee accounts on shareholder rights	Ch 4, Section 3
4.1.4 *know* which securities may be subject to UK stamp duty/SDRT	Ch 4, Section 4
4.1.5 *know* which transactions are exempt UK stamp duty	Ch 4, Section 5
4.1.6 *understand* the concepts, requirements, benefits and disadvantages of deals executed cum, ex, special cum and special ex:	Ch 4, Section 6
- timetable	
- effect of deals on the underlying right	
- effect on the share price before and after a dividend	
- the meaning of 'books closed', 'ex-div' and 'cum div', cum and ex rights	
- effect of late registration	
- benefits that may be achieved	
- disadvantages / risks	
- when dealing is permitted	
4.1.7 *know* what Continuous Linked Settlement (CLS) is and its purpose:	Ch 4, Section 7
- the sale of currencies across time zones	
- receiving and matching trades	
ELEMENT 5 SPECIAL REGULATORY REQUIREMENTS	
5.1 Takeovers and Mergers	
On completion, the candidate should:	
5.1.1 *know* the implications of the EU Takeover Directive:	Ch 5, Section 1
- that some countries continue with own rules as minimum standards directive and that takeover rules vary between states	
- application to all EU companies trading on an EU regulated market	
- requirement for a designated supervisory authority and scope for shared supervision	
- general principles of the Directive (Art. 3)	
- consequences of a mandatory bid and different mandatory bid thresholds	
- publication of information on the bid (Articles 6 and 10)	
5.1.2 *know* the legal nature and purpose of the UK Takeover Code (section 2 of the Introduction); the six General Principles; the definitions of 'acting in concert', 'dealings', 'interest in shares' and 'relevant securities'	Ch 5, Section 2
5.2 Disclosure of interests	
On completion, the candidate should:	
5.2.1 *understand* the principles behind disclosure of interest rules and why they are required	Ch 5, Section 3.1
5.2.2 *know* the following disclosure of interest rules:	Ch 5, Section 3.2
- EU under the Transparency Directive:	
- the disclosure thresholds	
- to whom disclosure has to be made and within what time scale	
- differing implementation of the Transparency Directive across EEA countries	
- US Securities and Exchange Commission:	

Syllabus Learning Map

Certificate in Securities and Financial Derivatives

Part 1: Securities

Workbook Edition 4 Comparison

- the disclosure thresholds	
- to whom disclosure has to be made and within what time scale	
- UK under the Companies Act 2006, Section 793, in relation to company investigations	
5.3 Specific regulations in US, Canada and Japan	
On completion, the candidate should:	
5.3.1 *know* that these markets restrict the promotion and sale of foreign equity	Ch 5, Section 4.1
5.3.2 *know* that foreign dealer-brokers must be registered with the local regulator in these markets before they can disseminate research	Ch 5, Section 4.2
ELEMENT 6 ACCOUNTING ANALYSIS	
6.1 Basic principles	
On completion the candidate should:	
6.1.1 *understand* the purpose of financial statements	Ch 6, Section 1.1
6.1.2 *understand* the requirements for companies and groups to prepare accounts in accordance with applicable accounting standards:	Ch 6, Section 1.2
- Accounting principles	
- International Financial Reporting Standards (IFRS)	
- IAS	
6.1.3 *understand* the differences between group accounts and company accounts and why companies are required to prepare group accounts. (Candidates should understand the concept of goodwill and minority interests but will not be required to calculate these)	Ch 6, Section 1.3
6.2 Company Balance Sheets	
On completion the candidate should:	
6.2.1 *know* the purpose of the balance sheet, its format and main contents, (including on and off balance sheet items)	Ch 6, Section 2.1
6.2.2 *understand* the concept of depreciation and amortisation	Ch 6, Section 2.2
6.2.3 *understand* the difference between authorised and issued share capital, capital reserves and revenue reserves	Ch 6, Section 2.3
6.2.4 *know* how loans and indebtedness are included within a balance sheet	Ch 6, Section 2.4
6.3 Income Statement	
On completion the candidate should:	
6.3.1 *know* the purpose of the income statement, its format and main contents	Ch 6, Section 3.1
6.3.2 *understand* the difference between capital and revenue expenditure	Ch 6, Section 3.2
6.4 Cash Flow Statement	
On completion the candidate should:	
6.4.1 *know* the purpose of the cash flow statement, its format as set out in IAS 7	Ch 6, Section 4.1
6.4.2 *understand* the difference between profit and cash and their impact on the long term future of the business	Ch 6, Section 4.2
6.4.3 *understand* the purpose of Free Cash Flow and the difference between Enterprise Cash Flow and Equity Cash Flow	Ch 6, Section 4.3
6.5 Financial Statements Analysis	
On completion the candidate should:	
6.5.1 *understand* the following key ratios:	Ch 6, Section 5.1
- Profitability ratios (Gross profit and Operating profit margins)	
- Return on Capital Employed	
6.5.2 *be able to calculate* the following key ratios:	Ch 6, Section 5.2
- Gross profit	
- Operating profit margins	
- Return on Capital Employed	
6.5.3 *understand* the following financial gearing ratios:	Ch 6, Section 5.3
- Investors' Debt to Equity Ratio	
- Net Debt to Equity Ratio	
- Interest Cover	
6.5.4 *be able to calculate* the following financial gearing ratios:	Ch 6, Section 5.4
- Investors' Debt to Equity Ratio	

Syllabus Learning Map

Certificate in Securities and Financial Derivatives

Part 1: Securities

Workbook Edition 4 Comparison

- Net Debt to Equity Ratio	
- Interest Cover	
6.5.5 *understand* the following investors' ratios:	Ch 6, Section 5.5
- Earnings per share	
- Diluted earnings per share	
- Price Earnings Ratio (both historic and prospective)	
- Enterprise value to EBIT	
- Enterprise value to EBITDA	
- Net dividend yield	
- Net dividend cover	
6.5.6 *be able to calculate* the following investors' ratios:	Ch 6, Section 5.6
- Earnings per share	
- Diluted earnings per share	
- Price Earnings Ratio (both historic and prospective)	
- Net dividend yield	
- Net dividend cover	
- Corporation tax	
ELEMENT 7 RISK AND REWARD	
7.1 Investment management	
On completion, the candidate should:	
7.1.1 *understand* the risk and reward of investment in equities:	Ch 7, Section 1.1
- medium- to high-risk/reward profile	
- effect of longer-term	
- can offer income and capital appreciation	
7.1.2 *understand* the risk and reward of investment in money market instruments:	Ch 7, Section 1.2
- lower risk	
- use as short-term investment	
7.1.3 *understand* the risk/reward profile of investment in debt (fixed interest, floating rate and index linked):	Ch 7, Section 1.3
- lower than equities	
- effect of holding to maturity	
- can combine low risk and certain return	
- can provide a fixed income	
7.1.4 *understand* the risk associated with investment in debt (fixed interest, floating rate and index linked):	Ch 7, Section 1.4
- inflation risk	
- interest rate risk	
- default risk	
7.1.5 *understand* the risk/reward profile of investment in property:	Ch 7, Section 1.5
- dependant on the property	
- normally a longer term investment	
- can offer income and capital appreciation	
7.1.6 *understand* risk/reward profile of investment in overseas shares and debt:	Ch 7, Section 1.6
- different domestic investments	
- exchange rate risk	
- diversification overseas	
7.1.7 *understand* how to optimise the risk/reward relationship through the use of:	Ch 7, Section 1.7
- correlation	
- diversification	
7.1.8 *understand* the risks facing the investor:	Ch 7, Section 1.8
- specific / unsystematic	
- market / systematic	
- currency	
7.1.9 *know* the role of hedging in the management of investment risk	Ch 7, Section 1.9

Syllabus Learning Map
Certificate in Securities and Financial Derivatives
Part 1: Securities
Workbook Edition 4 Comparison

7.2 Institutional Investment Advice	
On completion, the candidate should:	
7.2.1 *know* the differences between institutional client profiles including:	Ch 7, Section 2.1
- pension funds,	
- life and general insurance funds	
- hedge funds,	
- ethical funds	
- banks	

AIM OF THE EXAMINATION
The aim of the examination is to ensure that candidates have a basic knowledge of securities and financial derivatives market infrastructure, trading, operation, settlement, regulation and practice.

OBJECTIVES OF THE EXAMINATION
To test candidates' knowledge and understanding of:
- Securities and financial derivatives products
- New issues
- Primary and secondary markets
- Exchange traded and OTC derivatives markets
- Settlement
- Special regulatory and accounting requirements
- Investment strategies, risk and reward

ASSESSMENT STRUCTURE
An examination consisting of 175 multiple choice questions as follows:

Section 1 - Securities, markets and investment advice (100 questions) in 2 hours
Section 2 – Financial Derivatives (75 questions) in 1 hour 30 minutes

Note that each section of the paper is assessed separately. Candidates must satisfy the examiner in both sections in order to be awarded a pass overall.

Candidates sitting the exam by Computer Based Testing will have, in addition, a small number of trial questions that will not be separately identified and do not contribute to the result. Candidates will be given proportionately more time to complete the test.

SYLLABUS STRUCTURE
The syllabus is divided into **elements**. These are broken down into sections of **learning objectives**.

Each learning objective begins with the prefix *know, understand, be able to calculate* or *be able to apply*. These words indicate the different levels of skill to be tested.

Learning objectives prefixed:
know - require candidates to recall information such as facts, rules and principles
understand - require candidates to demonstrate comprehension of an issue, fact, rule or principle
be able to calculate - require candidates to be able to use formulae or tax rates to perform calculations
be able to apply - require candidates to be able to apply their knowledge to a given set of circumstances in order to present a clear and detailed explanation of a situation, rule or principle

Syllabus Learning Map
Certificate in Securities and Financial Derivatives
Part 1: Securities
Workbook Edition 4 Comparison

EXAMINATION SPECIFICATION

Each examination paper is constructed from a specification that determines the weightings that will be given to each unit. The specification is given below.

It is important to note that the numbers quoted may vary from examination to examination as there is an element of flexibility to ensure that each examination has a consistent level of difficulty. However, the number of questions from each element should not change by more than 2.

Element	Questions
1	22
2	18
3	28
4	6
5	5
6	13
7	8
TOTAL	**100**

EXAMINATION CONTENT

Candidates are reminded to check the 'Examination Content Update' (ECU) area of the Institute's website (www.sii.org.uk) on a regular basis for updates that could affect their examination as a result of industry change.

Syllabus Learning Map
Certificate in Securities and Financial Derivatives
Part 1: Securities
Workbook Edition 4 Comparison

NEXT STEPS

IAQ™ Programme:
Candidates who have passed three IAQ examinations achieve the IAQ Award and are eligible for Associate membership of the SII.

Certificate Programme:
Candidates who have passed two Certificate examinations achieve the SII Certificate Award and are eligible for Associate membership of the SII.

Visit our website to learn about the numerous career benefits SII membership will bring: www.sii.org.uk

After completing the IAQ or Certificate programmes, you are encouraged to progress your career by preparing for one or more of the SII Advanced examinations:
- Advanced Operational Risk
- Advanced Global Securities Operations
- Advanced Investment Schemes Administration.

You may also consider preparing for the SII Diploma qualification – the highest award for professionals in the securities and investment industry.

To sit the Institute's examinations or to purchase any of our publications please visit the our website at www.sii.org.uk or contact Client Services on 020 7645 0680. Details on all of these awards and further information can also be found on the Institute's website. Candidates are reminded to check the 'Content Update' area of the Institute's website on a regular basis for updates that could affect their examination as a result of industry change.

SII Membership Progression

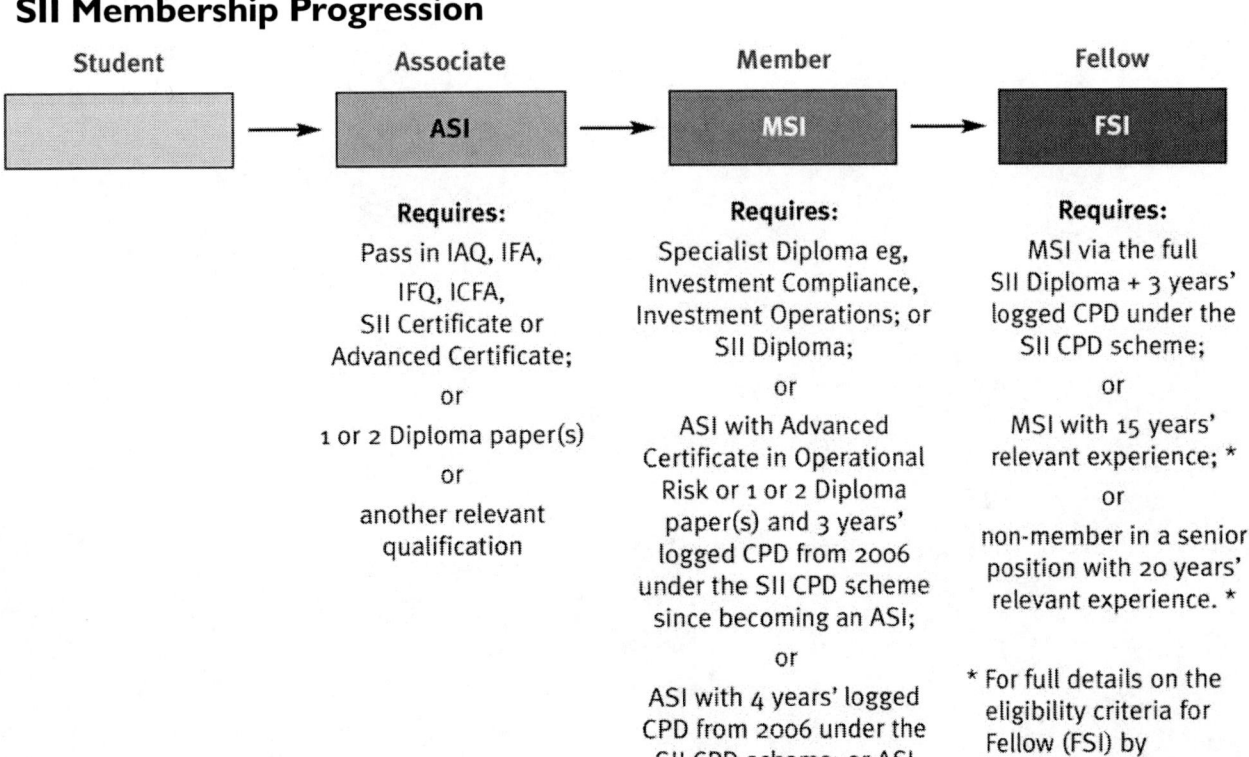

LEVEL 3 IAQ™ PROGRAMME

The *Investment Administration Qualification (IAQ™)* is a practitioner led programme for administration and operations staff. It equips individuals with an overview of the nature of the financial services industry and its regulation as well as providing a detailed picture of their particular industry sector. The IAQ is awarded on the basis of passes in any three modules (or two modules plus one exemption). Module selection depends on each candidate's individual circumstances, generally candidates fall into four groups:

1. Individuals presently in an overseeing role, working for a firm which is authorised and regulated by the FSA, are required to take the following modules recommended by the FSA:
   - Introduction to Securities & Investment
   - FSA Financial Regulation or Principles of Financial Regulation
   - A technical module relevant to the role.

2. Individuals working for a firm which is authorised and regulated by the FSA, who are not expected to take on an overseeing role, may, if their firm agrees, select any three modules.

3. Individuals working for a firm which is not authorised and regulated by the FSA, particularly in firms based offshore, may, if the firm agrees, select any three modules but are recommended to consider first passing Introduction to Securities & Investment and then selecting any two modules.

4. Individuals entering the IAQ examination privately are advised to take Introduction to Securities & Investment and FSA Financial Regulation (or Principles of Financial Regulation) as two of the three modules, but may select any three modules.

All IAQ modules have been recognised by the Financial Services Skills Council for "overseeing" functions as defined by the FSA. For details of the "overseeing" categories for which the IAQ is recognised, please refer to the Financial Services Skills Council's Appropriate Examinations list which can be found on their website (www.fssc.org.uk).

LEVEL 3 CERTIFICATE IN INVESTMENTS

The Securities & Investment Institute Certificate in Investments (previously the Securities Institute Certificate) is a series of examinations designed to satisfy the Financial Services Skills Council's examination requirements for advising on, and dealing in, securities and/or derivatives, and for managing investments.

In order to be awarded the Securities qualification, candidates must pass two modules:

- FSA Financial Regulation or Principles of Financial Regulation, and then one of:

- Securities - a two-hour, 100 multiple-choice question examination.
- Derivatives - a two-hour, 100 multiple-choice question examination.
- Securities and Financial Derivatives - this examination consists of two sections:
   - Section 1 (Securities & Markets) is a 2 hour, 100 multiple choice question paper.
   - Section 2 (Financial Derivatives) is a 1 hour 24 minute, 70 multiple choice question paper.
- Investment Management - a two-hour, 100 multiple-choice question examination.
- Financial Derivatives Module* - a 1 hour 24 minute, 70 multiple choice question paper.

(*If you have passed the Certificate in Securities and want to gain the Certificate in Securities and Financial Derivatives, you can do this through the Financial Derivatives Module. Please note that taking the Financial Derivatives Module after taking Unit 1 - Financial Regulation or Unit 6 - Principles of Financial Regulation does not lead to a Ceritificate).

Candidates can sit the modules independently of each other and in either order.

SECURITIES & INVESTMENT INSTITUTE

The Securities & Investment Institute is the professional body for qualified and experienced practitioners of good repute engaged in a wide range of securities and other financial services businesses. The Institute's purpose is to promote high standards of personal integrity, business ethics and professional competence and to create opportunities for practitioners to meet for professional and social purposes. Please call 020 7645 0600 or visit www.sii.org.uk for more information.

ASSOCIATE STATUS

Associate status is a professional designation offered by the Securities & Investment Institute in recognition of the achievement of a benchmark qualification. Through Associate status, the Institute offers practitioners the opportunity to meet regulatory requirements to maintain competence.

Upon achieving the Investment Administration Qualification (IAQ) individuals become eligible for Associate status. The use of the designatory letters 'ASI' demonstrates a high level of competency within the financial services industry and a commitment to high standards and professional integrity. For further information please telephone the Membership Department on *020 7645 0650*.

CONTINUING COMPETENCE

On successful completion of the IAQ, and to meet regulatory requirements, individuals will be required to keep their industry knowledge up–to–date by undertaking Continuing Competence. The Institute offers an extensive range of courses, conferences and workshops which provide excellent opportunities to keep in touch with industry developments. Telephone our Client Services team on 020 7645 0680 for more information.

Membership of the Institute provides access to a programme of free Continuing Professional Development (CPD) Events and information on a range of topics on the website. See the Membership section of our website (www.sii.org.uk) or telephone the Membership Department on 020 7645 0650.

LEARNING RESOURCES EVALUATION FORM

FROM: _____

FIRM: _____

OFFICE TEL. NO: _____

TITLE OF PUBLICATION: _____

MONTH OF PURCHASE: _____

Throughout this evaluation, please use numbers 1 – 4 to indicate your views.

1. Excellent / Strongly Affirmative
2. Good / Affirmative
3. Adequate / Slightly Negative
4. Poor / Strongly Negative

Q1. Are you satisfied with our speed of response to your order? ☐

Q2. Did your publication arrive in good condition? ☐

Q3. Do you find the layout and presentation helpful to your studies? ☐

Q4. Does the book cover everything you feel it should? ☐

Q5. Is it relevant to your training needs? ☐

Q6. Please expand upon your views here, or tell us anything that may help us with our continuous improvement programme:

....

....

....

....

....

When completed, please fax to *020 7645 0601* or post to the address at the bottom of the page.

We telephone a proportion of our customers to follow up on their evaluation. If you do NOT want to be contacted, please tick this box: ☐

Please fax this form to 020 7645 0601

Learning & Resources, Securities & Investment Institute,

8 Eastcheap London EC3M 1AE

Telephone: 020 7645 0680 Facsimile: 020 7645 0601 Email: clientservices@sii.org.uk